Columbus, Cortés, and Other Essays

Ramón Iglesia

Columbus, Cortés,

Ramón Iglesia

and Other Essays

Translated and edited by
LESLEY BYRD SIMPSON

University of California Press   1969

University of California Press
Berkeley and Los Angeles, California
University of California Press, Ltd.
London, England
Copyright © 1969, by
The Regents of the University of California
Library of Congress Catalog Card Number: 69–13727
Printed in the United States of America

Essays from
Cronistas e Historiadores de la Conquista de México (1942)
and from
El Hombre Colón y otros Ensayos (1944)
are here translated and printed with the kind permission
of El Colegio de México, México, D. F.

To my students of the
Centro de Estudios Históricos
of the Colegio de México

Translator's Preface

In 1939–1940, when refugees from the Spanish Civil War were finding sanctuary in Mexico, it was my great good fortune to know many of them, particularly the late Ramón Iglesia. He and I soon discovered a common ground of interest in our views of historiography, and our acquaintance ripened into a lasting friendship. We became so close indeed, and our thoughts harmonized so exactly that even today I do not know when or how his thought became mine, or mine his. I find echoes of his in my own work, and the reverse, less likely, may be true—less likely, because he was a much more learned man in his field and had devoted his life to it.

Iglesia's essays in this volume are arresting on several counts. They give us a sharp picture of the conflict among historians which was then (and still is) raging in the academic circles of Spain and Mexico, between the Positivists, who are wed to the notion that the accumulation of data will eventually solve the mysteries of the past, and the philosophical school, which holds that some kind of *a priori* scheme, however ephemeral, must be followed if we are not to lose ourselves in a sea of unrelated facts and divorce history from literature. This is the theme that Iglesia pounds away at relentlessly in his *Essays*, which are eloquent sermons directed at the young men of his seminar who, he hoped, would carry on his work.

All the longer pieces are concerned with the historiography of the Spanish Conquest. Like every good historian, Iglesia is at heart a detective. He methodically strips off the exuberant mythology that has grown up around the famous figures of the Conquest and re-examines the earliest texts. He is not interested in debunking, but in re-discovering the character of great men. That the resulting portraiture will at times distress dedicated hero-worshipers is to be expected. His *The Man Columbus*, for example, makes such a startling contrast with the Great Discoverer of our school textbooks and romantic histories that cries of anguish will be raised. And yet, Iglesia's Columbus, for all the discoverer's monomania about gold and his absolute refusal to believe that he has not found the western approach to Asia—his stubbornness was proverbial—is a more understandable human being and one for whom we can feel some sympathy.

Iglesia applies the same method to that crusty old conquistador, Bernal Díaz del Castillo, and to the *True History of the Conquest of New Spain*, a theme to which he devotes four of the *Essays*. There is necessarily some repetition among them, for they were written at different times and for different audiences, all in Mexico, where the subject has an abiding interest. As in his treatment of Columbus, Iglesia cuts through folklore and local *patriotismos*, and presents Bernal Díaz as a member of the human race, especially a member of the new aristocracy of Mexico, the conquistadores, with all their grandeur and pettiness. Under this treatment, the blind, deaf, poverty-stricken, and altogether pitiable Bernal Díaz of folklore (a caricature drawn by himself) disappears and is replaced by a sharp, angry, and envious man, who uses these very qualities to write the most memorable chronicle of the conquest. And this portrait of Bernal Díaz, far from detracting from his appeal, makes him somehow more appealing and even admirable.

The most brilliant of the *Essays* is that devoted to Hernán Cortés. In it he allows that enigmatic, slippery, sometimes ferocious, and immensely effective *caudillo* to reveal himself. Iglesia accomplishes this hazardous feat by sifting through the very large body of Cortés' correspondence and selecting those passages in which the conqueror lets down his guard, so to speak, and gives us a glimpse of the man beneath. The result is easily the best short life of Cortés that has thus far been written, altogether free from the nauseous adulation, on the one hand, and from the virulent denunciation, on the other, which the conqueror seems fated to excite.

The *Essays*, finally, constitute a kind of spiritual autobiography, poignant and self-revealing, of one of the most vigorous minds among the group of scholars gathered together by that great and humane Mexican, Don Alfonso Reyes, and incorporated in 1941 as the Colegio de México. The seminar in historiography that Iglesia conducted in the Colegio for the next three years attracted a brilliant company of students, whose critical work on the historians of the Spanish conquest put the Colegio far out in front in that vital and exciting re-assessment. Iglesia himself took a leading part in it, publishing in his *Cronistas e Historiadores de la Conquista de México* (Mexico, 1942), four essays on the historians of the conquest. I am including three of them in this volume (*Hernán Cortés, Peter Martyr*, and *Gonzalo Fernández de Oviedo*), where they most decidedly belong. For the same reason I am including Iglesia's last essay, his challenging and convincing defense of Ferdinand Columbus, which appeared as the *Prólogo* to his *Vida del Almirante Don Cristóbal Colón* (Mexico, 1947). I have omitted his very long piece on Francisco López de Gómara, because I quoted extensively from it in my introduction to Gómara's *Istoria de la Conquista de Nueva España*, published in translation as *Cortés: The Life of the Conqueror* (University of California Press, Berkeley and Los Angeles, 1966), to which the reader is referred.

Iglesia cherished no illusions about his importance or originality. He borrowed ideas freely from the great thinkers of this century and set himself the task of disseminating them. He saw himself as a teacher. He also saw himself as a kind of gadfly whose function was to sting the professors into an awareness of life and the intimate relationship with life that history must have to make itself meaningful. In Gonzalo Fernández de Oviedo he finds a made-to-order exponent of his grand theme, for Oviedo had the rare ability to select among his materials and bring them together in an organized whole. Iglesia might have added that Oviedo was writing in the sixteenth century, long before "scientific" history had been invented.

What lasting impact Iglesia might have had on his contemporaries if he had lived (he died in 1948), I cannot say, but I submit that his sane and courageous *Essays* could profitably be read by all students of history.

In their editing I have limited myself to an occasional footnote to guide the reader among unfamiliar subjects. Where footnotes might be intrusive, I have interpolated explanatory words in brackets and excised some redundant passages that seemed to clutter the text unnecessarily. To the same end I have omitted the preface that Iglesia wrote for his modernized edition of Bernal Díaz del Castillo's *True History* (2 vols., Mexico, 1943), which does little more than repeat the substance of his earlier essays on the same subject included in this volume. Finally, four of his critical reviews seemed to me marginal to the general stream of his thought, and I have omitted them.

I am offering this translation as a tribute to the memory of an old friend, whose bright passage through his adopted country dazzled it only too briefly.

LESLEY BYRD SIMPSON

University of California (Berkeley)
1969

Contents

Part One:
THE ESSAYS

Author's Preface

*"Everything has been said already, but,
since no one pays any attention to it,
we must always start over again
from the beginning."*
ANDRÉ GIDE

Dedicating this collection of essays to my students is not simply a gesture of courtesy or affection, for it would perhaps be more accurate to speak of them as my companions. Indeed, if any member of the classes in historiography of our Centro de Estudios Históricos has learned anything, it has assuredly been myself.

Anyone who devotes himself to teaching knows how frequently students embarrass their professor with questions that the professor cannot answer. Even now I am unable to answer several questions put to me by those to whom I dedicate this volume. I think that the questions which it raises are more numerous than the questions answered.

History—and I am speaking of historical writing, narrative history—cannot be considered apart from the crisis of our time, history less than any other study. In the face of the confident attitude of "scientific" historians which today dominates academic circles, a number of protesting voices are being raised, the chorus of which is continually growing louder.

This chorus grows more and more audible as the disproportionate accumulation of materials, which the study of history

3

has pre-eminently become, brings us no nearer, but rather drives us farther away from, the longed-for synthesis for which all historians claim to be preparing the ground. The coming of the synthesizing messiah, of which Benedetto Croce once talked, seems to be more and more remote.

There is dissatisfaction and uneasiness in the minds of many historians of today, who are dismayed to see this discipline becoming more ahistorical, more removed from living history, in proportion as those who cultivate it try to give greater reality to their findings, clinching them to the point of making them unanswerable.

They strive to make them immutable and definitive, that is, ahistorical. This is a strange paradox for our historical studies to have arrived at, in these days which are saturated with historicity, in the very moment when the sciences that once claimed to be least historical, namely, the physical-mathematical sciences, have made a complete about-face toward historical thinking.

There is dissatisfaction, uneasiness, and also insecurity, doubt, and a sharp awareness of a whole new set of conflicts and difficulties. From the peaceful shores of their thousands of volumes, the positivist historians look with the greatest scorn upon those of us who do not share their confident attitude, who do not regard the study of history as a work of stone and lime upon which history is being erected in changeless structures, rather than a play of perspectives, or a restless torrent of shafts of light among the clouds, behind which an airplane tries to slip away.

Insecurity, a panting after enlightenment, a fear of being misinterpreted, an effort to capture the expression of something fluid which refuses to let itself be captured. . . . The chorus of outcries raised against us is not small, either. We are "subjectivists," "relativists"—in short, we are dangerous persons who must be kept in check, because we imperil and threaten to crack the structure that "scientific history" has so painfully erected.

Well, what is to be done about it? The harm has been done, and those who rush in through the chinks in the wall which was believed to be so solidly built grow more numerous every day. Croce, Toynbee, Huizinga, Trevelyan—many are they who now proclaim the perishable and limited nature of the history that prevailed in the past century, and who loudly urge us to turn boldly away if we would avoid a complete and catastrophic ankylosis.

At such moments we must come to a decision, but we must also exercise caution. It has never been easier to be misunderstood. The desire to be original, a lack of serious preparation—all this and more they can tell us. And yet, and yet. . . . I should like to state here, once and for all, that I do not feel myself superior to, but rather, different from those who do not share my ideas; that my small effort is owing to eagerness, a tendency toward something which I strongly believe ought to be undertaken, but which I have not accomplished myself—far from it! When I say that history should seek a fresh contact with life, or that the historian should make an effort to reach the mind of the unspecialized reader by means of a greater attention to the form and quality of his writing, it is not because I believe myself possessed of such rare gifts.

Some day it may be more feasible for those who are now devoting themselves to the apprenticeship of history to acquire this ability, that is, if they are given the proper guidance and are not led off into blind alleys. The effects of their work will appear some day, but the work of those of us who now face these problems will remain as something truncated and immature, except in the odd cases of men of superior gifts who should serve as our guides and pilots, but with whom we can never hope to compete.

This, then, will be an essay, an adventure in the writing of history. Such is the nature of the studies gathered together in the present volume which were written over a period of fifteen years, from 1929 to 1943. Almost all of them have been published, but so feeble are our journals in these hazardous times, and so difficult of access in our looted libraries, that in this dress they may be better preserved from an oblivion which perhaps they do not altogether deserve.

To emphasize their character as essays I have stripped them of the scholarly apparatus with which some of them originally appeared. It would not have been possible now to annotate those that lacked such apparatus, because my many mischances and adversities have caused me to lose all my working materials. Besides, our generation has become so accustomed to seek, almost exclusively, in historical works the apparatus of notes and bibliographies, that perhaps it will be the gainer by seeing them thus naked, so that the attention of the reader may be concentrated on the content of the work. With this apology, the reader is begged to allow the author a margin of confidence in his intellectual honesty—which, perhaps, is a difficult thing to do.

I shall not engage here in a critical analysis of my own essays, for I have never been able to form a fixed criterion by which to assess their value. I find it amusing to see how my viewpoints have kept on changing as I grow older, including on occasion those I had about very limited and precise themes. Given my conception of history, this should not surprise me. The same thing happens to us when we repeat the same poem on different occasions, or see the same painting, or listen to the same piece of music.

In short, history is a work of art. I do not think it is lowered by our accepting fully a truth which has been so widely discussed. Ranke was a great artist, the archetype of the scientific historian, even though, perhaps, he would not have admitted it. All the great historians were great artists. Everything else, however strenuously it has been urged, however much it has been set before us as a desideratum, is only a mechanical work.

I hope that there will arise from among my students, whom I must now take leave of, some who will understand and sense what I have here so clumsily and painfully tried to express, and that it will yield fruit among them.

The arrangement of the book had to be somewhat arbitrary, given the nature of the materials. At the beginning are the four longest essays, followed by a section of "miscellaneous" pieces —lectures, articles, prefaces—including some sketches on general questions of history—to call them a theory of history would frighten me too much. These, perhaps, should have come first, but, if I had so placed them I should have given them more importance than I think they deserve. Indeed, they are hardly more than simple reflections on themes upon which brains better endowed than mine have been shipwrecked. In the last section, on the criticism of books, I have grouped my notes by subject, without regard to the date of publication.

Some of the journals in which these articles first appeared are no longer published. All my thanks to *Filosofía y Letras, Cuadernos Americanos, Letras de México, Revista de Historia de América, El Noticiero Bibliográfico,* to the publishing houses of *Seneca* and *Nuevo Mundo,* and to the editors of the *Homenaje a Don Francisco J. Gamoneda,* for giving me permission to reproduce them here.

Mexico, February, 1944

The Man Columbus

Let us try for a moment to imagine the astonishment of the inhabitants of a small island called Guanahaní one morning when they beheld three shapes out there in the water, three immense hulks, out of which issued several absurd beings who seemed human only in their eyes and movements, of light complexion, their faces covered with hair, and their bodies—if indeed they had bodies—covered with fabrics of diverse pattern and color. Since the Indians lacked any point of reference and saw everything in relation to objects they were used to, they placed the newcomers among the number of supernatural beings and worshiped them as coming from heaven, This immediate reaction of the Indians was accepted by the chief of those improbable beings and became the idea of many of those who for some four-hundred-odd years have interested themselves in the event we are about to relate.

It remained for an epoch as realistic as ours to see a little more clearly what happened before October 12, 1492, and to explain the discovery of lands hitherto unknown to Europeans.

The man who commanded those hulks . . . was a man of flesh and blood, an Italian born in Genoa in 1451. The commercial importance of that Mediterranean city is well known. The Genoese often migrated and engaged in commerce, but Christopher Columbus ... had no money. His father was a weaver of woolen stuffs. All his family were humble people, and, if he traveled at all, it was after the age of twenty, in merchant ships sailing the Mediterranean as far as the island of Chios, and the Atlantic as far as England.

Naturally, it has required an enormous amount of work to uncover the details of these first years of his life. A weaver's son who lived in Genoa? Try to find out something about him! His neighbors must have known him, and that's all. But wait a bit. This man of twenty-eight or thirty gets married in Lisbon, Portugal, where he had chanced to land, and some papers belonging to his father-in-law fell into his hands, although we do not know their contents. It seems that they were concerned with the subject of the day, the discoveries, which aroused as much enthusiasm then as trans-Atlantic flights do now. So our Genoese launches himself into the whirlwind of maritime explorations, as fascinating as a gambling game; he collects reports of them; he goes on voyages, no longer commercial but explorations. In 1484 he is received by King Juan II of Portugal and suggests to him certain projects which, it seems, were not welcomed. Then he goes to Spain. He has a brother, Bartolomé, ten years younger than he, but more experienced in nautical affairs, who is even less known than Christopher, for we have not a single paper written by him. Certain critics, notably Vignaud, allow Bartolomé a greater part in the making of plans of discovery than they allow his brother. But evidently our passage through such uncertain data is like that of a man clinging to the top of a greased pole, his fall expected at any moment.

This period in the life of our hero is treated exhaustively by Vignaud, in his *Histoire critique de la grande entreprise de Christophe Colomb*, an imposing, massive, and documented work. But what do we get out of this long and minute study, after all is said and done? We get the picture of a stubborn man, as boring as a commercial traveler, or a beggar who spends hours whining on our doorstep. Fernández de Oviedo, the cosmographer Santa Cruz, and Columbus himself, repeat the word "stubborn." What is the man after? He refuses to be explicit; he proposes nothing, but only begs. He wants to get funds with which to undertake a voyage of discovery and, when that is done, the results will speak for themselves. We do not know how he got himself listened to. It is possible that the information Columbus had, or thought he had, was given him in the privacy of the confessional by a friar of the convent of La Rábida, a friend of his. His success, of course, is owing to humanistic, not scientific, arguments. So it may be that because of his persuasion, his great assurance, and the firmness of his insistence, he was listened to merely to get rid of him. Columbus had no money but the small sums the kings had given him, and they soon ran out. And yet he kept on persevering, with astonishing stubbornness, for seven long and boring years, empty of accomplishment for him, and of data for us. The most we know of him is that he had a love affair with a certain woman, whose social status has been elevated by romantic critics, and lowered by the positivists to the level of a chambermaid at the inn where Columbus was staying—interesting only because their son, Ferdinand Columbus, wrote the first life of his father.

Columbus was not a learned man; neither was he a visionary, proof of which is that he was backed by merchants and Jews; also by King Ferdinand, a very suspicious man; also, that Santángel, Quintanilla, and other high functionaries of the Treasury took an interest in him, men to whom Columbus must have seemed trustworthy, bankers not at all given to letting themselves be swayed by dreams or vague fantasies. A reading of their negotiations suggests purely commercial matters: Columbus offers to pay part of the expenses, demands an excessive share of the profits, and does not come to an agreement with the Crown until he finds an associate in his enterprise, a Spaniard, a practical man, a sailor, who uses his influence and lends his ships to launch the expedition. And, just to make our desperation total, this man [Martín Alonso] Pinzón, dies just as he returns from the voyage, having fallen out with Columbus, and leaving us with no real knowledge about the part he played in the discovery.

And now we come to the dramatic moment, pleasing alike to readers and romantic historians: Friday, August 3, 1492, a moment that moves the scholar in his study and brings to his horrified imagination the littleness and fragility of three vessels which were about to brave the *Mare Tenebrosum* of the ancients, which was peopled with monsters and the like. Here the scholar tells us of medieval imaginings about the Atlantic which he details, in order to underscore the mad audacity of Columbus and his men.

Although we do not know what that moment was really like, it must have been less complex and hair-raising than it has been described. Columbus says only that he had readied "three *navíos* very well suited to their purpose." The monsters had retreated quite a bit in the popular view since the Portuguese expeditions of discovery and the alluring prospect of treasure promised in a certain saying of Solomon pointed out to one of the Pinzón brothers by a friend in the Pope's library in Rome.

This must be emphasized, because historians tend to give us a picture of Columbus overcoming formidable objections and terrors. Terrors there undoubtedly were, and proof of their existence seems to be in the breaking of *La Pinta's* rudder; but the collective hallucination, as the sociologists would call it, rather favored the enterprise than otherwise. That there was such hallucination is proved by the following paragraphs:

"The Admiral says that many honest Spaniards, who were in Gomera with Doña Inés Peraza, settlers of the Island of Hierro, swore that every year they had seen land to the west of the Canaries, toward the setting sun, and others of Gomera swore to the same thing. The Admiral says here that while he was in Portugal in the year 1484, a man came from the island of Madeira to ask the king for a caravel in which to sail to the land he had sighted; and this same man swore he had seen it every year, always in the same way; and he also says he remembers they were saying the same in the Azores, and the land was always in the same direction and always of the same size."

Hallucination, popular enthusiasm, the assurance of the chief, who knows where he is going, or thinks he does—which amounts to the same thing—who sets his course first for the Canaries, then follows the 28th parallel, and expects to sight land within 700 leagues. He is sure of everything.

Thursday, September 6, the little fleet puts out from the Canaries. Columbus's log written on board is laconic and despairful: "The sailors were frightened and suffering, from what, they did not say." A little later, "all were very cheerful, and the fastest ship went on ahead to be the first to sight land." Monday, September 17: irritating bits, as unsatisfactory as an interesting conversation heard over a bad telephone. Again we are left in ignorance. We have the declarations of some sailors who took part in the expedition, made many years later (1515–1535), which objective historians have seized upon. But these declarations are delightfully contradictory, as always happens when simple men are interrogated. According to Fernán Pérez Mateos, eighty years old in 1536, and Francisco García Vallejo, who belonged to the crew of *La Pinta*, Columbus was the one who became discouraged when he failed to sight land, and the Pinzón brothers made him go on. According to Francisco Morales, Columbus was the one who would not give up and it was the others who weakened. Las Casas gets angry with Fernández de Oviedo because the latter admits the possibility that Columbus lost heart. We, being more human, should admit the alternative: that all had hope and that all lost it. Some must have found the courage not to retreat, some at one time, some at another.

They had time for it: thirty-five days at sea without sighting land, which was always felt to be at hand, as evidenced by flocks of birds, a whale, a live crab, grass. September 17, more than 300 leagues out from the Canaries: "At the break of day that Monday they saw more grass, which seemed to come from rivers, and in it they found a live crab, which the Admiral kept, and he said that these were certain signs of land, because they are not to be found 80 leagues from land."

Thursday, September 20, 450 leagues out from the Canaries: "At daybreak two or three little land birds alighted on the ship, singing, and disappeared after sunrise." Every day the same. They observed the birds that came to the ship, and the direction of flight of those that passed. "All night long they heard little birds passing," not to read their fortune, like the Cid when he left Vivar, but "because the Admiral knew that most of the islands held by the Portuguese had been discovered by the flight of birds."

They see a light on October 11th and sight land on the 12th. This is the climax of accomplishment, Columbus's landing to take possession of the land in the name of his sovereigns. Elementary psychology, the end of the reel, where historians come into their own. The crews of the caravels embrace the Admiral; they ask his pardon for their doubts; they all weep and give thanks to the All-Highest. (See Washington Irving.) We know, nevertheless, that such moments, as we have experienced in our own lives, exist only as elaborations after the fact. It may be believed that the first impression of the Spaniards, very different from that of the Indians, was one of disappointment. In those days one did not undertake such a long voyage, as we do today, to break a record, or prove the endurance of a man or a machine, but made it for an immediately utilitarian purpose. They were seeking lands rich in gold and jewels, putting into practice the very human and very Spanish notion that what is distant is always best.

There was a complicated and fantastic fabric in the minds of Columbus, Pinzón, and the rest of the company, and reality had to coincide with it. But reality, as untamed as ever, instead of proud countries, magnificent edifices covered with gold and silver, presented them with wild Indians, "all as naked as their mothers bore them," good people who "came to the ships' boats where we were, swimming and bringing us parrots and balls of cotton thread, and many other things, which they exchanged for things we gave them, such as glass beads and hawk bells. In short, they took and gave of what they had very willingly, but it seemed to me that they were poor in every way." "They bore no weapons, nor were they acquainted with them, because when I showed them swords they seized them by the edge and so cut themselves from ignorance. They have no iron; their javelins are reeds without iron points, although some of them are armed with fishes' teeth, and others with other things." Disillusionment, a pause. First impressions in such cases are usually wrong, but rectifiable.

October 13th. Columbus observes. He carefully examines the

canoes of the approaching Indians. "They rowed with oars shaped like bakers' paddles, with marvelous speed, and if a canoe upsets they all jump into the water and set it upright and bail it out with gourds that they bring along." This is all very interesting and curious. Let's go on: "They brought balls of spun cotton, and parrots, and javelins and other trifles which it would be tedious to describe, and they exchanged it all for whatever was offered them. And I was alert and strove to learn whether they had any gold, and I saw that some of them wore small pieces of it hanging from their noses, and by signs I learned that by going to the south, or by sailing around the island to the south, we should find a king who had great vessels made of it, very many of them. I tried to make them lead us there, but afterward I saw that they did not know how to return, so I decided to wait until the afternoon of the next day, and then sail off to the southeast . . . , and so continue to the southwest to look for gold and precious stones."

And that's all. During the next three months of exploring—they set sail for Spain on January 16th—the scene is repeated at each landing: Columbus sets free one or several Indians—he had captured six on Guanahaní—to talk with those of the country. If these do not run away he offers them some of the trifles with which he is well supplied. The Indians give him everything they have in exchange, but he will accept nothing from them save only gold.

"And when they were convinced that no harm would come to them, they felt safe, and soon more than sixteen *almadías* or canoes came to the ships with cotton yarn and other little things of theirs, but the Admiral ordered that nothing should be taken, so they might know that he sought nothing but gold, which they call *nucay*." When the Indians are asked about gold, they bring some: "Many Indians came asking for hawk bells and other trifles, but we would give them nothing unless they brought gold; and when this was told them, they made off to the beach and in less than an hour each of them brought a leaf or a snail shell full of gold dust." (Bernáldez). They bring a little of it, but by signs all of them insistently point to other lands where there is much more. In the minds of Columbus and his men the most absurd information is good.

Monday, November 12th. "He left the port and *Río de Mares* at the end of the morning watch, in search of an island the Indians called Baveque, where they insisted that the people picked up gold on the beach at night by firelight, and afterward hammered it into bars, they said. . . ."

Tuesday, December 18th. "Today we got a little gold by trade, it is said; but the Admiral had heard of an old man who owned many neighboring islands, a hundred leagues distant and more, as he understood it, from which came a very great deal of gold, and he even heard that one of the islands was all of gold, and that in others there was so much that it was picked up and sifted as in a sieve, and was melted down and made into bars and a thousand different kinds of jewels, and he indicated their workmanship by signs."

Columbus had occasional doubts: "And about sunset I anchored near the said cape to learn whether there was any gold there, because the men I had seized on San Salvador told me that the people there wore very wide gold circlets on their arms and legs. I well believed that everything they said was false, so that they could run away." Still, on Tuesday, November 27th, he says: "And also I do not understand the language, and the people of these lands do not understand me; nor do I nor any of my men understand them. And with these Indians that I have I often take a thing for its opposite; nor do I trust them very much because they have often tried to escape."

But doubt and certainty become eagerness to carry on the search. Whether this greed is a characteristic of the Admiral, or whether it is owing to pressure from the Crown, we shall not discuss. The expedition must be justified by finding gold. It is not necessary to discover lands. It is not necessary to convert Indians—a subject to which we shall return later on—. Mines are necessary; *the* mine must be found. The rest is of no importance. "These islands are very green and fertile, the air is soft, and there may be many things that I don't know about, because I do not wish to stop and wander around a lot of islands merely in search of gold. And since these islands give evidence that it is worn on arms and legs, and it is gold, because I have seen some pieces of it and have them in my possession, I cannot be mistaken, and with the help of Our Lord I shall find out where it comes from." "Our Lord in His mercy has shown me where I may find this gold, that is, the mine, because I have many people here who tell me they know of it." "And I have no desire to see things in detail, which I could not do in fifty years, because I wish to see and explore as much as I can, and to return to Your Highnesses, God willing, in April. The truth is that if I find where there is an abundance of gold or spices, I shall stop there until I have got as much of it as I can, and for this reason I shall do nothing more than proceed and see if I can come across it."

To multiply such quotations would make this as boring as the log of Columbus. So let's get on, with the speed of his impatience, to the realization of his desires. In the last week of December there are more certain tidings of gold. It seems that in Cibao, very near our men, there are mines. On Tuesday, December 25th, Christmas Day, the *Santa María* runs aground. In this accident Columbus sees the hand of Divine Providence: "He knew that Our Lord had caused the ship to strike so that he might make a settlement there." Others, apparently less pious, thought they saw in this the hand of the Admiral. Thus Oviedo: "The flagship ran aground . . . and sprang a leak; but nobody was endangered; rather, many thought that he had slyly let it strike, so that he might leave part of his men on land, as he did."

In this regard the words of the priest of Los Palacios, Bernáldez, are also of interest: "And it was necessary, it seemed, to leave them behind, because, now that a ship had been lost, there was no way for them to return; and this was concealed here [in Spain], and it was said that they remained behind only to make a beginning of a settlement."

Martín Alonso Pinzón protested so strenuously against the abandonment of the men that Columbus was on the point of having him arrested, as Oviedo also informs us. Columbus does not mention it. "Now I have ordered built a tower and a fort, very strong, and a large cave dug, not because I think it is necessary for these men. . . . But it is reasonable that such a tower should be erected and built as it should be, since it is so far from Your Highnesses."

His haste to impart the good news is as great as his impatience to find gold had been. On December 27th he noted in his log: "The Admiral endeavored, with all the speed he could muster, to ready his return to Castile." But was not the return voyage to have been in April? There is an accelerated tempo in these pages. Columbus, more expansive now in view of his success, indulges in hyperbole: "He says that tonight [January 9th], by the grace of God he will set sail and not stop on any account, since he had found what he was looking for." Isn't it clear? Columbus, satisfied, lets his imagination run and again dreams his old dreams, now that he is sure they have come true. "And he says that he hopes in God that upon the new voyage he was planning to make from Castile, he would find a cask of gold got in trade by those he had left behind, and that they would have found the gold mine and the land of spices, and all this in such abundance that within three years the Monarchs would be able to undertake and prepare the conquest of the Holy Temple, for I declared to Your Highnesses that all the profit from this enterprise of mine should be spent in the conquest of Jerusalem, and Your Highnesses laughed and said they would be pleased, and that they had that desire in any case."

Sound the trumpets! Now indeed the great moment has arrived! And how he fulminates threats against his companions in the expedition, those annoying impediments holding up the time of the sharing! "And afterward I shall not suffer the deeds of evil men of small virtue, who presume to set their impudent will against those who have brought them this honor!"

Gold, gold, gold! Which is called *tuob, caona, nozay.* Their Highnesses have it all at home. The king of the country has ordered a statue made of pure gold as large as the Admiral. He will bring it within ten days. One of his own men has said so. (The news flies about as it does among visionaries.) There is another island beyond Juana [Cuba], where the nuggets are as large as beans. Here in Española they are no bigger than grains of wheat. . . . *Tuob, caona, nozay.* . . .

Here we might end the account of the first voyage, but we must undertake the monotonous and despairful task, as labori-

ous as towing a boat on the Volga, of attacking the castles of
sand and cloud erected by historians, by the most serious historians, such as the foolish and insipid Washington Irving, the
more profound but ingenuous Humboldt, and our own magnificent Don Marcelino [Menéndez y Pelayo], always so precipitate
and headlong.

What does Columbus think of the Indians? For a tempera-
ment like his, so simple, dry, unemotional, hard, egotistical
(whose supposed complexity of character exists only in the
spiritual myopia of the erudite, or in the hypercritical Byzantin-
ism of today), he sees the Indians as objects, as things that can
be exploited for profit. He is neither kindly nor cruel in himself.
His attitude changes with the circumstances. At bottom he is
very energetic and hard, as he is revealed in the speech he made
to his men when they threatened him on the outward journey:
"The said Admiral told them to desist from their intentions,
because if they killed him and his servants, who were few, they
would not accomplish much, but they might be sure that they
would be called to account by the King and Queen, our Lords.
(Deposition of Francisco Morales, in the *Pleitos.*) And especially in the log for Wednesday, October 10th: "Here the men
could stand it no longer. They complained of the long voyage;
but the Admiral encouraged them as well as he could, holding
out the hope of the good profits they might make. And he added
that it was useless to complain, for he had set out for the Indies
and, with the help of God, would go on until he should find
them."

This was the essential Columbus: it was useless to complain.
A man like him, tested in misfortune, hunger, mockery—what
could make him weaken? Right and reason belong to the strong-
est. He despises the Indians because they yield to the "cannibals." "The said Indians informed him by signs of other things,
very wonderful. But it is said that the Admiral did not believe
them and thought that the Indians of the island of Bohío
[Española] must have been more clever and astute than they,
for they captured them because they were very weak-spirited."

Such observations are frequent in the log. "The Admiral says
that he well believes it [that is, that the Caribs ate the other

Indians] but that since the Caribs were armed, they must have been more intelligent." Speaking of new tribes: "And if they are not Caribs, at least they must be their neighbors having the same customs, and fearless people, not like those of the other islands [the Bahamas], who are cowardly and unarmed beyond reason."

We shall see Columbus later as a conqueror, but in this first voyage it is the merchant in him who dominates. He tries not to frighten the Indians; he tries to win their confidence, to coax them, treating them with extreme friendliness, as alluring and insistent as a commercial traveler. Here he is the peddler of raffle tickets on the streetcar or train, who hands around caramels before the drawing. And how he displays his commercial ability, how he rubs his hands! Let him speak for himself: "I ordered each of them to be given something, that is, a few beads, ten or twelve on a string, and a few brass rattles worth in Castile a *maravedí* each—all of which they hold in the greatest esteem."

On another occasion: "And I who was on the poop deck of the ship and saw everything, sent for him and gave him a scarlet cap and some small green glass beads, which I put around his arm, and two hawk bells that I hung on his ears, and I ordered returned to him his canoe which he also had on the ship, and sent him back to land . . . , and I gave him the said things so that we should be held in esteem when next Your Highnesses should send us here, and they would not be hostile to us; and anything, everything that I gave him would not come to four *maravedís*."

It would detract from the performance of the picturesque history now in vogue to relate how our men dressed and adorned the Indian women who came on board, and describe the presents that Columbus made to King Guacanagarí, among which stood out a shirt and a pair of gloves. "The lord was now wearing the shirt and gloves that the Admiral had given him, and he made more fuss over the gloves than over anything else the Admiral had given him." And so on. Our cacique was as proud of his shirt as the king was in the story of Count Lucanor.

And now here is a painful and suggestive question for those

of us who travel, who have a sense of the landscape, who have been educated for generations in nature worship and the open air. We bow in awe before Columbus, the discoverer of a new world, about which he had no previous knowledge. What did he see, what did he feel, when he came into contact with such strange realities? An exploitable object, such as he saw in the Indians? Let's listen to the romantic historians. For Humboldt, the Admiral, "in spite of a burden of material and minute cares that chilled his soul, retained a profound feeling for the majesty of nature." He praises his animated descriptions. "In these pictures of nature (and why not use this term for these descriptive bits full of charm and truth?), the old sailor at times displays a talent for narration that will be appreciated by those who are initiated into the secrets of the Spanish language, and who prefer vigor or coloration to a severe and formal correctness." Menéndez y Pelayo introduces Humboldt's ideas among us, so now we have Columbus consecrated as a writer and admitted into the anthologies of classical Castilian.

Men of our time, less given to enthusiasms than Humboldt and Menéndez y Pelayo, have quite a different opinion. For Filson Young, the English critic and writer, author of a life of the Admiral (*Christopher Columbus and the New World of his Discoveries*, London, 1911), "Columbus was not a very lucid or exact writer, and he has but two methods of comparison: either a thing is like Spain, or it is not like Spain. . . . The essay written by a cockney child after a day at the seaside or in the country, is not greatly different from some of the *verbatim* passages of this Journal; and there is a charm in that fact too, for it gives us a portrait of Columbus who, despite his search for gold and precious stones, roams, still a child at heart, through the wonders of the enchanted world to which he had come."

Although Young's first observation seems just enough, I cannot accept his second. Columbus's descriptions are naïve only in their form, because he is self-interested in their purpose. They are the first example of a literature that today is abundant: the propaganda leaflets published by touring clubs and travel agents. All the islands, all the landscapes are like the women in Don Quixote's tavern: if one is beautiful, her neighbor is more so; not to mention such exaggerations as: "And among other things there was anchorage and shelter for all the ships of Christendom." "At the end of the cape was the mouth of a big river . . . and in it there was room for all the ships in Spain." "And he certifies to the King and Queen that the mountains he has seen along this coast since day before yesterday, as well as those of these islands, have not their equals in height in the world." Not to mention either such wild guesses as: "And he said he believed that there were very great riches and precious stones and spices among them." "He saw a very wide valley, all sown with something like barley, and he felt that in it there should be some large towns." "And here also there is a very beautiful beach, and a grove of many kinds of trees, all loaded with fruit, which the Admiral thought to be spices and nutmegs, but, since they were not ripe, he could not identify them." "And they found many mastic trees and brought some of it in, and they said there was a great deal more of it, only this is not the season to gather it, for it does not coagulate [until ripe]."

If we leave all this to one side, what have we left? Praise of the softness of the air and the purity of the water—as villagers do when they have nothing else to boast of—praise of the meadows, as green as those of Andalusia in April and May. He changes provinces, sometimes saying Seville, sometimes Córdoba, sometimes the *Vega* of Granada, and pronounces eulogies of the Indians, although we know by now that he despises them. "The people of the islands make war on each other, although they are very simple and handsome men." Everything is idyllic. He even eulogizes the singing of the frogs and crickets at night: "The singing of the crickets all night long, to the pleasure of all."

Never, as I have said, does Columbus give us a disinterested description. When he finds no gold, he goes on about nature, and even in this he always implies: "My eyes never tired of gazing upon such beautiful verdure, so different from ours, and I even believe there are in it many herbs and many trees which would be valuable in Spain for making dyestuffs and medicinal spices; but I am not acquainted with them, to my great regret. All the trees were green and loaded with fruit, and the herbs were all very tall and in flower; the roads very wide and good; the air like that of Castile in April; the nightingales and other birds were singing as in the said month in Spain, and they say it was the sweetest music in the world. By night little birds sang softly; crickets and frogs were heard in numbers; the fishes were like those of Spain; many mastic trees were to be seen, and aloes and cotton plantations. They found no gold, which is not surprising in such a short time."

In these commonplaces the fine sensitivity of certain historians has detected a great poet, "the first and greatest of American poets," it has been said. They have uncovered the surprising spectacle of a superior man astonished by a never-before-seen nature, writing a Pastoral Symphony. No. My attitude will be called censorious, when it is only a desire to see things clearly. Columbus was a business man, and it is useless to demand of him lyrical delicacies which he did not feel.

Let us leave *La Niña* on her way to Spain with the good news. The Admiral is on *his* way to glory and the honors he has always dreamed of, and periods of contentment are usually the most boring. It is for this reason, when the happy moment for the principal actors arrives, that the accounts end. Let's get on to the year 1500. Christopher Columbus—not yet Admiral—goes to Spain. *La Niña*, that swift and graceful ship, has yielded her place to another with an ugly name, *La Gorda*. Columbus has been removed from the command he exercised in Española, and his feet are in fetters. Next to him are his brothers, Bartolomé and Diego, also fettered.

In this passage of almost two months, Columbus, caught in the dullness of immobility, recalls many things: his arrival in Spain upon his return from the first voyage, when the people gathered along his way; the King of Portugal granting him an audience in Lisbon; the Catholic Monarchs, in Barcelona. He had been seated next to them, had shown them his Indians, and he, the son of a weaver, had been given a coat of arms, on which it was inscribed that he, and he alone, had given a New World to Castile and to León.

It was a glorious moment also when, with drums beating and

banners flying, his men discharging their pieces in the air, he had sailed away to take possession of the gold mines of Cibao, where he had ordered a fortress built and had given it the name of Santo Tomás, to the confusion of the unbelievers, some of whom had thought he would find no gold, and especially when those lazy Spaniards who had so laughed at him had to go to work opening roads and making bread. They had thought that gold would be waiting for them, "washed up on the beaches," as Las Casas would say later on, and that they were going to get it without having to wait years and years, as he had. One was Fermín Zedo of Seville, who has such a large part in the second voyage "because he was a man of much knowledge about gold," and who began by saying there wasn't any, but it later turned out that "he knew very little about it." Then there was Father Buyl, and Bernal de Pisa with his servant Roldán, all against Columbus, whom they accused of being hard, his brother also, as if the conditions at Isabela, the colony he had founded, had not justified the most violent measures.

If only the Monarchs, if only Queen Isabella, who had so strongly urged the gentle treatment of the Indians, and who demanded so much gold—if she had only been there to see how much work it took to get it! Because the Indian is indolent and would rather kill himself than make an effort, however slight! And King Ferdinand, that old fox, apt to agree with everyone and with no one, suspicious, most uneasy, capable of issuing the severest orders against the Admiral, and then receiving him with open arms and a thousand excuses!

Did Columbus really think that way? Alas for the poor devil of a historian, forced always to guess! We don't know what Columbus thought. He was a prisoner. Why? Historians of a parliamentary bent have accused him of bad management. Columbus, the great mariner, shows himself to be incapable of governing the colony. And so on. We cannot say the same today. Columbus was the best manager when he was given an end to pursue that did not allow the slightest deviation in its means, just he had allowed no deviation in the route of his first voyage. The apparent contradictions and weaknesses observed in his conduct originate in a power superior to his own, that of the Crown, with which he had to temporize. When he is on his own, the consistency of all his acts, his hardness, his lack of humanity, are exemplary. Upon his return from Spain on his second voyage, the first thing he and his companions saw when they landed, after certain indications that cannot be explained, was two corpses, "one that of a young man, the other apparently of an old man, and the old man had about his neck a rope of esparto grass, such as is made in Castile, and his arms were outspread and his hands tied to a beam, as on a cross." They are Spaniards. In *Thomas l'imposteur* Jean Cocteau remarks: "A miracle, if it continues, ceases to be considered as such. This is why apparitions disappear so quickly." The thirty-eight men of the Trinidad garrison had been in contact too long for them to be adored as gods. They had wandered off, stolen women, gold, and anything else they had taken a fancy to. The Indians had killed them to a man. And what does Columbus do when he hears of the disaster? Does he weep? Does he mourn? Does he consider reprisals? "The Admiral ordered the whole site searched where the Christians had been fortified, for he had ordered them to bury all the gold they had." Cruelty? No. A unilateral, exclusive act. He does the same with the Indians. In his instructions to Captain Pedro Margarite, commandant of the fortress of Santo Tomás, he recommends that "they be not harmed or illused; nor shall anything be taken from them without their consent; rather, that they be honored and reassured, to keep them from taking offense." And then he adds: "And since on the journey I made to Cibao it happened that an Indian stole something and I had his nose and ears cut off, if you should learn that one of them is stealing you will punish him in the same way, because these are members that cannot be concealed; and in this fashion trade with the people of the whole island will be made safe. And you will give them to understand that such Indians were punished for the thefts they had committed; and you will command that the good Indians be very well treated, and the bad ones punished."

Cruelty? To be sure, from the Indians' point of view. When Columbus imposed barbarous and excessive tributes in gold, he was doing neither good nor bad, but only his duty. "He then ordered that a kind of copper or brass tag be struck, on which a mark should appear, and this mark should be changed with each tribute payment, and that each Indian tributary should wear one about his neck, so that we may know who has paid his tribute and who not."

For some centuries now stupendous things have been told of this meticulous man, of this great organizing talent, which reach their apogee in Jacob Wassermann's book, *Columbus der Don Quichote des Ozeans* (1929), where one reads paragraphs like the following: "He knew not what he did. He will be brought before the Highest Judge, and the Lord will forgive him. At no time, in good things or in bad, did he know what he did."

We wonder whether Wassermann had read the report that Antonio de Torres, captain of the *nao Marigalante* and commandant of the fortress at Isabela, made to the Catholic Monarchs in 1494. Was the writer of this careful report a dreamer, a poet, a man who lived in the clouds and understood nothing of reality, the writer of a report in which all loose ends are tied up? In which he speaks of the animals needed: "We want live sheep, preferably young ones, with more ewes than rams, and some small calves, male and female, to be shipped over in any caravel sailing this way, and some asses, male and female, and mares for work and breeding, for there are none of these beasts here which can be used by man." He tells how the vessels should be loaded. It is more profitable and less expensive to load such ships as the merchants load them for Flanders, by *toneladas* (by volume). He tells about the wine wasted through faulty cooperage. He asks that ore-washers be sent over "like those of the mines at Almadén." He suggests sending to Castile a few Indians to learn the language, "who are not to talk to each other or see each other except very infrequently, and who will learn faster there [in Castile] than here." It will be better if these Indians are cannibals [Caribs], "because the islands of the cannibals are very large and well populated. So it seems to us here that it would do only good to capture some of them and send them to Castile, because they would thus be cured at once of their abominable habit of eating human flesh, and there in Castile they would very soon be baptized, to the profit of their

souls; and even among the people here who have not such customs we should gain great credit, since we had seized and captured those from whom they commonly suffer, and of whom
they are so afraid that they are terrified at their very name."

"He knew not what he did?"

Wassermann's notion no longer holds. Modern opinion, reflected in the most diverse books and authors, is that Columbus
was a visionary, a mystic, and that as such he obeyed strange
forces, which, in the eyes of the romantics, came from Providence, but which, according to the positivists, were the result
of his scanty learning. All insist, with praise or with censure,
upon the sincere religious feeling of Columbus. For the romantics he is God's messenger, and as such we see him, not only
in Washington Irving and Roselly de Lorgues, who consider
him impeccable, but in Humboldt and in our Menéndez y
Pelayo, who follows Humboldt's lead and says: "Neither the
scientific ideal by itself, nor much less self-interest and calculation, would have sufficed to produce the discovery; and it was
providential that the discoverer should possess within himself
such diverse qualities of the mystic. . . ." The positivists accept
Columbus the mystic by denigrating him. Thus Ruge, perhaps
the best of them all, says: "He was a fantastic dreamer, living
in his own self-created mystic world, in his belief in authority,
which he conceived to be above all things." Sophus Ruge was
a professor of geography in the century of enlightenment, and
his attitude cannot surprise us today. But it is also Vignaud, who
is always so careful in his judgments, who does not doubt the
religiosity of the discoverer. There was no priest in the first
voyage, "which is rather surprising, in view of the great piety
of Columbus and the religious character that he attributes to
his work."

Despite these opinions, I believe that Columbus was not at
all a religious man. The piety that is claimed for him was fabri-
cated, conscious, extroverted, ritualistic. Just as in materialistic
periods, our own, for example (I am writing in 1929), those
who have religious sentiments tend to conceal them, because the
archetype of today is the "strong man," the "self-made man," the

industrialist, the flyer, Henry Ford, Stinnes, and the like, who calculate everything and leave nothing to chance or supernatural forces. Columbus, who was that same type of the cool strong man, set down in the fifteenth century, saw himself, in speaking of his work, as the agent of God, impelled by supernatural forces that guided his steps. But this does not extend beyond a form of expression to which we could assign a date—which takes away from it all the meaning it would have today. The religiosity of Columbus is as secondary in his spirit, is as self-interested and dependent upon practical results, as his supposed feeling for nature.

In his first voyage he completely forgets the religious purposes of the expedition and limits himself to planting crosses on several promontories along the coast. If he mentions the conversion of the Indians, it is only in passing. Take, for example, the following passage in his log: "This is a very green, level, and very fertile island, and I have no doubt that they sow and harvest grain all the year long, and so with everything else. And I saw many trees very unlike ours, and many of them had their branches loaded with fruit of all kinds, all growing from one trunk, and one little branch has one appearance, and the next a different one, so unlike that it is a most marvelous thing to see how unlike they are. For example, one branch had leaves like those of [sugar] canes, and another like those of the mastic, so that on a single tree there are five or six like that, all very different. Nor are they grafted, as one might think, rather they are in the forests and not cultivated by the people. I saw no evidence of religion among them, but I believe they could be converted, because they are of good understanding. The fishes here are so different from ours that it is an astonishing thing. Some look like cocks, with the finest colors in the world, blue, yellow, red, and of all colors; others painted in a thousand different ways; and the colors are so fine that there is not a man who does not marvel at them and take great pleasure in looking at them. There are whales also, but on land I saw no cattle of any kind."

Note the space he devotes to plants, to fishes, and to religion, and the conclusion can be drawn. The following paragraph can also serve us as a guide: "I take it for granted, Most Serene

Princes, that if devout religious persons should learn their language, they would soon all become Christians, and so I hope in God that Your Highnesses will diligently apply yourselves to it in order to bring such numerous peoples to the Church and convert them, just as you have destroyed those who refused to believe in the Father, Son, and Holy Ghost. And after your death (for we are all mortal), you will leave your kingdoms in a very peaceful state, free of heresy and wickedness, and you will be well received in the presence of the Eternal Creator, whom I pray to grant you a long life and a great increase of your kingdoms and seigneuries, and the desire to magnify the Holy Christian religion, as you have done in the past, amen. Today I cleared the *nao* and am readying her to depart, with the help of God, on Thursday, and sail to the southeast in quest of gold and spices, and to explore the land."

It is needless to emphasize the difference in tone of this last paragraph and the sudden transition. Poor Columbus here suffers the same vagaries that he had suffered when he discovered the beautiful landscapes of the tropics: "And so, Your Highnesses should decide to make Christians of them, for I believe that once they begin, in a short while a multitude of people will be entirely converted to our Holy Faith, and you will acquire great seigneuries and riches, and will add all their people to Spain, because doubtless there is in this land a very great quantity of gold, for these Indians that I am bringing say, not without cause, that there are places in these islands where they dig it up. . . ."

The historians call this an astonishing mixture of sentiments. Does the attitude of Columbus toward Father Buyl, as described by Fernández de Oviedo, mean nothing? "There were many disputes between the Admiral and the reverend father, Fray Buyl. And these came about when the Admiral hanged several men, especially one Gaspar Ferriz, an Aragonese, and had others whipped, and began to show himself more severe and cruel than he had been before." In the opinion of the friar the Admiral was guilty of cruelty and, since he was the Pope's vicar, he opposed him. "And so, when Columbus, in the administration of justice, did anything the friar thought unjust, he at once proclaimed an interdict and stopped divine services. And then the Admiral ordered his ration cut off, and ordered that neither Fray Buyl nor any of his staff might be given anything to eat. Mosén Pedro Margarite and the other gentlemen tried to make peace between them, and they became friends again, but only for a few days, for as soon as the Admiral did any of those things that have been mentioned the father opposed him and again proclaimed an interdict, and stopped the prayers and divine services; and the Admiral again imposed an interdict on the rations, and would not allow the friar or the clerics or their servitors to be given any." In such cases religion had to give way before his will. But then, as if afraid of being punished by the Crown, he lets his beard grow and assumes the Franciscan habit. "And so," says Bernáldez, "a few days later he [Buyl] told the Admiral to ready himself to return to Spain, which the Admiral felt to be a grave matter, so he dressed himself in brown like a friar and let his beard grow."

Humboldt sees in this a typical mark of Columbus's piety. As I do. How can one explain that he had the miners purified when they went off to look for gold? Says Oviedo: "Admiral Don Christopher Columbus . . . would not allow the Spaniards to seek gold until they had first confessed and taken communion. And he said that since the Indians went twenty days without having intercourse with their wives (or other women), and stayed away from them and fasted, in the belief that otherwise they would find no gold; therefore [he said], since the barbarous Indians observed that rite, it was all the more reason for the Christians to desist from sinning, and to confess, and that, being in a state of grace with God, Our Lord would more fully grant them temporal and spiritual goods. This sanctimony did not please everybody. They said that, as for women, they were farther away from them than the Indians were, since their wives were in Spain; and as for fasting, many Christians were dying of hunger and were eating roots and other evil dainties, and drinking water; and, as for confessing, the Church obliged them to confess only once a year."

Up to this point I [formerly] had no doubts concerning the piety of Columbus; but, after his arrest, when I learned that on his return voyage to Spain he busied himself composing his

Book of Prophecies, I was led to accept the judgment of Menéndez y Pelayo, who found in that book "the philosophy of discovery as Columbus understood it, and a greatness of spirit that should move the most skeptical to a respectful veneration." Like everyone else, I thought I saw here a profound crisis, a complete change in the spirit of the Admiral, and I even went so far as to sketch out a theory *more germanico*, according to which Columbus had two personalities: the one practical, the Genoese; the other mystical, the Castilian. And then I made comparisons with Charles V and El Greco, typical cases of Castilian absorption. My satisfaction was great when I discovered the same idea in Humboldt: 'The theological fervor characteristic of Columbus did not come to him from Italy, that republican, commercial country, avid for the wealth that had given birth to her. He had imbibed it during his sojourn in Andalusia and Granada, and in his intimate conversation with the monks of La Rábida, his dearest and most useful friends. Such was his devotion that upon his return from the second voyage in 1496, he appeared on the streets of Seville wearing the habit of St. Francis. Faith for Columbus was the source of various inspirations: it sustained his courage in the midst of the most menacing danger; it made endurable his long adversities with the charm of ascetic reveries. . . ."

In short, I had to resign myself bravely to reading the *Book of Prophecies*, which was anything but a pleasant task, and I found myself lost in a dark night, as is to be expected in any apprentice mystic, when Las Casas' book showed me the light —I shall explain why later on—. In all these apparent moments of delirium and these wanderings of a mind tormented and overwhelmed by suffering, and so on, Columbus was seeking a practical and immediate advantage, as he always did. This otherworldly and visionary book was a plea for the restoration of his rights. In this view the following sentences become completely understandable: "I have navigated every sea that up to the present time has been navigated. I have associated with and consulted learned men, ecclesiastics and laymen, Latins and Greeks, Jews and Moors, and many others of different sects." "I say that I am giving up all my navigating in this new age, from this time on, as I am giving up the intercourse I have had with so many people in so many lands and of so many sects, and all the books of instructions and writings that I have spoken of, and shall cling only to the Holy and Sacred Scriptures, and to certain authoritative prophecies of certain holy men, who by divine revelation have said something about this matter." "For the execution of the enterprise of the Indies, I have said that I did not rely upon arguments or mathematics or maps of the world, but upon the fulfillment of the prophecy of Isaiah, and this is what I wish to write here, to bring it to the attention of Your Highnesses."

Here we have it. If he has succeeded in demonstrating that he and no other was called to be the discoverer of the Indies, the Monarchs will not fail to reinstate him in the dignities snatched from him by Bobadilla. Proof that Columbus was not wasting his time is afforded by his letter of September 13, 1501, to Father Gorricio, in which he speaks of the prophecies, and on the 28th of the same month and year comes the order for restitution: "The Comendador de Lares is ordered to restore to Columbus and his brothers all the gold and jewels and cattle farms and stocks of bread and wine, and books and clothing and personal adornments, which the Comendador Bobadilla had taken from them, and to send his officers [to him] with the tithe and the eighth part of gold, and all the other gains and profits described in the capitulations."

The Monarchs should restore his privileges and annul the licences they had issued to other explorers. It was God, not Columbus, who demanded it. One doesn't know what to admire most in this idea, its ingenuousness or its audacity. Columbus still maintains, as he will maintain to the end, his attitude of pleader, his continuous importunation which we mentioned in his first steps, and which now turns away from earthly courts and toward the celestial, bringing God into service for his purposes. Rather than Columbus's being the servant of God, as has been said, God was the servant of Columbus. His vision at Veragua (so designated by Humboldt) means nothing else: the voice that the Admiral hears in moments of extreme peril on his fourth voyage, that apologetic and laudatory voice which

enumerates his services with his usual insistence: "O thou foolish one, slow to believe in thy God and serve him, the God of
all. . . . When He saw thee to be of an age pleasing to Him,
He made thy name marvelously to resound in the world. The
rich Indies, which are part of that world, He gave them thee
for thine, and thou didst distribute them as thou didst please,
and He gave thee authority to do so. . . . I have told thee what
thy Creator has done for thee and what He does for all. Now
He shows thee thy reward for thy sufferings and the perils
through which thou has passed in the service of others." Now
that God is so clearly on the side of Columbus, it follows that
his enemies and Satan are one and the same thing.

In sum, all the supposed mysticism, the prophesying power
and the illumination of Columbus, are no more than a partial
manifestation of that mania of his for lawsuits in his last years,
made famous in the words of Don Francisco de Zúñiga, the buf-
foon of Charles V. If what I have said is not convincing enough,
it will suffice to think of the activity of the Admiral which he
displayed in that same period, when he was preparing a new
expedition. In the words of Angelo Trivigiano, secretary of the
Venetian legation in Spain: "Columbus is making preparations
for another expedition of discovery, and he says he wishes to
make another voyage, more beautiful and profitable than any
other that has been made. I believe he will soon depart. He
will be accompanied by many of my friends, who upon their
return will give me an account of the whole affair. Many caravels have been readied at Cadiz which at any time now will sail
for Española with 3,000 men." Las Casas tells us the same, although he reduces the figures of the Venetian: "The Monarchs
finally sent the Admiral off, and they ordered him to be given
all the provisions in Seville and Cadiz necessary for the preparation of his fleet or armada. He left the city of Granada for
Seville with them in the month of October, and there busied
himself in their shipment very diligently. He bought four ships
. . . and got together a crew of 140 men, young and old. . . ."

A Dios rogando y con el palo dando [which may be translated, "Praise God but keep your powder dry"]. Once the cloud
of mysticism has been dissipated (for "Everything uncertain is

frightening"—Croce), we have the Columbus we already know, the seeker after gold, who in the midst of the horrors of his last voyage finds strength enough to cry: "Gold is most excellent. With gold we have wealth. He who possesses it does what he will in the world, even to the point of sending souls to Paradise."

Revista de Occidente. Madrid, February, 1930.

Two Studies on
the Same Subject

*"In any piece of historical writing,
arrangement is the thing. Explanations of fact,
each of which is true, may be arranged in many
ways, and, since some arrangement is always
necessary, no historian can be truly impartial."*
SHOTWELL, *History of History*

The present situation of those of us who have
been trained in historical studies within the cheerful and com-
fortable framework of the postivist creed is not to be envied. In
it we dozed, while we devoted ourselves to an unhurried search
for documents and the accumulation of "facts," and tried to
smother our scruples under the belief that interpretation and
synthesis would come later on, a task for future generations,
who were to build upon the solid foundation that we would
bequeath to them.

What a carefree life, that of our professors, in their painstaking quest! No philosophical worries, no visions of a common
goal, not a shadow of disturbing or contradictory ideas! Unearth the facts, publish new documents, refine your philological
techniques, pile up materials, and the truth will drop into your
laps like a ripe fruit!

And today? By chance does anything remain of those innocent dreams? Have we truly learned so much from the heaps of
materials that our predecessors accumulated so diligently? Or,
on the contrary, do we not find ourselves overwhelmed, tired

out, and faced with the prospect of suffering the fate of Anatole France's scholar, who was buried beneath the avalanche of his own reference cards?

Unfortunately, we must accept this last possibility as true, for, lulled by the confident and persuasive attitude of the positivists, who, when all is said and done, limited themselves to repeating, consciously or unconsciously, *Après moi le deluge*, we find that the deluge has already begun and threatens to drown us.

At first glance the prospect could hardly be more discouraging. Positivism dehumanized history and, what is worse, dehumanized the historian. It prescribed for him a total indifference in his research and demanded of him that he hold himself aloof from all the conflicts and ideas of his time, and that he rid himself of all subjective content. Only in this fashion could the historian analyze and evaluate the productions of epochs and cultures different from his own, and acquire difficult historical knowledge.

Has he succeeded? No. When the historian emptied himself of humanity, he also emptied his work of meaning. Instead of gaining greater breadth, what he has done is to lower its level, with the evident result that today, as a general rule, people do not read history. The historian little by little has reduced himself to the point of exchanging notes with his colleagues, as he might exchange postage stamps, or solve chess games by mail. At best, the man in the street thinks of the historian as a poor creature, incapable of facing life, taking refuge in the past because there he has no competition, no conflict, beyond his power of confronting. Today, as always, the man in the street is avid to read history and eagerly scans the productions of those who, having taken an active part in the whirlwind of their own time, give the story of their participation a pulse, a breath of passion, which is never to be found in the works of the professional historians.

It seems undeniable to me that, if any historical writing has survived at its full power in our day, it is biography, cultivated —with a greater or smaller degree of mystification—by men outside the field of history proper, men who in their writings have carefully avoided the coldness, the solemnity, the stench of death, which are so apparent in the productions of "scientific" history.

Does this not indicate to us the road we should take? Is it not clearly to be seen in the success of certain biographies published in recent years in which a grateful public perceives the elements that have always been considered essential to history, that is, a well-told story, an intelligent selection that brings out certain aspects of it and, in turn, sets aside everything useless and confusing? But there is more to it than that. Among historical writings biography is the only genre that has managed to keep in touch with human life, rejecting the indifference of which the "scientific" historians make such a parade. This is what has rescued history from catastrophe, because history is, as Huizinga tells us, the one discipline that maintains closest contact with life, and it will be killed out of hand if this intimate relationship is destroyed.

It may be, then, that all is not lost, that there is an escape route open to the historian, only it lies in a direction opposite to that which he has been taking lately. The historian will have to humanize himself again and accept the lowly fact that he too is a limited being, a complex of ideas and passions and instincts—a man, in short, with all the grandeur and humility implied in the word, and that only in this fashion, by accepting beforehand all his limitations of time, place, culture, in a word, the way of life of his own time, will he be able to focus his attention upon the past, fertilize his vision with his own vital experience, and in turn allow himself to be fertilized by the past itself.

These and other considerations which today worry and vex many students of history, were forcibly brought to my attention by the contradictory impressions made upon me by certain studies that I was engaged in, and by the vicissitudes of my own life. I am aware that it is not quite the thing for a historian to talk about himself; but I cannot avoid it, nor do I wish to do so. Before the Spanish Civil War I was preparing a critical edition of the *True History of the Conquest of New Spain* by Bernal Díaz del Castillo. Having been invited to read a paper before the XXVI Congress of Americanists at Seville, in 1935, I was obliged to summarize pretty drastically—as one is always forced to do—my notions about some aspects of Spanish historiography, especially the work of Bernal Díaz. That summary comprises the first of the two studies presented below. In it I accept as true the story of the conquest as given by Bernal, that is, that it was the men of Cortés' company, and not Cortés himself, who carry its whole weight and who take the initiative and responsibility in its most critical moments. Cortés is only one man among many.

If the Civil War had not intervened, the prologue that I planned to write for my edition of Bernal, of which the study I mentioned is only a sketch, would have been conceived and oriented in similar terms. But the war broke out, I was caught up in it, and so acquired a direct and living experience of military problems, an experience that all the history books in the world could not have given me. I saw at first hand what war is, a touchstone for all human values, because in war we are always under the pressure of death, which in ordinary times is kept out of sight. I saw the part played by commanders who knew how to command, and the part played by soldiers who knew how to obey and die, and I saw the deep need of hierarchy and discipline in an army, something that we had been forgetting, or perhaps scorning, in our civilized, liberal, and individualized society. And this is what made me review my whole concept of a number of historical problems, including the work of Bernal Díaz. After the war I re-read his book and studied more carefully than before the text of Gómara. I compared the two and derived conclusions that will be found in the second of the studies offered below. In them, although I do not accept the exclusive importance that Gómara gives to Cortés, I recognize now that Cortés' part in the conquest was much more significant than Bernal allows.

Would I have experienced this change in my point of view if the Civil War had not affected my life so tremendously? Surely not. For this reason it occurred to me that the simultaneous publication of the two studies might be of interest to those trusting believers who think that the simple accumulation of data in a straight line is the best approach to historical knowledge. This may give them something to think about, for what occurred with me was not a simple accumulation of data, *but a change in my point of view*, brought about, not by reading and reflection, but by a living experience, an *Erlebnis*. One and the same person—if it is allowable to say that I am the same person I was before the war—this person, studying the same theme, using the same method, can derive different and even opposite conclusions if his life has suffered a change. Is this not a theme worthy of the attention of the scientific historians? I believe it is. . . .

Is it possible, then, as we have been told lately, for the historian to put aside his personality completely? If it is not possible, to what extent can or should his personality and the feeling of his time and circumstances affect his vision of the past? What complex of ideas and sentiments does the historian use, consciously or unconsciously, to analyze the facts and select and interpret them, now that the need for selection, interpretation, and synthesis is so urgently recognized? Will not this subjective element upset the unity and cohesion of the historical knowledge that was acquired with such a deal of effort? I submit these pressing questions to awaken the positivist historians and interrupt their endless siesta of publishing documents. If it is true that such questions complicate horribly the mission of the historian, it is also true that his work risks sterility if he does not try to answer them honestly and straightforwardly.

I. Bernal Díaz del Castillo and Popularism in Spanish Historiography (1935)

"Of all disciplines, history is the one that most closely approaches life. To this indestructible relationship history owes her weakness and her strength. It makes her norms variable and her trustworthiness doubtful. At the same time it gives her universality, significance, and sobriety."

These words of Huizinga very likely have general application, but I consider them more applicable to Spain than to any other country. In Spain history is so intimately linked with life that our most valuable historical works were written, so to speak, on the wire edge of events, works that sprang from a direct knowledge of those events, from living with them.

It frequently happens that a Spanish scholar, composing a history of a lofty and scientific kind based upon documents and reading, fails in his purpose. It will suffice, for example, to recall what happened with the official history of the Indies. On the other hand, any witness of, or actor in, significant events commonly has among us Spaniards a capacity and a plastic power of description, a directness of style and accuracy of detail, which I do not believe are equalled in the historical works of other nations.

Historical works flourish on our soil. The medieval chronicle had the purpose of relating the deeds of kings, as we are told in the Chronicle of Alfonso X, which, in the opinion of Fueter, is a model of the genre. Indeed, after Alfonso X each Spanish monarch has one or more chronicles devoted to the events of his reign, the authors of which are not always known.

In the fifteenth century, when the royal power declines under the feeble kings of the House of Trastamara, the chronicles relate not only the deeds of kings, but also those of the nobles. nificent one of Don Pero Niño, Count of Buelna, that glass of chivalry. Next to the Chronicle of Don Juan II appears that of his favorite, Don Alvaro de Luna; next to that of Henry IV appear those of the Constable Miguel Lucas de Iranzo, his favorite, and Don Alonso de Monroy, Treasurer of the Order of Alcántara, and others, while kings and nobles are paraded in the stupendous gallery of portraits by Pérez de Guzmán, entitled *Generaciones y Semblanzas*.

It was in the fifteenth century also that the travel book made its appearance in our country, such as the delightful *Andanzas* of Pero Tafur, knight of a noble Andalusian family, who, taking advantage of the truce with the Moors of Granada, made a journey to the Holy Land and visited various countries. Tafur, who fills his book with tall stories of prodigies, nevertheless tells us: "I learned a great deal about the city of Damascus, but, since I did not see it, I shall leave its description to someone who did."

At the height of the Renaissance, during the reign of the Catholic Monarchs, when historians were trying to raise their tone by imitating models of classical antiquity—and succeeded only in swamping their works with windy ramblings, as in the Chronicle of Hernando del Pulgar—we have a fine example of popular, direct narrative in the *Memoirs* of Andrés Bernáldez, priest of Los Palacios. Bernáldez is not ashamed to confess that he is writing his book at the urging of his grandmother: "I, who wrote these memoirs at the age of twelve, read in the journal of my late grandfather that he had been a notary public in the *villa* of Fuentes, in the *encomienda mayor* of León, where I was born, and there I found accounts of some great events that had taken place in his day; and his wife, my grandmother, a widow, who was then approaching her dotage, said to me: 'Why do you not write of the events of today, which are just as great as those of olden times? You should not hesitate to describe the things happening today, so that they may be known to those who come afterward, and who, stricken with wonder when they read of them, will give thanks to God.'" Bernáldez even tells us how Queen Isabella tore her hair when she learned of the defection of Archbishop Don Alonso Carrillo, "Who had unwisely advised the Queen to inquire whether or not he was really in Alcalá, telling her that when she should enter by one gate, he would escape by the other. And, after Mass, when the Queen learned that he had actually done so, she was so furious that she tore her hair."

Bernáldez reflects the dawn of the emerging Spain in the lines of a children's song: "After the wars had broken out in Castile between King Henry and the nobles of his kingdom, and before the marriage of Don Ferdinand and Queen Isabella, a song was sung by the new people of Castile, who are charmed by music, to the tune of *Flores de Aragón, dentro de Castilla son.* And children waved little flags, and knights curvetted on their horses, and they shouted: *Pendón de Aragón, Pendón de Aragón!* And I myself shouted it more than a few times, so that one might say: *Domine, ex ore infantium et lactantium per-fecisti laudem.*" In the same familiar vein Bernáldez pens un-surpassed pages about the taking of Granada, the expulsion of the Jews, and the discovery of the New World. His portrait of Columbus is justly famous.

While in Spain erudite historians are wreaking havoc, writing extravagant accounts of the life of *El Gran Capitán*, Latin screeds on the life of Cisneros, a vast lot of sketches about Charles V, and collecting documents about him, the unlettered Spaniard of the Indies, with his delight in contemplating never-before-seen wonders and in performing fantastic exploits, over-flows his banks in a boundless flood. His subject is no longer the heroic deed of kings and nobles, but those of any captain or soldier in an expedition of conquest, thereby lowering the so-cial level of author and subject. Fernández de Oviedo makes it clear that he is concerned with a typically Spanish trait: "This is a rare and precious gift of nature, not to be seen so fully and generously conceded in any other nation as in the Spanish peo-ple, because in Italy, France, and most of the countries of the world, only the nobles are especially trained in, or naturally in-clined to war, for of the common people and those engaged in the mechanical arts and agriculture, and plebeians, few are those in foreign nations who take up arms or have any desire to do so. But in our Spain it seems that all are commonly born to, and principally dedicated to, arms and their exercise. And so true is this that everything else is merely accessory, and they willingly abandon it in favor of a military life. And this is the reason why, although they are few in number, the Spanish con-quistadors have always accomplished in those parts what the men of other nations have failed to do."

It is a foreigner, Friederici, who tells us that there is no other country with so large a number of soldier-chroniclers as our own. It is characteristic of them that they despise book learn-ing, even though they tend to display, ingenuously and fre-quently, the little that they do possess. Gonzalo Fernández de Oviedo offers a prime example of this attitude, informing us at every step that erudition and elegance of style are worthless unless the author has lived through the events he describes.

His target is Peter Martyr, the court chronicler, who wrote his *Décadas de Orbe Novo* without leaving Spain, "Especially since the said authors relate what they please, not as actors, like our Spaniards, but as mere armchair spectators." "I did not gather my materials from the two thousand volumes I might have read . . . , but got everything I have written here from the two thousand travails and hardships and perils I underwent in the past twenty-two years and more, in which I witnessed and experienced these things in my own person." Outbursts like these are frequent in the pages of Oviedo.

If, deep down, Oviedo feared that his culture was insufficient, even more fearful was Captain Bernal Díaz del Castillo, one of the fighting men who distinguished themselves in the conquest of Mexico. He tells us himself that he abandoned his writing when the chronicle of Gómara, the chaplain of Cortés, came to his hands. Nevertheless, and happily for us, he took up his task again when he became convinced of the misstatements made by the priestly panegyrist of his chief. Bernal Díaz has the same attitude toward Gómara that Oviedo has toward Peter Martyr. Even so, although his book possesses unique and marvelous qualities, posterity has not done justice to its merits, but rather has accepted the adverse judgment of Antonio de Solís, the eighteenth-century chronicler, who, buttressed behind his excellent prose, has given us the classical version of the Spanish conquest of Mexico. Solís says of Bernal's work: "Today it is accepted as true history, owing to the very slovenliness and unadorned simplicity of its style, which has the effect of establishing its verisimilitude and convincing some readers of the writer's sincerity. But, although he is favored by the fact that he has witnessed the events he wrote about, it is evident from his work that he is not so free of prejudice as to keep it out of his pages. He shows himself to be as satisfied with his simplicity as he is querulous about his own fortunes. In his lines his envy and ambition are undisguised, and often his ill-tempered feelings turn into complaints of Cortés, the principal character of his history, whose designs he tries to fathom, for the purpose of belittling and amending his counsels, frequently asserting as fact, not what his commander had ordered and planned, but the grumblings of the soldiers, in whose republic there is as much of mob spirit as there is in any other, all republics being equally endangered if those who were born to obey are allowed to express their opinions."

Historians, in their evaluation of the chronicle of Bernal, usually follow the lead of Solís. All of them speak of his crudity of style, his arrogance, and the animosity toward Cortés he shows in his chronicle. All of which is inexact. It would be difficult to surpass Bernal's style in its descriptive force and grace of narration. He has a feeling for effective detail, aided by an astonishing memory. When Alonso de Grado, a captain who had fallen foul of Cortés, spends two days in the stocks, Bernal tells us of it, and adds: "I remember that the wood of the stocks smelled something like garlic or onions." In his desire to attain the greatest credibility he does not think it beneath him to relate the smallest details. He never forgets to count the steps of the temples. "And then we descended the steps, and, since there were a hundred and fourteen of them, and since some of our soldiers were sick with the buboes or humors, their thighs hurt when they climbed down." Nor did the heaps of skulls escape his attention. "I remember that in a square, where there were certain shrines, a great many rows of skulls were piled up in such wise that they could be counted, for they were regularly arranged, and it seems that there were more than a hundred thousand of them. In another part of the square there were so many rows of shinbones and bones of dead men that they could not be counted."

It is not in relating the minute details, however vigorous and savory they may be, that Bernal is the great artist, but in his wider pictures, where his pen retains its precision and strength. He describes the reversals in a combat with as much care as he gives to the fight in the great market of Mexico, or to the life that Moctezuma led. Here is a scene chosen at random:

"And after these exchanges they told us in sign language that we should go with them to their village, and we wondered whether we should go or not, and we decided to go, but cautiously. And they took us to some very large houses, which were shrines for their idols, well constructed of stone and lime, and on the walls many figures of serpents and great snakes were painted, and other pictures of ugly idols; and around them, beyond the idols, on something resembling an altar, there were objects like crosses, all painted, at which we were astonished, as by something never-before-seen or heard of. And it seems that at that time they had sacrificed some Indians to their idols, to induce them to give them victory over us, and many Indian women were laughing and enjoying themselves, apparently very peaceably. But so many Indians were assembling that we feared we might be in for a row like the one we had at Cotoche. And while they were standing around in this fashion, many other Indians came up, dressed in very ragged blankets, carrying dry reeds, which they deposited on a flat place. And after them came two companies of Indian bowmen, with lances and shields and stones, clad in cotton armor, in formation, each company with its captain, and they took their stand a little apart from us. And then at that moment ten Indians emerged from another house, which was also a shrine for their idols, wearing long white blankets that came down to their feet, their hair very long and tangled and matted with blood, so matted that it could not be separated with a comb, but would have to be cut. These last were their priests, who in New Spain are commonly called *papas*, which is what I shall call them from now on. And these papas brought pots of incense, somewhat like resin, which they call *copal*, and with earthen braziers full of burning coals they began to perfume us, and told us in sign language to leave their country before the wood they had there should catch fire and be consumed; otherwise, they would make war on us and kill us. And then they ordered the reeds to be ignited, and the papas left us without another word. And those in the companies who were in fighting trim began to whistle and sound their conches and rattles."

After reading passages like the above, it is hard to understand the verdict of a historian of the stature of Prescott: "The literary merits of the book are slight, as one might expect, given the class of the author." Prescott also speaks of the vulgar vanity of Bernal, who erupts in truly comic ostentation on every page of his book. The great North American historian must have had a strange notion of human nature if, according to him, exploits like the conquest of Mexico would fail to arouse pride in those who participate in them. The conquistadors were fully aware of the historic significance of their acts, and remarks like the following are frequent in Bernal:

"In reply to what you say, gentlemen, that no famous Roman captain ever did such great deeds as we did, I say you speak truly. And now and henceforth, with the help of God, histories will give them greater importance than they gave to those of former times. Since the beginning of the world what men have dared to invade, with four hundred soldiers, and we were even fewer, a strong city like Mexico, which is as large as Venice, more than 1500 leagues from our Castile, and seize such a great lord and execute his captains in his presence?"

If the reader doubts the active participation of our chronicler in the great enterprise, he should read the final chapters of the book, especially the astonishing "List of the battles and skirmishes in which I took part." A man with such exploits to his credit could well afford to talk about them without being accused of vulgar vanity. "And among the stout conquistadors my companions, many of whom were very brave, I was counted as one and the oldest of all. And I say again that I, I, and I, and I repeat it many times, was the oldest of them and have served His Majesty as a very good soldier."

The attitude of Bernal toward Cortés, and the relationship between the soldiers and their commander, poses an extremely delicate question, nothing less than the relationship between an individual genius and the masses. Solís, with his aristocratic bias, answers it bluntly in his words quoted above. Nevertheless, expeditions of conquest may well convince us that he is wrong, that those who participated in them played a very different part from that of the common soldier of our day, and that they were consulted in the most serious decisions. This reduces the singular and outstanding greatness of the leader and makes the mass a principal actor in the epic; it is the mass itself that is endowed with extraordinary and unique qualities. In Bernal's pages this breath of the mass is always throbbing strongly in the urge toward a common goal:

"And this is where the chronicler Gómara tells us that when Cortés ordered the ships scuttled, he did not dare to let the soldiers know that he intended to go to Mexico and seek out the great Moctezuma. But this is not so. Does he imagine that we Spaniards are such as would hesitate to march on to war and riches? And while we were in that *villa* [of Vera Cruz] and had nothing to do but finish the building of the fort, most of us soldiers told Cortés to let it go as it was, since it was now ready for timbering, and we also told him that, now that we had spent more than three months in that country, it would be a good thing to go and find out what kind of person the great Moctezuma was, and to seek booty and adventure."

According to Bernal, Cortés would call together a council of his captains and distinguished soldiers whenever a matter of importance had to be decided: "Our captain resolved to call a meeting of certain captains and a few soldiers who he knew were favorable to him, because they were as intelligent as brave, and because he never did anything without first getting our opinion about it." This should not surprise us, if we bear in mind that when expeditions were planned, the soldiers themselves had a voice in the election of their leader. "And all of us soldiers there present said that Juan de Grijalba should be in charge, since he was a good captain and there was no fault in his person or in his ability to command." Vargas Machuca confirms this state of affairs in his *Milicia y descripción de las Indias*: "The soldier must accept this obligation, he being under the orders of his chief, although this is a duty that the soldiers of the Indies observe very badly, in the arrogant belief that they know as much as their chiefs and that they, being experienced, have no need of anyone to tell them what to do, and, convinced of this, they fall into a thousand errors for which they should be punished."

Bernal never displays malice toward Cortés. "No captain was ever obeyed with as much respect and promptness as Cortés," he tells us, and he adds that he will call Cortés only by his name, with no other title, because the name of Cortés by itself is above all panegyrics. "And, since our captain was bold and daring, I shall omit from here on such epithets as valorous, or brave, nor shall I refer to him as the Marqués del Valle, but only as Hernán Cortés, because the unadorned name of Cortés was held in as much esteem and respect, in all the Indies as well as in Spain, as was the name of Alexander of Macedonia, or, among the Romans, that of Julius Caesar, or Pompey and Scipio, or Hannibal among the Carthaginians, or Gonzalo Hernández [de Córdoba] in our Castile. And the valiant Cortés himself did not wish to be known by those lofty titles, but only by his name."

What Bernal gives us is a living portrait of Cortés, a man of flesh and blood, not a character in an academic tragedy. In Bernal's pages, Cortés, without lessening his heroic stature, purges himself, and laughs and jests with the Indians. He does not use lofty speech, but an ordinary and popular one. "And Cortés said he could not rest, because siestas are not for the lame goat, and that he wanted to be with his men in person." "And Cortés answered them half angrily, saying that it was better to die bravely than in dishonor." Nor will Bernal fail to tell us that, in the division of the spoils, Cortés and his captains took the lion's share, especially when the captive native women were distributed, leaving for the soldiers only the old and ugly. The ponderous Solís apparently had this kind of thing in mind when he wrote: "[That he would not] waste his time in insignificant details, which either soil the page with indecencies, or fill it with what is least worthy, thus adding more to the thickness of the book than to its merit."

I don't believe that today this opinion is shared by anyone. The greatness of a history rests precisely on the fact that its personages are men, not gods. And Solís, who has Cortés wear the buskin of tragedy, must have known that the footgear worn by the chief, as well as by the soldiers, was the alpargata.

The greatest significance of the work of our chronicler is for America, especially for Mexico and Guatemala. The Mexican historian Carlos Pereyra has written pages warm with admiration for the work of Bernal. But it is also a Mexican, Genaro García, the editor of Bernal's chronicle, who levels a new charge against our author. He says of Bernal that he depresses the Indians and exalts the Spaniards more than he should,

"To make a contrast, or, perhaps, to weaken somewhat the interest that the Indians might awaken in the reader." That García is mistaken is apparent from a careful reading of Bernal's pages. Our chronicler greatly admires the warlike virtues of the Mexicans. He speaks with immense respect and affection of Moctezuma and his qualities of a great lord. He loves the Indians of his encomienda and is happy to hear that they will become good Christians.

The conduct of the conquistadores [of Mexico] was more humane than that of any colonial force of our day, as is well proved by the punitive expedition of Gonzalo de Sandoval against a subject town of Texcoco:

"In that town a great deal of blood was found splashed on the walls, blood of the Spaniards they had killed, with which they had sprinkled their idols. Also there were two faces they had flayed, the skins of which were dressed like glove leather, complete with beards, and placed as an offering on one of their altars. There were also the skins of four horses, tanned and very well preserved, with hair and shoes, hanging as an offering to their idols in the main temple. And there were many garments of the Spaniards they had killed and offered to the same idols. And on a wall of the house where the Spaniards had been held captive, these words were written in charcoal: 'Here the luckless Juan Yuste was imprisoned, with many others of his company.' This Juan Yuste was one of the horsemen killed there, one of the persons of quality that Narváez had brought. All of this filled Sandoval and his men with pity, but there was nothing to be done about it except to treat the people of the town with kindness, for they had not waited, but fled, taking their wives and children with them. And some of the women they had captured were weeping for their husbands and fathers. And Sandoval, seeing this, set them free, with four nobles he had taken, together with their wives, and sent them to summon the people of the town, and they all came and begged forgiveness."

I have already spoken of the process of democratization in the chronicles, a process that concerns content rather than style.

There is more popularism and a more direct style in the early royal chronicles than in those of the fifteenth-century nobles. The tendency toward elegance that had blended harmoniously with popularism in Pero López de Ayala—less in Alonso de Palencia—breaks openly with popularism beginning with the Renaissance days of the Catholic Monarchs. By that time the conflict between the vulgar and the learned had become irreducible in historiography. And while the so-called mob opens the way in its own fashion in the splendid flowering of the chronicles of the Indies, which reached its height in the work of Bernal, the learned scholars of the Peninsula lose themselves in collecting materials and polishing their prose. Only direct contact with living events will enliven chronicles such as those of Hurtado de Mendoza and Mármol Carvajal, who wrote of the war with the Moriscos of Granada. This preoccupation with form, which is so pronounced in these two authors, in the seventeenth century will go to the extreme of abandoning the writing of history altogether, in favor of treatises on how history should be written, and discussions of qualities that the historian should possess—Cabrera de Córdoba, for example, and Fray Jerónimo de San José. The baroque school will distort the facts in its quest of interpretations and moral sentences. Scholars of the stature of Nicolás Antonio will introduce the niceties of the seventeenth century. But popular historiography will not raise its head again, for it is buried in America along with the soldiers who wrote it.

II. *Bernal Díaz del Castillo's Criticism of López de Gomara's* History of the Conquest of Mexico (1940)

According to Prescott, the two pillars upon which rests the history of the conquest of Mexico by the Spaniards are the chronicles of Gómara and Bernal Díaz del Castillo. To me, however, these two pillars, with their inimitable symmetry, are not pillars as much as sensitive barometers that register continual changes in the prevailing climate of opinion.

At the moment we are witnessing a rise in the stock of

Bernal Díaz, and he seems definitely to have passed Gómara, who has little hope of regaining his lost ground. I myself, in the XXVI Congress of Americanists held in Seville in 1935, broke a lance in support of Bernal, whose chronicle I was then editing. I repeated the criticisms of Gómara then in fashion, calling him a panegyrist of Cortés, a servile adulator, and heaven knows what else.

The trouble with me was that I had not read Gómara with sufficient attention. I do not suggest that all those who shared my attitude in 1935 feel the same way. No indeed. But the fact is, that having read Gómara more carefully, and compared his work with that of Bernal Díaz, I have formed opinions quite at variance with those I then held, so much so that the present essay turns out to be a lance broken in defense of Gómara, or at least an effort to establish a balance between the two, which today has veered strongly toward Bernal Díaz.

It is well known—and here I accept the current version, for which see the following essay—that Bernal Díaz, then an old man, undertook to write the history of the conquest. He had already completed several chapters when Gómara's book came to his hands. Upon reading it his first feeling was one of discouragement. He thought that his own narrative could never compete with that of the secular priest, and he was on the point of giving it up; but he continued his reading and discovered, according to his account, that Gómara's work was so full of falsifications that he felt encouraged to proceed with his own work, for the purpose of disproving them. "I shall use my pen as a good pilot swings his lead, to discover the shoals that he suspects lie ahead of him—which is what I shall do with the errors of the chroniclers, not all the mistakes, to be sure, for if I should note them all the cost of gathering the gleanings would be greater than that of the harvest itself."

Today, generally speaking, Bernal Díaz' opinion is accepted. His *History of the Conquest* is the "true" one, as he entitled it—which seems to imply that Gómara's is not, a matter to which I wish briefly to call the reader's attention.

I shall preface my remarks with an observation, to wit, that I do not believe in historical impartiality, in the sense given to it by positivistic historiography, that is, the existence of a definite and unique truth that can be established. When I studied chemistry as an undergraduate—and I make this plea because I am not up on the present state of the question—we were taught that there existed a certain number of elements over and above those that could be identified in a body supposed to be unique. In like fashion what I understand by historical truth might be explained. Beyond a doubt events occurred in a certain way, in a unique way; but to establish them, as in the analysis of elements, we cannot go beyond the viewpoint of those who witnessed them, lived with them, and observed them. The narrator's viewpoint is the simple element of our investigation. When the actors in the events are various, or the witnesses, we can gather together their viewpoints in homogeneous groups; but if there is disagreement among them, there will be a new factor in our selection, which will be, whether we like it or not, our own viewpoint as conditioned by, or limited by, a series of factors as complicated as those we are examining. Contrary to the view that is commonly accepted, I do not believe that observing historical events from a greater distance gives us a clearer picture of them.

A typical illustration of what I am saying occurs in the history of the conquest of America by the Spaniards. Depending on who is doing the writing, and his race and beliefs, opinions clash fiercely, and pens carry on the quarrel as they write. In the Congress of Americanists just mentioned, there was one session in which the members almost came to blows in the discussion of the person and works of Father Las Casas. "What a deplorable spectacle!" said some. "What an inevitable spectacle!" I thought, for if life consists of strife and conflict, the account of such strife and conflict, that is, history, must be impassioned and biassed. We may consider ourselves lucky if passion is kept within noble bounds and if the account of events is not deliberately falsified; but what we can never avoid is that the account of the events studied will vary according to the viewpoint of those who witness and analyze them.

I'm afraid that this introduction is getting to be too long, but I think it is necessary if we are clearly to see what I am driving at. When we admit the relativity and contingency of historical knowledge we gain a greater freedom of movement, a greater validity in our conclusions, since we recognize *a priori* its limitations.

Let us, then, face directly the problem raised by the historiography of the conquest of Mexico and by an appreciation of the two basic texts. In the name of so-called historical impartiality, today the work of Bernal Díaz is preferred to that of Gómara. Why? Is Bernal really more sincere and less impassioned than Gómara in his narrative? I propose to demonstrate that he is not. Is this preference owing to literary and stylistic excellence? Again, no, because, although Bernal's work is evidently unique in its freshness and spontaneity, it is also evident that Gómara's is one of the most beautiful products of the Spanish language. Well, then, why this preference? Why is it that Bernal's book is frequently reprinted, while Gómara's, which had an unprecedented success at the time it appeared, is now rare and is read by few—outside the specialists, of course —in Spain or Mexico.

This preference is owing to what I have already said about viewpoint, that is, to that fact that in the pages of Bernal, despite his protestations of loyalty to and admiration for Cortés, there runs a barely concealed resentment and a furious urge to belittle his merits, while in Gómara the conqueror is glorified. Bernal's viewpoint, indeed, coincides with that of an epoch which strives to bring everything down to a common level, an epoch which looks with suspicion upon men of genius, especially in the field of political and military affairs. Please understand that I am not anti-democratic—if I were I shouldn't be here. What I am doing is to point out certain tendencies of democratic thought which in the terrain of historical investigation have led us to assume attitudes that are patently demagogic. I haven't the slightest doubt that the conquest of America was carried out by common men, who played an outstanding part in it; but what these same masses do when they lack superior leaders to give them ideals and guide their energies may be seen in the conquest of the West Indies, in the civil wars of Peru, and in a whole series of episodes that we needn't go into here.

Cortés, with all his defects—and he wouldn't have been human if he hadn't had them—was a superior man, although Bernal refuses to admit it, that is, the exceptional character of Cortés' personality. For Bernal, Cortés was a good captain and nothing more, a type that abounded among the Spainards of those days. For Gómara, Cortés was a genius. Today's historians look with approval upon the testimony of Bernal, for the same reason that makes them solemnly repeat any gossip of any servant girl in Cortés' *residencia* unfavorable to the conqueror—all this, of course, in the name of historical impartiality.

Things would be clearer, perhaps, if we should recognize that Bernal Díaz is just as biassed as Gómara, but that their viewpoints are opposed, which is apparent when they assess the work of Cortés. Gómara, chaplain of the Marqués del Valle and closely associated with him during his sojourn in Spain, writes a life of Cortés and is paid for it. Bernal, on the other hand, a common soldier who would have remained anonymous but for his own testimony, resents Cortés because the latter quite unabashedly uses the first person singular and passes over the merits of his companions. Bernal attacks him head on: "And I say this, that when Cortés first wrote to His Majesty his pen dripped with pearls and gold, all in praise of himself, without a word of praise for our brave soldiers. To my knowledge, he makes no mention of Francisco Hernández de Córdoba, or of Grijalba, but speaks of himself alone, taking the credit for everything, the discovery and the honor. And he even said at the time that all this were better left unsaid and not transmitted to His Majesty; but there must have been someone who told him that our King and Lord would certainly be informed of what was going on."

According to Bernal Díaz, Cortés falsified the truth for his own ends, in order to win concessions from the Emperor, and ignored the rest of his men completely. When Cortés was in Spain, "He did not take the trouble to solicit anything for us which might have been to our profit, but only for himself." This is a pretty startling accusation coming from the mouth of Bernal, who was not precisely a model of disinterestedness, and had few scruples himself about falsifying the truth. He continually bemoans his poverty and neglect—this contrary to the documentary evidence we have concerning the closing years of his life, when his lamentations become loudest. "And I say this, with sadness in my heart, because I am poor and very old, with an unmarried daughter on my hands, some of my sons grown up and bearded, and others still to be reared, and I cannot go to Castile to tell His Majesty things necessary to his royal service, or to beg well-deserved favors for myself."

If we compare Bernal's statements with the evidence supplied by the documents mentioned, we shall see the need of picking our way very carefully among them. He is afflicted with the same unrestrained greed that afflicts all his companions, and he does not disguise it, but makes the quest for booty one of the motives of the conquest: "They died that cruel death [that is, sacrificed by the Aztec priests during the retreat of the Noche Triste] in the service of God and His Majesty, to spread light among those who dwelt in darkness, and also to gain riches, which all of us in common came to seek."

Bernal's attitude is that of a resentful man. He reproaches Cortés always for taking the lion's share of the booty of the conquest. Nor does he allow his own name to remain obscure in his narrative. Since his part in the conquest is secondary, he has to raise the level of all the men and depress that of Cortés, in order to place himself in the foreground, for it was not only the thirst for riches that motivated Bernal, but the thirst for glory, typical of the men of the Renaissance. At the end of his book he includes a brief dialogue, not fully realized, between himself and "the good and illustrious Fame," in which he does not conceal his resentment at all. "Fame cries loudly, saying that it would be just and reasonable for us to enjoy a good income. She asks where our palaces and mansions are, and what coats of arms do we carve on them different from the others, as a memorial to our heroic deeds of arms." Fame also asks where are the tombs of the conquerors, and Bernal answers: "They are in the bellies of the Indians, who devoured our legs and thighs and arms and fleshy parts, burying the rest, except the intestines, which they tossed to the tigers and serpents and falcons, which were kept at the time for show in the great houses. These were their sepulchres and there their coats of arms." Greed, thirst for glory, and resentment join hands at the end of the dialogue: "In reply to my request the most virtuous Fame answers and says she will grant it most willingly, for she says she is astonished that we do not have the best allotments of Indians in the country, since we conquered it, and since His Majesty has commanded that they be given us, just as they were given to the Marqués del Valle, although it is understood that they will be not so great, but moderate."

If Cortés deprives his companions of their just reward, Gómara removes their last hope of getting it, for he makes no mention of their deeds. Hence Bernal includes the two of them in his reproaches. He frequently repeats that if Gómara wrote as he did, praising only Cortés and failing to mention the deeds of the other captains and soldiers, it was because "his palm had been greased and he had been paid for it." Gómara's account is false, but the real falsifier is Cortés. "He [Gómara] is far from the truth in what he writes, but in my opinion it is not his fault but that of his informer."

According to Bernal, Cortés is as much to blame for falsifying the truth as Gómara is for relating what he has not witnessed. In all wars the scorn of the fighting men for those in the rear is typical, as is their indignation when the latter describe military actions in which they have not participated. Bernal, in his soldier's pride, continually scolds Gómora for so doing. His "I am not surprised that he is wrong in what he says, for he knows it only at second hand," and his "He was badly informed" are sharply contrasted with the precision of his own recollections: "As I write this I can see everything before my eyes as if it happened only yesterday." A certain licentiate, to whom Bernal showed his manuscript, "and who was very rhetorical and had a great opinion of himself," reproaches Bernal for using the first person so much. Bernal replies that only one who had been in a war was fit to talk about it; "But one who had not been in a war, who hadn't seen it or understood it, how could he talk about it? While we were fighting could the clouds or the birds passing overhead have informed him? Or should he not take the word of the captains and soldiers who were there?"

This for Gómara, who, to Bernal's despair, possessed a style that lent great luster to his narrative. Bernal affects to give it no importance, but he has misgivings: "And whoever reads his history will believe it to be true, such is the eloquence of his style, although it is quite contrary to what really happened." "And let the reader disregard his rhetoric and polish, which is evidently more pleasing than this coarseness of mine." That this modesty of Bernal's is false, and that he was not as indifferent to literary grace as he pretended, is apparent in the dialogue he had with the licentiate, who said of his manuscript "that it is written in our popular speech of Old Castile, which these days is held to be the most pleasing, for it does not indulge in pretty sayings or gilded phrases, such as are employed by some writers, but is plain and open, which is the foundation of all good speech."

Gómara, who was not in the conquest, Gómara, who possesses literary talent, is, to cap it all, a secular priest. And Bernal shares the opinion of Cortés himself and that of so many other conquistadores concerning the part played by the secular clergy in the Indies. All the respect and veneration he has for the friars turns into strictures on the secular clergy. One need not delve very deeply into his book to unearth such remarks as these: "I wish to bring this to mind so that the curious reader, as well as the priests who now have charge of administering the holy sacraments and doctrine to the natives of these parts, may see how that soldier who stole two chickens in a peaceful village almost lost his life for it, and see how the Indians should be treated and not stripped of their goods." "And the Indians treated the secular priests with equal courtesy, but after they came to know them better and had seen some of them, nay, all, and how greedy they were, and how they commit excesses in the villages, they turn away from them and will not have them for priests, but only Franciscans and Dominicans; and it is of no avail for the poor Indians to appeal to the bishop, for he will not listen to them. Oh, what I could say about this business, but it will have to remain in the inkwell!"

In view of this cargo of phobias he has against Gómara, it

is not to be expected that the pilot's lead he spoke of should function with any precision. In fact, most of Bernal's commentaries are nothing but violent outbursts, such as: "Neither in the beginning, nor the middle, nor the end do they [Cortés and Gómara] relate what truly happened in New Spain." "They lie in everything they write, so why should I bother to correct each individual lie, which would be only a waste of paper and ink? Be damned to him and his style!" "And if everything he writes in his other chronicles of Spain are in the same vein, why, I say, damn them also for old wives' tales and lies, however beautiful his style!"

All this is of interest as an index to a state of mind which we cannot ignore if we wish to assess at their true value the valid criticisms that Bernal levels at Gómara. The purpose of my study is not to make an exhaustive confrontation of the two, which would be useful, but out of place here. I wish simply to call attention to the problem.

Well, then, what exactly are the objections that Bernal makes to Gómara's account? On many occasions Bernal remarks at the end of his chapters: "This is what happened, not what is told by the chronicler Gómara." "This is where the chronicler Gómara repeats many things of which he was given a false account." And so on. But Bernal's own narrative becomes suspect as we compare the two texts. Let us examine in both authors the account of Cortés' preparations for his enterprise, or his meeting with Jerónimo de Aguilar, or his interview with the emissaries of Moctezuma at San Juan de Ulúa. I frankly confess that I see no essential difference between them which would justify Bernal's strictures. Bernal, who possessed a great sense of detail and a memory of astounding fidelity, was doubtless able to note discrepancies that escape our attention, but his commentary is always out of proportion. His boasted skill in heaving the lead is not good enough, as is proved by two episodes that I should like to emphasize.

In his desire to contradict Gómara, Bernal not only disagrees with him in his relation of fundamentally identical events, but he makes Gómara say things that Gómara did not say anywhere, as when he speaks of the Spaniards' stay in Cempoal.

According to Bernal Díaz: "This is the place where the chronicler Gómara says Cortés spent many days, and where he plotted the rebellion and alliance against Moctezuma. But Gómara was ill-informed, because, as I have said, we left there the following morning. And I shall tell later on just where the rebellion was planned, and why." Well, in Gómara's account there is no mention that the alliance against Moctezuma was made in Cempoal. What Gómara does say is that the cacique of Cempoal, "the fat cacique," complained to Cortés of the dreadful slavery they were suffering, which is just what Bernal says, and that the rebellion and alliance against the Aztec monarch was plotted later on at Quiahuiztlán, as Bernal also says.

The same thing occurs at the occupation of Cingapancinga. Bernal states: "And this affair at Cingapancinga was the first military exploit of Cortés in New Spain, and it was very useful to us, not, as the chronicler Gómara says, that we killed and seized and destroyed so many thousands of men in the action at Cingapancinga." Now, Gómara says nothing at all about the fight, for the simple reason that there was no fight, since the natives offered no resistance and the forces of Moctezuma had abandoned the place. "And Cortés [says Gómara] begged the soldiers and guards not to harm the inhabitants, but to let them go free, although without arms and banners—which was a novel thing to the Indians." The killing of thousands of Indians does not appear anywhere in Gómara, but only in Bernal's head in his frantic anxiety to discredit the other.

Up to this point Bernal's criticisms are not justified, but they have another aspect that deserves more careful consideration, that is, his objection to Gómara's account of the part played by Cortés. Here, beyond a doubt, Gómara's pen ran away with him. His book would have gained in stature if he had entitled it *The Life of Hernán Cortés*, instead of *The Conquest of Mexico*, for he concentrates his attention exclusively upon the Extremaduran hero and always credits him with every kind of exploit, which justifies this indignant outburst of Bernal: "Cortés never said or did a thing without first consulting with us and obtaining our agreement, even though the chronicler Gómara says: 'Cortés did this, went there, and returned from yonder.' And he says many other things that won't hold water, for, even if Cortés had been made of iron, as Gómara tells us in his history, he could not have been everywhere at once."

We must admit that Bernal is right in this, as he is right in his detailed knowledge of events. For example, it was not Cortés who entered the Alvarado River, but Alvarado himself, who penetrated that country for the first time shortly after the landing of the Spaniards. All this is very well, but what we cannot accept is Bernal's constant use of the first person plural: "We agreed, we ordered, we acted," which reduces Cortés to nothing but a tool in the hands of his captains. "It seems that God gave us soldiers such favor and good counsel so that we might advise Cortés in the things he did so well." "And let us say that all of us who were there unanimously encouraged Cortés and told him to take care of himself." However one-sided Gómara's vision is when he ignores the companions of Cortés, I think it is more acceptable than that of Bernal, who portrays a Cortés ruled by the opinions of a junta.

I regret that I have no exact knowledge of the organization of the military hierarchy in those days. What we now call a general staff did not, of course, then exist, with its specific duty of preparing the decisions of the commander. But then, as now and always, the decision, with or without previous advice, was the responsibility of the chief and not that of his subordinates. Bernal contradicts himself here, for when he describes the character of Cortés he insists that Cortés was a very stubborn man. "And he was very stubborn, especially in matters pertaining to war, for, no matter what advice and arguments we gave him about things he had not considered in the combats and forays he ordered us to undertake, as when we marched around the lake or attacked the rocks that are now called Los Peñoles del Marqués and told him that we ought not to climb up to the rocks and forts until we had them surrounded, because of the many stones that came bounding down from the forts and knocked us off and because it was impossible for us to defend ourselves because of the speed and violence with which they came, and it would mean risking the lives of all of us, since we lacked the strength, knowledge, and skill [for it], nevertheless he stubbornly insisted, against the advice of all of us, and we had to undertake the ascent. And we were in great danger, and eight soldiers died there, and all the rest of us were bruised and wounded, and we accomplished nothing worthy of mention until we changed our plan."

All this against Cortés, but it runs counter to the allegation that Cortés was pulled this way and that by the opinions of his captains. Exactly the contrary must have been true, that is, that Cortés was so able and had such address in explaining his plans to his men that they came to believe that they had made them. In this regard Orozco y Berra, when speaking of the seizure of Moctezuma, makes a very just observation: "The general had made his plan, but, as he always did, pretended to accept the opinions of others, so as not to be saddled with the sole responsibility if the question should arise."

This is the truth, and Bernal's attempt to twist it is in vain. At the time the ships were destroyed, Bernal himself admits that it was Cortés' idea. "And, as I understood it, Cortés himself had already planned it when we proposed it to him; but he wanted it to appear as coming from us, because in the event that he should be asked to pay for the ships, he could say that he did it on our advice, and that we should all share in the cost." Bernal is very indignant with Gómara for stating that the conqueror kept his plan under the greatest secrecy, and he gives us to understand that the soldiers knew of it. "This is where the chronicler Gómara tells us that when Cortés ordered the ships scuttled he did not dare let the soldiers know about it who wished to go on to Mexico and seek out the great Moctezuma. But it did not happen as he says. Does he imagine that we Spaniards are such as would hesitate to march forward to war and riches?"

This appreciation of the courage (and the greed) of the Spaniards is all very well, and it's a pity that Bernal should once again contradict himself. When he describes the reactions of the soldiers who want Cortés to give up the enterprise, he has them say: "It would be a good thing if we had all those ships we scuttled, or at least two of them, to use in case of need, if the need should arise; but he, without telling us about it, or about anything at all, on the advice of someone who knew nothing of the risk, ordered them all scuttled."

Really, this famous impartiality and this tested veracity of Bernal Díaz confuses things terribly. If the soldiers knew that the ships were to be destroyed, why do they complain that they had not been told of it? Lying, friend Bernal, requires a good memory. It would have been better for you to content yourself with saying that Cortés at times had followed the advice of some of his captains, but without implying that it was they and the soldiers who decided everything, as if Cortés did not exist. War is not decided by committees and votes, as Bernal would have us believe when he tells of the celebrated meeting of the Spaniards at Cholula, when they thought they were going to be attacked by the natives. "That very night Cortés asked our advice about what we should do, because he had very outstanding men of good counsel, and, as commonly happens in such matters, some said it would be well to veer off and go by way of Huejotzingo; others, that we should make peace in any way we could; still others of us gave it as our opinion that if we allowed those treacherous acts to go unpunished, we should be inviting worse trouble everywhere, and, since we were in that large town [Cholula] and had plenty of supplies, we should fight them there, where we could punish them more severely than in the open country, and that we should at once warn the Tlaxcalans who were there. And this last advice was approved by all."

Cortés says not a word. Apparently Bernal fails to note that Cortés is the one who makes the decisions at critical moments, as he did at the forking of the roads leading to Mexico. "Cortés then said we should take the road that had been obstructed." But this is the exception. Bernal's Cortés is as dense as his companions are in Gómara's account; but where Gómara omits, Bernal deforms.

A final example, the accounts of the seizure of Moctezuma. In Bernal's narrative he tells us who composed the junta of Cortés, the junta which is the conqueror's advisory and executive organ, without which Cortés does not take a step. Naturally, Bernal himself is a member of it: "Four of our captains, all told, and some twelve soldiers whom he trusted, and I was one of these." It is they and not Cortés who thought up the plan to seize Moctezuma, and it is they who work out the smallest details of the daring exploit. Cortés—such an irresolute man, of course—does not clearly see how they can arrest Moctezuma when he is surrounded by his warriors. "And our captains, who were Juan Velázquez de León, and Diego de Ordaz, and Gonzalo de Sandoval, and Pedro de Alvarado [told him] that if Moctezuma should make a disturbance or shout when he was informed that they were going to arrest him, he should answer for it in his person, and that if Cortés did not wish to carry it out immediately, he should give them permission to do so."

I doubt that there is a better commentary on the effrontery of Bernal, which, as we are beginning to see, was in no sense inferior to that of Gómara, than the paragraph in the second *Letter* of Cortés, referring to the lost first *Letter*: "And I remember, with respect to the search for this lord, that I offered to do much more than was possible for me to do, because I assured Your Majesty that I would have him either a prisoner, or dead, or subject to the royal crown of Your Majesty." That is to say, the idea of seizing the sovereign had been conceived by Cortés from the moment he learned of his existence.

With regard to the statements of Bernal concerning the group of captains—the matter of the soldiers seems more difficult now—whom Cortés consulted before taking important decisions, this we may admit, but not that this group was the center of the conquest, the inspiration and encouragement of Cortés, as Bernal informs us. In any event, the criticisms I have noted do not justify the burial, the oblivion, and discredit of Gómara. It should be borne in mind that Bernal does not refute Gómara's account in the large, but only in the violent attacks mentioned above. He admits without demur Gómara's description of the main episodes of the conquest: the war with Tlaxcala, the massacre at Cholula, the entrance into Mexico, the fight with Narváez, the escape from the capital, the march to Honduras. And please don't tell me that this is because Bernal tells us that he will never mention Gómara again, for he does so a little after describing the entrance into Mexico: "And since I am sick of noting how far the chronicler Gómara strays from what really happened, I shall not mention it again." But this is beyond Bernal's power and he returns to the attack whenever he finds, or thinks he finds, an excuse for it, as, for example, when he comments of "Alvarado's Leap": "I say that at the time no soldier stopped to see whether he leaped much or little, because we had enough to do to save our own lives."

Before closing, I should like to make an observation which I offer to the attention of some patient student. Let him give more thought to a comparison of the texts of Bernal and Gómara, and perhaps he will find that Gómara gives valuable assistance to Bernal, helping him to give tone to his work, to organize his chapters, and the like. This is a suggestion that I cannot fully defend at the moment, but I believe that Gómara not only stimulated Bernal, but provided him with a model to follow in his narrative. This by itself would be to the credit of Gómara, an author who deserves our attention on many counts. By all means let Bernal be edited and studied—no one could be less suspect than I in so saying, since I spent almost four years working on an edition of his book, which the Civil War prevented me from completing. But don't let a passion for Bernal and the oblivion of Gómara be the fruit of resentment, because Gómara's work, like that of Cortés, can be disputed as much as you like, but it can never be ignored.

Introduction to the Study of Bernal Díaz del Castillo and his *True History*

In our time Bernal Díaz del Castillo has taken over the place that Gómara occupied in the sixteenth century. He is the author to whom specialists, and even laymen, interested in the conquest of New Spain first turn, when, indeed, he is not the only one they turn to.

The *True History* is very frequently reprinted. It has been translated, in whole or in part, into French, English, German, Danish, and Hungarian. Its author is the center of a genuine cult, and his book has become the touchstone by which to judge all writers who treat of the conquest.

The interest in Bernal Díaz has brought into being a very large number of studies concerning his person and his book. It has also tended to modify an attitude which has been with us for a long time now, and which reached its most definite and highest pitch about the beginning of this century, in Genaro García's Introduction to his edition of the *True History*, based on the manuscript preserved in [the Municipalidad of] Santiago de Guatemala. If we compare his Introduction with that of another Mexican historian, Joaquín Ramírez Cabañas, in the

1939 edition, we can see how much ground has been gained toward a truer and more thoughtful appreciation of the character of Bernal and his work.

I myself was once a member of the enthusiastic cult of Bernal. I too was indignant with those who pointed out—not always justly—the defects of his book. Today I take it more calmly, having learned by a painful experience [the Spanish Civil War], which some day may occupy a higher place, perhaps, than that of the conquistadores of New Spain. And because I no longer accept Bernal unconditionally I think I understand him better and admire him more.

Bernal's life is apparently known to everyone now. In these past years new documentary materials have been published which complete or rectify the image of his person as we had glimpsed it in the pages of his chronicle. But such studies fail—as always happens—because of their excessive dispersion and because they do not properly assemble their results. We must, therefore, clear away the rubbish, first by establishing a few dates indispensable for a knowledge of the period in which Bernal wrote his book and for that of the very genesis of its composition.

We do not know for certain the year of Bernal's birth. Genaro García, in his above-mentioned Introduction to the *True History*, says he was born in 1492, which Ramíra Cabañas repeated in his edition. Genaro García bases his opinion on an error, believing that Bernal Díaz was twenty-four "at the time he decided to come to New Spain." This error arises from a mistaken interpretation of Bernal's text. The passage that Genaro García bases his opinion on goes like this:

"And God was pleased to save me from many deadly perils in that painful expedition, as well as in the very bloody wars with the Mexicans—for which I thank God and praise Him mightily—so that I might write and relate what happened in those same wars, and, besides, so that the curious reader might ponder and think how I, being at that time twenty-four years of age, and how the Governor of Cuba, Diego Velázquez by

name, and a relative of mine, promised that he would give me
[an encomienda of] Indians, of the first to be vacated, and how
I did not wait for them to be given me."

The passage is obscure, as very frequently happens with
Bernal. Genaro García interpreted it in the sense that Bernal
said he was twenty-four when he refused the encomienda offered him by Velázquez and decided to go to New Spain. But
García fails to take into consideration Bernal's peculiar style
and lack of experience in writing, for Bernal always puts his
ideas down hit-or-miss, wanders about from one theme to another, scrambles their chronology, and never separates them
properly. Bernal tells us of "the very bloody wars with the
Mexicans" and of his purpose to write their history. He mentions as a personal merit having fought in them as a young
man—only twenty-four or so—and, to give his account greater
emphasis, he adds that he had rejected the profitable offer of
Diego Velázquez.

That is to say, Bernal is thinking of his twenty-four years,
associating them with the Mexican wars and not with the offer
of the Governor of Cuba, which follows in his text, but which
in fact had preceded them. So we can fix Bernal's twenty-four
years between 1519 and 1521, the end dates of Cortés' cam-
paign, or perhaps in 1520, when the "wars with the Mexicans"
were at their bloodiest for the Spaniards, the disaster of the
Noche Triste.

At first glance this conjecture may seem doubtful, but it will
not be so for a person who has familiarized himself with Bernal's style, and it allows us to fix the date of his birth between
1495 and 1497—which agrees with statements he made at different moments of his life. In his affidavit to the *probanza de
servicios* of Don Pedro de Alvarado (June 4, 1563), he says he
is sixty-seven, which places the year of his birth about 1495.
We are thus able to state with some assurance that Bernal was
born in 1495 or 1496 and discard completely the date of 1492
proposed by Genaro García.

We have yet another source of confusion to be got rid of:

On the first page of his chronicle of the conquest Bernal says: "I am an old man of more than eighty-four." Those who have concerned themselves with his biography have tried to reconcile this statement with what he says elsewhere, that is, that he is making a clean copy of his book in 1568:

"Of the 500 soldiers who came with Cortés from the Island of Cuba, in this year of 1568, in which I am making a clean copy of my chronicle, only five of us are alive in all New Spain."

The problem is not easy, for if Bernal is more than eighty-four in 1568, he must have been born as early as 1484. Those who try to reconcile Bernal's two statements fall into a very common error; that is, they consider books to have been produced all at once, and finished just as we see them. They forget that behind the finished product there is hidden a slow process of elaboration, with retouches, contradictions, additions, and eliminations. When the author is unskilled in writing, the process is disclosed more clearly, as he fails to organize his materials properly. Bernal's is a typical case. His work is a conglomerate—as are all works that are produced collectively—and in it we can trace the different strata. Only if we accept the fact that Bernal is the author of a single book, the work of his whole life, can we avoid the errors of those who suggest these comments.

Bernal worked for a long time on his history—I shall go into more detail about this later on—and there is no doubt that he left his prologue to the last, as happens with all of us. He was unable to write it to his satisfaction, as he tells us himself, and did not get beyond a short note, in which he indicates that he is over eighty-four. He may well have written this note toward 1579 or 1580, in one of the revisions of his work. It should be borne in mind that his remark about his age does not appear in the prologue to Remón's edition, which is doubtless by the hand of Bernal. In this prologue, which is perhaps that of the copy he sent to Spain before 1579, he speaks of his purpose to continue working on his book: "I have to finish writing certain things that are lacking, which have not yet been completed."

So we must discard the notion that Bernal was more than

eighty-four in 1568. The two dates occur at different moments, and no one who is acquainted with Bernal's mentality will be surprised that he did not bother to bring into agreement statements made at different times in his life.

The fact is that the bothersome statement in the Guatemala rough draft is the one that has most troubled those who have studied Bernal's work. They have striven to put back the date of composition as much as possible, in order to bring it close to the year 1568 and justify the notion that the author was writing at a very advanced age. As Bernal also states, when speaking of his eighty-four years, that he had lost "his eyesight and his hearing," the resemblance to Homer becomes tempting. The ancient conquistador, "with his noble desire to correct the errors of ill-informed chroniclers, seizes his pen, as once he had seized his sword," says González Obregón. "He dedicated himself to writing his *True History* when he was going on seventy-odd years of age," says Genaro García. "We know that Bernal Díaz del Castillo began to write his *True History* about the year 1568," Carlos Pereyra roundly declares, without telling us where he got the information.

The data that we now possess make it possible to correct all these statements. Bernal was working on his history before the age of sixty. Alonso de Zorita, *oidor* of the Audiencia de los Confines [Guatemala], who had traversed the lands of Guatemala between the spring of 1553 and the end of April, 1557, says, in his *Historia de la Nueva España*: "Bernal Díaz del Castillo, a *vecino* of Guatemala, where he has a good encomienda, a conquistador of that country and of Nueva España and Coatzacoalcos, told me, when I was serving as *oidor* of the Royal Audiencia de los Confines, that he resides in the city of Santiago de Guatemala and is writing a history of that country, and he showed me the part he had written. It is not finished, nor has it been published."

Bernal, then, had not finished his history when Alonso de Zorita was *oidor* of the Audiencia de los Confines. We find a new reference to his book, made this time by Bernal himself in 1563, when he was not yet seventy, in the *probanza de servicios* of the Adelantado Alvarado already mentioned:

"Many things [happened] which this witness has described in his account of the wars, as a person who was present in all the actions. . . ."

Here Bernal speaks of his work as already in existence, although not entirely completed. In fact, he never did complete it. He hesitates when he tries to bring it to a close, as I have indicated when he began his prologue. Perhaps he thought initially that the most adequate ending would be the "List of battles and engagements" in which he had taken part, following Chapter 212. The Remón text ends with this list, and Bernal's signature appears at the end of the list in the Guatemala manuscript. But then he adds two more chapters, of the appropriateness of which he is doubtful, for the following note appears at the head of Chapter 214: "Omit what follows." His lack of decision goes farther, for at the end of the same chapter he announces: "It will be well for me to list in another chapter the archbishops and bishops there have been." This chapter does not exist, and it does not look as if the Guatemala manuscript has been mutilated. Most probably Bernal never got around to writing it.

These notes will suffice to give a notion of how slow the process of elaboration of the *True History* was. The first mention of it is before 1557; others are between 1563 and 1568; and the last one we can date is toward 1579 or 1580. The book is patched up throughout the life of the author after the middle of the sixteenth century.

Another factor has been at work in the tendency to set back the date of composition of Bernal's history, and that is the close association established between his work and the *Conquest of Mexico* by López de Gómara. "Bernal Díaz, who was living tranquilly in his encomienda of Chamula, could not see without anger that that writer [Gómara] was attempting to exalt Cortés at the expense of all his companions, and attributing to him alone the glory of the conquest, so his indignation made him an author. From that time onward he doubtless began to sharpen his memory and recollection of those events." This opinion, expressed long ago by [Enrique] Veytia, is still floating about, although it has been necessary to modify it, because Bernal himself tells us that he was already at work on his history when Gómara's book came to his hands. "He had written a little of the *True History* when there came to his hands the chronicles of Paulo Jovio, López de Gómara, and Gonzalo de Illescas," says Genaro García. Carlos Pereyra gives us more details: "He had about twenty chapters well along and was narrating the events of the voyage he had made with Juan de Grijalva, when three books fell into his hands. . . ."

These statements also require revision. We cannot know on what date exactly, or at what moment in the composition of the *True History*, these three books came to his attention. On the other hand, the fact that he mentions them in Chapter 18 of his history does not mean that it was precisely then that they came to his knowledge, nor does he say such a thing. The only thing he does say is: "While I was writing this chronicle of mine, I saw by chance what Gómara and Illescas and Jovio were writing about the conquests of Mexico and New Spain." The passage quoted fits best where it is, because it follows the account of the expedition of Grijalva and precedes that of Cortés, where the corrections of these chroniclers were to be most frequent. But Chapter 18 could hardly have been interpolated by Bernal, for in the manuscript he clumsily changed their order, giving the previous chapter the number 16, which did not correspond to it, probably in order to make it part of the account of Grijalva's expedition and to make a place for his animadversions on the three chroniclers.

There is still more. Those who believe that Chapter 18 marks the moment in which Bernal learned of the other chroniclers seem to forget that already in Chapter 1 he states: "Speaking here in reply to what has been said and written by persons who did not know what they were talking about, or who did not see, or had no information about the matter." In case the allusion to the chroniclers whom Bernal proposes to refute is not clear, we find it more explicit in Chapter 13, in which he speaks of the gold acquired by trade by Grijalva in the Río de Banderas: "And this must be what the chroniclers Gómara, Illescas, and Jovio say was acquired in Tabasco." In the next chapter he again corrects Gómara.

If Bernal, from the beginning of his book, mentions the three chroniclers, as he also does in the prologue to Remón's text, what this shows us is not that he knew them shortly after beginning his history, but that he modified it after having read them. It should be kept in mind that part of his book was already written in 1557, and that possibly the first version had been completed by 1563, when he could hardly even have seen the above-mentioned chroniclers, with the exception of Gómara, for the first edition of Illescas appeared in 1564 and the Spanish translation of Paulo Jovio in 1566.

We must, therefore, resign ourselves to admitting that his indignant accusations leveled against the chroniclers' errors were not the germ of his book, as we have repeatedly been told. There is indignation and polemic in Bernal, but they were not the motives of his attitude.

At first glance there is nothing very surprising in the paradox that Genaro García, that enemy of the conquistadores, should make an exception in favor of Bernal, converting him into the archetype of virtues and drawing an entirely false picture of his character.

"And so, then, rather poor but well loved and esteemed, he dedicated himself to the writing of the *True History* when he was approaching the age of seventy-odd years. He feared no one, and was convinced that in the history of the world nothing more heroic than the Conquest had been recorded; nor were there men more heroic than the conquistadores. He accepted his lot of being less rewarded than he justly deserved. He was free of pessimisms, animosities, and remorse. His conscience was perfectly clear. His extraordinary memory and his exceptional mind were at their most vigorous. Now and then he would interrupt his work to visit the towns of his encomienda, sometimes accompanied by friends."

This idyllic picture of a quiet and tranquil Bernal, who visits his Indians and cherishes his memories, who interrupts his peaceful life to defend, with a quixotic gesture, the glory that Gómara is trying to snatch from him and his companions—this picture collapses when we read attentively Bernal's book and the documents we now possess relating to his person. The edition of Ramírez Cabañas is the one that is most widely circulated today, and there is no point in repeating here what he says in his prologue about Bernal's character and his real economic situation in the years in which he was composing his chronicle of the conquest. What indeed is fitting is to place these new data into their relationship with the genesis of the *True History*.

Bernal is a turbulent man, discontented and litigious. He is never satisfied with the rewards he receives for his services. He is always peevish and resentful. In 1550 permission was given for him and two of his servants to bear arms "offensive and defensive," because "he has several enemies in that country [of Guatemala]." And to judge by the tone of his two letters of 1552 and 1558, Bernal has a wicked temper; he grumbles, and is terribly pleased with himself. "I well believe that in your Royal Council of the Indies they must have heard of me," he writes the King in 1552. "I believe that your Lordship cannot have heard of me, for I see that I have written to you three times and have never had a reply," he writes in 1558 to Father Las Casas, and brazenly demands that when the latter "writes to the Dominican Fathers he ask them to send him a letter or collect that will favor me."

No. Bernal is not a man who "accepts his lot of being less rewarded than he justly deserves," as his Mexican editor [García] would have us believe, the man "free of pessimisms, animosities, and remorse." He is an immensely ambitious man, profoundly dissatisfied, a true representative of that turbulent generation of conquistadores who, when they stop fighting the Indians, spend the rest of their lives bombarding the Crown for favors that will allow them to live without working.

Ramírez Cabañas, in the prologue to his edition, hits the mark when he points out this attitude which explains all Bernal's conduct. [Francisco de] Icaza, in the introduction to his authoritative *Conquistadores y pobladores de Nueva España*, refers to our author repeatedly as the most outstanding exponent of the dissatisfaction and endless complaints of the conquistadores who feel they have not been sufficiently rewarded for their services. Carlos Pereyra stresses the need of being on one's guard "against accepting the whining literature of the affidavits of the merits and services of the conquistadores." But none of these authors brings out clearly enough that this atmosphere of dissatisfaction, resentment, and greed of the conquistadores, this formidable and exceedingly long suit against the Crown in the matter of their interests, the distribution of lands and Indians, is the foundation, the very root, of Bernal's *True History.*

Not everything about Bernal's life is entirely clear. If his merits were as great as he informs us, why did he not achieve a more outstanding place among the companions of Cortés? Indeed, if it were not for his own account we would know next to nothing about his part in the conquest. In his book he portrays himself with all the characteristics of the conquistador: he is very brave and yearns for adventures and riches. Nevertheless, it may well be that Bernal is a soldier of fortune and that army life has no attraction for him as a career. He has hardly landed in Mexico when we see him interested in getting his share of the booty, not in gold or jewels, but in land and Indians. Sandoval gives him an encomienda in Coatzacoalcos, and from that moment on he is angry whenever Cortés requires his presence in some military expedition. He is always sorry for the soldiers who "already had their homes and leisure" and find themselves thrown against their will into new adventures. Take, for example, his commentary on the Honduras expedition:

"And when we wished to rest from our great hardships and get together a little property and money, he [Cortés] orders us to undertake a march of more than 500 leagues, and all the territories through which we passed were warlike and we lost everything we had."

This intense desire for rest, manifested when Bernal was not yet thirty—the Honduras expedition began in 1524—is sharply at variance with his tone when he relates his part in the campaigns of Cortés: "And those who held these opposing opinions [i.e., opposing Cortés' plans] were those who had estates

in Cuba, for I and the other poor soldiers always offered our
souls to the God who had created them, and our bodies and
wounds, until we should die in the service of Our Lord God
and His Majesty."

   That is to say, Bernal ingenuously confesses that the conquistadores fought well when they had nothing to lose, but as
soon as they had acquired some wealth it took a deal of persuasion to get them to take part in new military adventures.
And so it was that Bernal ended his soldier's career very young.
He goes with Cortés much against his will, because he had no
choice. The expeditions in which he later took part were not
very dangerous. He himself repeats on several occasions that
the Guatemalan Indians "were not warlike, but were given to
shouting and screaming and making noise." He is not tempted
to go to Peru, for he is not attracted by the risky and profitless
expeditions organized by the government of Viceroy Mendoza.
   While still quite young Bernal gives up the life of a conquistador to become an encomendero. And in his struggle for reward, which was not the less violent than that he made against
the Indians just because it was less noisy, he spends the greater
part of his life. He makes two voyages to Spain. In the council
held at Valladolid in 1550 he offers his opinion about the perpetuity of the encomienda. The letters and documents of his
that have come down to us concern that subject exclusively.
I shall not analyze them in their more definite and juridical
aspects. It will suffice to underscore that the fixed idea of all
Bernal's life is that he has become part of the new aristocracy
composed of "the true conquistadores," who because of their
heroic deeds have put the Crown in debt to them for all manner of favors.
   "Besides our ancient claim to nobility, which we earned by
our heroic deeds and great exploits in the wars, fighting day
and night, serving our King and Lord, exploring these lands
and winning this New Spain and the great City of Mexico and
many other provinces, all at our own expense, being so far from
Castile and having no help whatever except that of Our Lord

Jesus Christ, who is our succor and true help, we achieved more glory than we had before."

Bernal expresses an idea then current among the conquistadores, that is, that the wars with the Indians were a continuation of those waged in Spain against the infidels—the Reconquest—and he demands that those who have taken part in them receive the same rewards as the medieval warriors:

"And I have also noted that some of those knights, who rose high enough to be given estates and the title of 'Illustrious,' did not go to those wars, nor did they engage in battles except when they were paid their wages in advance, and that even so they were given *villas* and castles and great estates in perpetuity, and privileges and exemptions which are still enjoyed by their descendants. Moreover, when King Jaime of Aragón conquered and won from the Moors many parts of their kingdoms, he distributed them among the knights and soldiers who had taken part in their winning, and since that time they have their coats of arms and their title of 'Valiant,' and the same thing happened when Granada was taken."

The *True History* has clusters of passages like this one. Sooner or later, all the conquistadores would file *probanzas* of their merits and services, sometimes collectively, acting on superior orders, as happened during the administration of Viceroy Mendoza. It was a stroke of genius on Bernal's part, when he filed the *probanza* of his own merits, to give us at the same time "the chronicle of the wars," as he called them, which is the best and most complete account of the conquest of New Spain. The egotist Bernal has also a very pronounced feeling for the group, which is so highly developed during war, and hence he cannot conceive of relating his exploits without including among them those of all his companions, "because ever since I began my narrative my purpose has been none other than to relate the deeds and exploits of those of us who came over with Cortés."

The germ of Bernal's work must be sought, then, in the struggle for encomiendas and in the accounts of merits and services. See the air of a notarial document at the beginning of his chronicle:

"Bernal Díaz del Castillo, a *vecino* and councilman of the very loyal city of Santiago de Guatemala, one of the first discoverers and conquistadores of New Spain and its provinces and the Cape of Honduras, and everything else in this country . . . , a native of the noble and illustrious *villa* of Medina del Campo, son of Francisco Díaz del Castillo, former councilman of that *villa*, otherwise known as the Gallant (may he rest in glory!). . . ."

The last chapters are devoted to the listing of all the conquistadores who accompanied Cortés and the merits of each. One of the versions—the one used by Remón—concludes with a list of all the battles and skirmishes in which Bernal had a part.

The *True History* kept on growing beyond reason because Bernal was incapable of selecting from among his recollections and, once he had begun his chronicle of the conquest, could keep nothing back. So what started out as a simple account of his merits and services took on greater and greater scope. We know that Bernal showed what he was writing to persons he thought competent to judge: the *oidor* Alonso de Zorita and the *licenciados* he mentions in Chapter 212, who doubtless encouraged him to go on. His reading of Gómara did the rest, and Gómara may have helped give definitive form to his history.

It was, therefore, the personal interests and suits of Bernal Díaz the encomendero which originated the stupendous narrative, in its first version, of the exploits of Bernal Díaz the conquistador and his companions. If Bernal had been a more modest man, one capable of adjusting himself to the new conditions of labor required by the colony, he would not have defended so stubbornly the rights of the "true conquistadores" and we should not have his *True History* today.

In the vast polemic attendant upon the discovery and conquest of the Indies, the historical work of Bernal is at the opposite pole from that of Las Casas: in Las Casas, the defense of the rights of the Indians; in Bernal, the defense of the rights of the conquistadores.

It is a curious paradox that such an obvious counter-position has not been clearly established. This is owing to the fact that Bernal's work became the favorite weapon in the attack against Gómara and, above all else, in the attack against Hernán Cortés. This failure to understand the origins of the *True History* has made the unconditional partisans of Las Casas the unconditional partisans of Bernal Díaz—which doubtless would greatly have astonished both of them.

Filosofía y Letras
Mexico, January–March, 1941

The Disillusionment
of Don Carlos*

The feeling of a person who finds himself in unfamiliar surroundings takes two directions. On the one hand, he especially notices everything that strikes him as different from the things he is used to; on the other he looks for points of contact and analogies. We find this dual attitude among the conquistadores who, when they see in Mexico things that evoke their readings in the romances of chivalry, are reminded of scenes in Spain, as we continually note in the names they give to the towns they see. Examples of this kind of double attitude occur in the chronicle of Bernal Díaz. This tendency toward assimilation and recollection reaches its height when Cortés proposes that the new lands be called New Spain: "From what I have seen and learned of the similarity between this country and Spain," [he wrote the Emperor Charles V], "in its fertility, its size, its climate, and in many other features of it, I thought

---

* [The Spanish title of this essay, *La Mexicanidad de Don Carlos de Sigüenza y Góngora*, defies translation and, moreover, fails to indicate the tragic theme of Sigüenza's life, that is, his violent about-face from an antiquarian's love of all aspects of pre-conquest Mexico to his bitter contempt for the Indians of his later days, when he saw his youthful dreams destroyed in the terrible popular uprising of June 8, 1692. So I have

that the most suitable name for it would be New Spain of the Ocean Sea."

The Mexican lands, then, are a Spain, but a New Spain, somewhat different from the other. How does this New Spain come to realize that it is different from the Old; not only different, but as great as the Old, or superior to it? This is a theme which for some time past has been exciting interest, and in which I believe there is much still to be done. In the minds of all, the culmination of this feeling of difference, fully mature, comes at the moment of Independence. And before that? I wonder whether there has not been here that distortion so frequent in historical studies, in which one sees the events of the past through the eyes of today, the past projected into a present that we are familiar with, and sees the direction and tendencies of previous events thus determined. As I ask myself this question, I think of the Mexican historian, Don Luis González Obregón, in whose studies the idea of Independence is always present and, as he points out, had been alive and working since the sixteenth century.

How far can this idea be accepted? At what moment can it be said that a Mexican is aware of being different from a Spaniard and of being even superior to him? At what moment is the idea and feeling of being Mexican born?

At this point I should like to make it clear that I do not share the attitude so firmly rooted among the intelligentsia of our day, a kind of Germanizing attitude, according to which problems must be involved and complex, if they are to achieve the

---

adopted the present English title as more suggestive of the profound crisis suffered by one of the great figures of seventeenth-century Mexico.

Sigüenza y Góngora was Professor of Mathematics and Astrology (Astronomy) at the *Real y Pontífica Universidad de México* in the late seventeenth century, until his death in 1700. He was a vastly learned man for his time, interested in all manner of things: cartography, history, and particularly Mexican antiquities. He wrote voluminously, although few of his works have survived. He achieved considerable repute, and caused no little scandal, by denying the supernatural origin of eclipses and comets and their portents, which brought him into conflict with the famous Jesuit, Father Eusebio Kino.

(For Sigüenza and his times, consult Irving A. Leonard, *Don Carlos de Sigüenza y Góngora, a Mexican Savant of the Seventeenth Century*, University of California Publications in History, vol. 18, Berkeley, California, 1929.)—*Tr.*]

dignity and loftiness of being "prestigious." I do not agree with that attitude. Things can be complicated and simple at the same time. I fully share the view of Professor Crane Brinton, who, in his *Anatomy of Revolution*, says that the dread of falling into a commonplace has led many intellectuals to have an equal dread of the self-evident.

In this talk I shall endeavor not to complicate things, but shall allow commonplaces to frisk about in it, if such commonplaces strike me as being true. I shall not, for example, attempt a definition of "Mexican." To set up a basis for mutual understanding, it will suffice for us to agree that "Mexican" is an idea, more or less clear, or it may be simply a feeling, that "Mexican" has its own personality, that it is something different from, or superior to, "non-Mexican."

When and how did this idea arise? I had already wondered about it. I have had neither the time nor the means to make a deep study of the subject, so I shall limit myself here to pointing out a few aspects of it that have come to my attention in readings that are not as abundant or as continued as I should have desired. I shall only call to my defense an ancient truth, that in games the spectator sees more than the players. I hope that in this case the players, who know more about the game than I, who am merely an interested onlooker, will help me with their comments in the discussion that will follow my talk.

The first idea, that America is something radically different from what was known before, lies in its very name of the New World. I shall not attempt here to trace how this idea developed after the initial confusion of Christopher Columbus. Rather, I wish to indicate the moment in which it culminates, in which it is fully expressed. We find that moment in New Spain seventy years after the conquest of the Aztec capital by the Spaniards, in the *Problemas y Secretos Maravillosos de las Indias*, by Dr. Juan de Cárdenas [Mexico, 1591]. Cárdenas is a Spaniard, an Andalusian, who, when he takes up his pen in praise of a foreign land, interrupts himself and exclaims: "What am I saying? Foreign? I can with reason call it my own." The doctor is an ill-tempered young man, who writes his book when he is twenty-six and publishes it at twenty-eight, who suffers with his stomach—a thing which, as he tells us, happens to all Spaniards who go to the Indies, especially the intellectuals— who has a hard time earning a living, and who misses no opportunity to scold those who, with more means and knowledge than he, have not proclaimed to the world the excellences of the new part which has lately been added to it:

"I also offer as an excuse the small number of the authors from whom I take what I am writing, for, since this is a matter never written by or discussed by another, the kind of reply I must make is only in my poor imagination, and that incurs the risk that many—possibly those of my profession—will grumble and complain of me. I shall take comfort, however, in the thought that whether I am good or bad, and whether they were born and reared in the Indies and have greater prospects, age, and experience than I, they have not been up to doing what I have done, since they are more concerned with the pomp and adornment of their persons than with proclaiming and bringing to the light the mysterious grandeurs of this fertile, magnificent, and opulent land."

Cárdenas knows that his book will be imperfect, because it treats of a new world, a new history, and its author is also new and young. But, as the laudatory pieces at the beginning of the book proclaim, he wishes to complete with his pen what Cortés undertook with his sword, that is, to make a spiritual conquest of the New World by giving it expression and a written form.

Cárdenas displays his youthful impatience when he laments that so much has been written about the Old World and so little about the New: "I say again that in this land of the Indies we can deplore the fact that, although there is an abundance of material and plenty of strange and excellent grandeurs, there is no one to herald them and bring them to light; nor would Asia, Africa, and Europe have anything to complain of if they were, for they have and have had more writers to tell about them than there are things to write about." Our author thinks he will say things which, "if only Pliny had heard them he would have been amazed and astonished." "In the Indies everything is portentous, everything is surprising, everything is different and on a larger scale than in the Old World. It rains in summer but not in winter; the earth trembles frequently; there are immense volcanoes. . . ."

Cárdenas mentions numerous properties of minerals and plants, and he especially points out the decisive differences between the inhabitants of the New World and those of the Old. This is what interests us here. He is not concerned with the natives, for whom he has nothing but contempt—"nasty, filthy specimens, the Indians and Negroes entirely so," he tells us—a contempt which comes from an absolute lack of comprehension, frequent among his compatriots. He is concerned with the Spaniards born in America, the Creoles.

According to Cárdenas, the Spaniard born in America is superior to the one born in Spain in many respects. He notes the traits that are typically Mexican, a nationalism that you may have thought appeared later—at least, I thought so. The element of racial difference, which has frequently been adduced to account for the difference between Spaniards and Mexicans, for Cárdenas is nonsense. The differences [for him] are between *gachupines* and *criollos*, between the Spaniards of Spain and those of Mexico.

"In order to demonstrate and make clear that all those born in the Indies are alike in sharp, penetrating, and keen wit, I should like to compare one of those born here with one recently arrived from Spain, to wit: Let the one born in the Indies not be one of those reared in any of these great and famous cities of the Indies, but in a poor and barbarous Indian village, in the company of only a few farmers; and let the *gachupín* or recent arrival from Spain also be reared in a village [there], and bring the two together for discourse and conversation.

"We shall hear the Spaniard born in the Indies speak with such polish, urbanity, and clarity, with so many preambles of delicacy and rhetoric, not taught or artificial, but natural, that he will seem to have lived all his life at court in the company of well-spoken and eloquent men.

"The *gachupín*, on the contrary, unless he has been reared among city people, you will find to be more rude and stupid than an untrimmed log.

"So if we observe how different the manner of the one is from that of the other, the one so brutish, the other so lively, there is no man however ignorant who will not see immediately which of them is the *gachupín* and which was born in the Indies.

"Or take a woman from Spain and let her enter a convent with many ladies of the Indies, and they will at once display this difference, if only in the advantage that those born in the Indies have over those who come from Spain.

"Or let [a Criollo] make a witty remark, a speech, or a well-turned and polished argument, and on my life you will not find a courtier reared in Madrid or Toledo who will do it better. I remember one time, when a Mexican gentleman remarked to me, thinking I was a physician, how little he feared death, and made his argument in the following manner: 'Let the Fates spin out the thread of my life however they please, for when they wish to cut it I shall take your Worship's hand and you will tie it together for me.' Another, offering me his person and service, said to me: 'Take this house, your Worship, for you know that it is the storeroom of your Worship's pleasure.'

"Such is the fashion and such the delicacy of the men born in the Indies. And this only with respect to their speech, for in understanding and subtle argument they are no less superior, for truly I think that in everything they undertake and do (if they persevere in it to the end), they have the advantage. And this is clearly to be seen in the pretty wit they all display in these schools of the Indies, where, if they should not win the prize for their efforts, they would be [considered] freaks of nature."

Cárdenas, as you have seen, limits himself to pointing out the differences, but a somewhat later writer, the Englishman Thomas Gage, who was a Dominican friar when he traveled through this country, where he arrived in 1625, not only points out the differences, but the hostility and bad blood between Spaniards and Creoles. Gage wrote his book to encourage England to seize the American colonies of Spain, an enterprise he thought feasible, because the Spaniards in the Indies had neglected the exercise of arms and because of the hatred the Creoles had for them, and so would be disposed to give their support to anyone who would free them from the Spaniards. "In all the states of America that belong to the King of Spain there are two classes of Spaniards who hate each other more violently than the Spanish and French do in Europe. This hatred is so bitter that I dare say nothing could contribute more to the conquest of America than this division, for it would be easy to win over the Creoles and induce them to take a stand against their enemies, to break the yoke, emerge from the slavery to which they are subjected, and avenge themselves for the cruelty with which they are treated, for the unfairness with which justice is administered, and for the favoritism and partiality that the natives of Spain always enjoy."*

I am aware that Thomas Gage's notes have been challenged and that it is held against him that he spoke too freely of corruption in the colony, especially among the religious. We may allow that this corruption was not so general as he indicated, but we have no reason to believe it did not exist, for he is not the only witness to it. He mentions numerous instances of the conflicts within the religious communities occasioned by the opposition and animosity between Spaniards and Creoles.

This is the atmosphere in which Don Carlos de Sigüenza y Góngora is born and lives—an atmosphere that we cannot easily capture in the history books, which, like modern reporters, are on the lookout for news wherever important events occur and then present them to us in rapid succession, making history seem to us extremely mobile and dramatic, full of significant episodes.

---

* [Thomas Gage, *A New Survey of the West Indies, 1648: The English American*. There are many editions of this famous book, which is not always to be taken seriously, for it is a frank piece of propaganda written at the instigation of the Long Parliament. In 1654 Cromwell directed Gage to prepare a plan for the best way to attack the Spanish Indies, his "Western Design," which led to the taking of Jamaica. Despite Gage's unsavory character (he earned immunity from persecution for being a renegade Catholic by betraying two Jesuits to their death), his book is still a unique and delightful account of colonial life in the seventeenth century.—*Tr.*]

The atmosphere of the seventeenth century in Mexico is best seen in the leisurely pages of the *Diarios de Sucesos Notables*, which several conscientious men of the time have left us: Guijo, Robles, Gemelli Carreri. In their pages one can appreciate how thin was the historical density of life in those days. If, as we are told, those countries are happiest which have no history, New Spain was a happy land in the seventeenth century.

It was a slow, soporific life, disturbed by only a few lawsuits which today strike us as foolish—disputes over the proper place in which to seat various officials—a life stimulated by masques, bullfights, and *autos de fe*, by cruel punishments, doubtless meant to teach a lesson to the victims, who are almost exclusively mestizos, Indians, mulattoes, and Negroes.

Sails have been sighted off Campeche; sails off Tampico; sails off Acapulco. The dispatch boat arrives; the China galleon departs. Theses are defended; poetic contests are held: insipid rhetorical exercises and colossal displays of memory. Notable events like the following may be worth mentioning:

"At the beginning of this year [1665] came a foreigner who took from his mouth lettuce, radishes, wine, orange-flower water, and other things.

"At the end of this year came a flying acrobat, extremely dexterous, called Francisco de Morales, who is said to be from the Canary Islands."

And in these years that begin with a foreigner who extracts lettuce from his mouth, and end with a flying acrobat, there occur bits of news like this: "Today [May 6, 1675] a Moor killed his mother-in-law by plunging a sword into her belly." September 6, 1676: "Marcos the constable, at nine o'clock, in the Cathedral bakery, arrested the Negro Pinacate, who had helped Cascabel to escape from jail." April 6, 1697, during a religious ceremony, "the Vicereine wished to take a little wine, and when it was brought to her by an acolyte, he tumbled down the stairs still holding the carafe, to the laughter of the populace." Saturday, December 2, 1684: "About the hour of prayers there fell a dust cloud of salt or saltpeter all over the city, very thick, which lasted until eight that night. The bells were rung everywhere for prayers; there was a great deal of sneezing; it is said that the dust came from Lake Tequesquite [Tequesquitengo]."

In this slow and leisurely atmosphere lives Don Carlos de Sigüenza y Góngora. He is of noble family, son of a tutor of Prince Don Baltasar Carlos; he is a man of unlimited curiosity, a genuine encyclopedist, interested in everything: mathematics, philosophy, literature, history. Although he is satisfied with himself, his satisfaction does not lead him to the extreme of having a facile complacency in his own work. Friends of his, such as Don Sebastián de Guzmán, reproach him for his excessive versatility, for getting interested too speedily in every kind of subject, and losing his interest just as speedily. "I do not know," Guzmán tells us, "whether he is quicker to plan a book than to forget it. I advise him as often as I can, to sit at his writing desk, which he thinks is a sufficient reward for his trouble. The writings that are not written may be deemed fortunate, for the others are carried off by the curious, or they die torn up by the hands of their author."

Guzmán mentions Sigüenza's carelessness, and also his "foolish modesty and humility." This last note may not be accurate, for Sigüenza is not at all modest. To be sure, he can be too exacting with himself; there may be in him an uneasiness that makes him scorn his finished or half-finished work. His nephew and editor says of one of his books, *Oriental Planeta Evangélico*, that Don Carlos had composed it at the age of twenty-three, "and, although a license to print it had been issued since that time, he did not want the book to appear because it was not properly polished in its astrological terminology, for this was at the beginning of his application [to be admitted] to that faculty."

This same nephew, Don Gabriel López de Sigüenza, rebuts the charge of carelessness made by Guzmán and bemoans the fact that his uncle lacked the means to publish his books, which is what Don Carlos himself says in the prologue to his *Paraíso Occidental*: "If there had been someone in New Spain to defray the cost of printing (as the Convento Real de Jesús María has just done), there is no doubt that I should publish various works which I have written under the stimulus of the great love I have for my country, and in them might be found most singular bits of information. . . . These are things, and others like them, which require a great deal of space, so they will probably die with me, for in my great poverty I shall never find the means to publish them."

I think there is some exaggeration in this, a kind of excuse that Don Carlos makes for himself. According to the data that Pérez de Salazar supplies us in his biography of Sigüenza, it is not accurate to consider him as totally lacking in resources. Rather, Guzmán's explanation seems to me more plausible, that is, the tremendous intellectual voracity that led Don Carlos from subject to subject, as well as the trouble he took to perfect his works, as Guzmán himself and Sigüenza's nephew both tell us.

However it was, we cannot justly appraise Sigüenza, because the bulk of his work has been lost. On the other hand, the things he wrote by commission have been preserved. These he finished and delivered to the press, but they are very likely of less consequence. I have not been able to consult all his extant works, in which some carelessness is evident, which indicates that there was as much or more in the others that were lost, or in the manuscripts that were dispersed—carelessness in allowing them to disappear, or self-interest in considering them lost, in order to make better use of them. Surely, if a few works of the eighteenth century are examined, no small part of the materials collected by Sigüenza may be recovered, but this is a task that I have not been able to undertake.

In all the work of Sigüenza there occurs a theme to which he gives a most outstanding place: that theme is Mexico, his fatherland, the love of which is his motive for writing, as he tells us so many times. Sigüenza is a tireless collector of Mexican antiquities; he is the first to draw a complete map of New Spain; he is the first to scrutinize its past in all its aspects; but he does so not in the spirit of a missionary, as the religious had done who before his time had dedicated themselves to the study of languages and customs of the natives, such as Sahagún and Durán, who considered such studies to be antecedent and indispensable to the work of conversion. In Sigüenza the subject has in itself a feeling and a grandeur that give his work a radical novelty. The *mexicanismo* of Sigüenza seeks a solid base in the indigenous past.

Ermilo Abreu Gómez, in his edition of Sigüenza's poetry, has properly emphasized the realism of our author, who scorns the fabulous when he can find in historical sources examples of grandeur and pattern of conduct. But there is more in Sigüenza: His is not a universal realism, or an ample historicity, but an interest exclusively focussed upon the past itself, upon what is Mexican, as deliberately opposed to what is European.

In Sigüenza we do not find merely, as we found in Cárdenas, the balancing of the European against the American, but also a definite notion of what Mexican meant. "The great love I have for my country," as he tells us, dominates all his work—how far it dominates it we shall see later on. He refuses to accept excessive praise for what is European. On the contrary, he tirelessly seeks in the past of his own country grandeurs that will be equal to or superior to those of beyond the seas. He frequently bemoans the oblivion and disdain with which everything Mexican is regarded. "And if in the past the many examples of the Roman vestals stimulated the piety of Christian maidens, I do not see why [the examples of the Aztec maidens who lived in the temples], as I have proposed, should not be more efficacious and productive, unless their proper recognition has been prevented by the ill luck that has attended our name, and they have lost because of their being Mexican and local what others have gained elsewhere because of their being Roman and European."

A Mexican past worthy to be compared with that of Rome! And so, therefore, Sigüenza dedicates himself to the study of the past, of the indigenous past. Since in the present there are rivalries between Spaniards and Creoles, between mestizos, Indians, and Negroes, the fixed point of departure that Sigüenza needs for his idea of a fatherland must be sought in native life, although, to be sure, he does not deny the Spanish part in it. Don Carlos realizes to the full the beautiful aphorism of José Bergamín: *En México, lo Cortés no quita a lo de Cuauhtémoc,* that is, "In Mexico there is room for both Spaniards and Mexicans."

Cortés and Cuauhtémoc, the Spanish and the indigenous, seek an integration, which turns out to be very difficult, given the conduct of the Spaniards toward the natives. Sigüenza's rejection of it is vigorous, and his voice is accusing when he raises it against the cruelty of the Spaniards in their treatment of the Indians: "The people of Mexico, torn from their villages, merely because these are the most remote of their provinces; a people destroyed because they defended their country; a people broken by their poverty, patient in their affliction beyond any other, always awaiting relief from their misery, and always trodden upon by others." "The dreadful and repeated calamity of those days, when Mexico City was flooded; the great sickness of the Indians which destroyed their provinces, caused by the attempt to settle them elsewhere; the burning of their poor houses for that purpose; and the pitiful seizure of their goods, evident in the ruins of their villages—all this cannot be seen without one's eyes being bathed in tears."*

In the study of a people sacrificed and oppressed, Sigüenza finds a subject worthy of his complete dedication. His curiosity is not simply that of a scholar, but is born of a great love. "And although in others these may be the effects of excessive study, in me I wish them to be considered the consequence of the great love that my country inspires in me. Since the time I chose them [my people] as the object of my studies, I have become competent enough in their ancient lore, which is a very particular reason why I am able to illustrate them without having to use remote and unfamiliar materials."

Love of country as a stimulus to the study of history is an idea often repeated in Sigüenza. "Who can be so ignorant of his country's history that he has need of fabulous tales with which to link up his guesswork?" It is not strange, then, that

---

* [Sigüenza is referring to the vast resettlement of scattered Indians known as the *congregación*, which began in very early times and continued until the end of the eighteenth century. The *congregación* reached its climax long before Sigüenza's time. (For the *congregación* and its circumstances, see L. B. Simpson, *The Civil Congregation*, Ibero-Americana, No. 7, pp. 29–129, University of California, 1934.)—*Tr.*]

when Don Carlos was put in charge of planning the triumphal arch to be erected for the welcome of Viceroy the Conde de Paredes, he should seek examples for the guidance of the new Viceroy among the ancient Mexican emperors. "When the doors are first opened to admit princes and governors, let it be only when they have been instructed in the heroic virtues of their ancestors." "Among the Mexican emperors who actually lived in this most celebrated emporium of America, I had no trouble in finding what others have had to seek in the fables." Each emperor exemplifies a virtue, and those who fought the Spaniards are eulogized most. Thus Cuitláhuac "took upon himself the government of the empire, . . . a resolution as magnificent as his determination to defend his liberty and his fatherland at the time when its destruction was feared." Thus when he speaks of Cuauhtémoc: "I could relate deeds of this unconquered youth which, if they did not exceed those told of the ancient Romans, are at least the equal of the most celebrated in all nations."

Love for everything indigenous, admiration for its grandeurs —all this is in Sigüenza; but also, perhaps more deeply, there is his pride of the intellectual, his will to dominate, his satisfaction in manipulating a theme that belongs to him alone, that only he knows. Sigüenza bemoans the fact that the Mexicans are so little interested in writing of the splendors of their fatherland, so it is their fault if these splendors are not so well known as they should be. "The fault is ours, for, although we all boast of our love of the fatherland, what is known of it is owing to the pens of foreigners."

We should not be deceived by these laments. Deep down, Sigüenza is happy to dominate a field in which he knows he has no rivals. Pride frequently peeps out in his pages: "Those who do not know what is in it, and that means everybody, will pardon me for this digression, but I warn them that what I have said is but a small part of what I have learned in my study of the matter."

For years and years—his nephew says that Sigüenza had been devoting himself to the study of Mexican antiquities since 1668, when he was twenty-three—Don Carlos had been working hard collecting facts and materials. In 1690, Don Sebastián de Guzmán announced the publication of a series of books, now lost: "I can give an account of all of them, for I have read them with great pleasure, and if it so happens they should be lost through his negligence, I shall here set down their titles and recapitulate their contents, so that in that event this note of them will survive." The books are *El Fénix de Occidente*, which is concerned with the preaching of St. Thomas in America; *El Año Mexicano*, a study of the Aztec calendar, a work for which Sigüenza was especially fitted because of his knowledge of astronomy; and *El Imperio Chichimeco*.

Guzmán goes on to say: "I have not included his *Teatro de Grandezas de México*, for he has not yet finished it. When it is published, the citizens of this most noble city should not spare any pains to see that the work of this diligent son of an illustrious mother redounds to her honor. A great deal of it is completed, much remains in notes, and not a little, I think, is still to be done."

In 1680, Sigüenza was already saying that the grandeur of Mexico "will some day be a subject for my pen to glorify." His interest in Mexican antiquities made him an indefatigable collector. He assiduously researched all the codexes, all the paintings [picture writings], all the remains of a past now vanished and forgotten, which he felt called upon to bring back to life. "And if Fate decrees that the Mexican monarchs arise from their ashes, in which they lie forgotten, and be immortalized by Fame as Phoenixes of the Occident, this would be the most propitious moment for it."

To rescue the Mexican past from the ashes of oblivion is the task to which Sigüenza bends his whole effort—hence the passion with which in his will he speaks of the treasures he has been accumulating. In his opinion no precaution is too great to insure their safekeeping.

"Item. I order to be delivered to their Reverences all my books that treat of matters of the Indies, general and particular histories of their provinces, conquests, and the spiritual fruit that has been harvested in them, as well as moral, natural, and medicinal things, and the lives of the famous men who have flourished there, the collecting of which has cost me a vast amount of vigilance and care, for it was not easy to acquire such a store of books in all the Indies. And for this reason I most strongly pray . . . that they be kept in a place of their own, for my consolation.

"Item. I order to be delivered to their Reverences various books in manuscript contained in the same list, part of them in Spanish and part in the Mexican language, most of them originals, which up to the present have not been published. In the said list the subject of each of them is specified in detail, and so, because they are unique and treat of most singular matters, they should be cherished and guarded as a great treasure, which is why I feel obliged to beg that they be kept apart and in a safe place.

"Item. With the greatest assiduity and solicitude, and at a very considerable cost, I have obtained various original books or maps [picture writings] of the ancient Mexicans . . . and to the end that they be kept safely and never be allowed to be lost, and guarded from moths [termites], I order that, in some shelf or place or table that his Reverence may indicate, a very clean chest of Havana cedar be made, with its lock, the necessary cost of which to be defrayed by my estate.

". . . To be kept in their library and not allowed to be removed from it, a case of mathematical instruments, made in Flanders . . . which is to be kept and guarded in the said library, in the chest that I have ordered made at my expense, where other treasures are to be kept, and I state that the said chest cost 200 pesos."

In his very care, in this anxiety of Sigüenza to preserve what he thinks of as his treasure, we can see the distortion present among so many students of history: It is best that the past remain past and keep very quiet in its Havana cedar chest. The Indians are admirable in their codexes and picture writings, so long as these things are kept in a safe place. The ancient emperors are models of virtue, so long as Don Carlos de Sigüenza is the one to bring them to life with the magic of his scholarship.

But what happens if this patient race, downtrodden by every-one, stands up and demands bread and, if its anger overflows, breaks all its bonds and destroys all that lies in its path? What does Don Carlos feel then? What does he think? Ah, things are different then. Don Carlos gets furious, and his rage is in no respect inferior to that of the natives. This weakness of Don Carlos must be mentioned, as was his greatness, for it is not just to say of him, with his biographer Pérez de Salazar, that "whenever he had the opportunity he strove to aggrandize his fatherland, and always treated the Mexicans with words of praise and encomiums." Not always. Sigüenza's attitude changed radically after the riot of June 8, 1692.

The first years of the last decade of the seventeenth century were especially bad ones: floods, loss of crops, hunger among the people. The following item in the *Diario* of Robles is ter-ribly meaningful: "Sunday, March 9, 1692. An edict was read, forbidding the Indians to bake the communion bread, and al-lowing only the sacristans to do so, and ordered the Indians to procure it at the Hospital de Jesús Nazareno, for it was feared they might adulterate the wheat flour because of its high price."

Restlessness and discontent increase without pause until they turn into a riot, the riot of June 8, 1692, which shattered the slow rhythm and dull quietness of the viceregal capital.

"Dawn finally broke, as it should not have done, on that most fatal day of June 8th," writes Don Carlos in his account of the riot. True enough, such a day should not have dawned, espe-cially for him. He was working in the calm of his study in the Hospital del Amor de Dios when he heard a commotion in the street. He paid no attention to it, being accustomed to the noise the Indians commonly made when they got drunk. But a ser-vant burst into his room, shouting: "Sir, it's a riot!" Don Carlos left the house, and when he returned he was a changed man, the opposite of everything we know he was before. "The In-dians," [he wrote], "are the most ungrateful, ignorant, com-plaining, and restless beings that God ever made, the most fa-vored with privileges, under the cover of which they rush into iniquities and follies, and commit them. I will not set down here everything that my feeling dictates, when I recall what I saw and heard that night of June 8th."

Those long-suffering Indians, trampled upon and mocked by everyone—it is Sigüenza himself who tells us so—have risen without regard for his feelings. In the minds of those who fought the war in Spain, the attitude of the intellectuals, who had spent their lives praising the Spanish people, is too well remembered for it to be worth our while to dwell upon such changes in attitude. At least it may be said in Sigüenza's defense that he was not afraid but angry, as he ran to save the records of the city council from the fire, books which had for him more value than the lives of the Indians who were dying of hunger. Don Carlos was not afraid. "He ascended to the council chambers, where no one else wished to go, and he alone, by his own strength, endangering his life and those of his companions, spending out of his own pocket more than ninety-four pesos to pay those who with ropes climbed up to the balconies of the said chambers, he brought out the said books and saved them from the flames."

Don Carlos is not afraid, but neither is he compassionate. He stops thinking, as do so many others when they come face-to-face with a reality that runs counter to their opinions. The papers, the documents, are of more value to him than human lives. So he disowns his whole work, which will no longer be the fruit of love, but of "excessive labor."

A riot, which might have been insignificant, but which got so out of hand, was the fault of the cowardice and stupidity of the Spaniards whose duty it was to maintain order, and it seems to him "like what happened in Troy when it was burned by the Greeks." We must, of course, judge Sigüenza's impressions against the background of soporific calm of colonial life to which I have alluded; but that does not suffice to excuse the torrent of abuse which he pours out upon his beloved Indians in his account of the riot.

How different from this attitude of Don Carlos is that of a contemporary and friend of his, the presbyter Don Antonio de Robles, who says in his *Diario*: "The causes of this disaster are said to be our faults, which God wished to correct, using as His instrument the weakest and frailest, that is, the naked, impovident, and unarmed Indians." And he has the generosity to admit that on the night of June 8th the Indians spared the lives of the Spaniards, "for it was not observed or learned that they [the Spaniards] tried to put up a defense or temporary barricades." The only ones who dared to come out during the riot were the friars, who displayed the Host "in the streets of Escalerillas and El Reloj, followed by a numerous throng, and not a white face was to be seen in the attendance and defense of Our Blessed Lord, nor a devotional lamps in any window, as is customary, even less at the doors to relight the torches, which had been blown out by the strong wind."

When at last a few gentlemen went to the square to learn what had happened, they saw "that by nine o'clock in the evening everything was quiet, the square empty of people, but with many dead bodies." Indeed, the lampoon that some joker had scrawled on the ruins of the burned palace of the viceroys could hardly have been more apt: "This pit is to let for the cocks of the country and the hens of Spain."

But all this was a poor reason for such a radical change of heart. And so that nothing should be missing in this painful fall of Sigüenza, there is a document penned by his own hand in the Archivo General de la Nación [of Mexico], which has never been published because of its shameful implications, so far as we know. It is the opinion of Don Carlos on the troubles that arise from having the Indians live in the center of the city, intermingled with the Spaniards. He wrote it at the command of the Viceroy, who clearly accepted it. Sigüenza had not spent his life in vain studying native questions: no one better fitted than he to draw the dividing line and brandish the fiery sword that would prevent all contact between Indians and Spaniards —a sad finale to his zeal for all things Mexican.

In his opinion he mentions the notes made by old chroniclers on the separation of Indians and Spaniards ordered by the Marqués del Valle. And then he adds:

"A great deal more of this business of ordering the Indians to be separated from the Spaniards will be found in the first volumes of the minutes of the council of this city (which I rescued from the flames on that fatal night of June 8th, when the archives were burned, together with the council chambers). In them it is recorded that the most wise councilmen, not satisfied with keeping the Indians at a distance in their own districts, request at various times that the City of Mexico be walled and fortified, if only to protect it from the Indians, who in any movement induced by their constant inconstancy in good behavior, and by the innate malice with which (in their hatred of the Spaniards, especially when they are well treated), always so act.

"As a result of the failure to put this plan into effect, and of allowing the intermingling of the Indians with the Spanish population, occurred the attempt of the Indians, aided by the Negroes, to seize the city in 1537, and they would have succeeded (such were their numbers at that time) if their plan almost by a miracle had not been discovered.

"Juan Ramón, a stocking maker by trade, made use of the Indians living in the city when in the year 1549, he plotted to seize it.

"It was the Indians who, in the riot of January 15, 1624, gave such vast scope to a thing that had been begun by boys.

"And it was these same Indians who, living in almost all the houses of the Spaniards and, what is more ominous, in the square itself, in permanent camps they had there, and in the *pulquerías*, where in their hundreds they assembled day and night, wrought the havoc that we see before our eyes, to our everlasting grief.

"For all these reasons, considering it just, holy, good, and necessary to withdraw them from the main part of this City of Mexico, putting into practice again what was done at its founding, I recommend, after having studied in detail the topographic plan of this city, and after having traversed its districts and outlying parts three or four times these past days, that [he here traces the limits of the zone to which he thinks the Indians should be restricted].

"And lest there be any confusion whatever, Your Excellency may order, if it is your pleasure, that the ministers in charge of the Indian parishes, and their governors in the districts of San Juan and Santiago, and the persons who shall be given the execution of this resolution, shall have a copy of [the map of] their boundaries, so that, after studying them and making themselves familiar with their directions, they may observe infallibly whatever Your Excellency shall command, which will always be for the best."

Don Carlos de Sigüenza y Góngora

Mexico, July 5, 1692

Don Carlos omits nothing to insure the acceptance of his plan, to interrupt the harmony between Cortés and Cuauhtémoc, which is the essence of *mexicanidad*. We should not be surprised, therefore, that his life, which had been so laborious and fruitful before the fateful day of June 8, 1692, should seem empty to us from that moment onward. If he again interests himself in the Indians, it is to defame them, as he does in his brief account of the expedition to New Mexico.

Thereafter his work will not be one of love, but of "excessive study."

(A discourse read before the Sociedad Mexicana de Historia, October 14, 1943.)

The Historian's Dilemma*

These gatherings of itinerant professors, who descend upon you like the gentle rain from heaven to address a public they know not at all well, are exceedingly hazardous, for the professors could easily suffer the fate of the parachute troops who are dropped into a strange country and become the victims of their own foreignness, and fail where other soldiers, possibly more familiar with the terrain and the country, might succeed.

This figure is only partly valid, because our auditors are not hostile. On the contrary, they come with a lively curiosity and a hope to learn new ideas and new theories—a hope, to be sure, that may be frustrated by the professors' lack of familiarity with their listeners.

When I was considering the subject of these lectures I tried

---

* [Two lectures by Ramón Iglesia, read at the University of Guadalajara, Jalisco, Mexico, in May, 1940. He originally entitled them *La historia y sus limitaciones*. His purpose was to clarify the heated discussion over the definitions of history which agitated the Congress of Americanists held in Morelia a few months before, referred to in the text as the Morelia Congress.—*Tr.*]

to adapt myself to the reality of certain facts that I have en-
countered during my brief Mexican experience. Your reception
of my remarks will determine whether I have succeeded or
failed. . . .

Four months ago I attended a Congress on the History of
Mexico at Morelia and heard certain opinions and points of
view expressed, which gave me my first inkling of the state of
historical studies in this country. I may have got the wrong
impression, of course, which suggested my comparison with the
parachutist, but it gave me a jumping-off point for these casual
observations.

At the Morelia Congress I saw with marked, I may say with
exaggerated, clarity, that today there are visible divergencies
among the historians of the whole world regarding the proper
focus of their studies. While the majority of the historians attending the Congress read papers of a strictly monographic
kind, on very precise and limited questions, with an abundance
of data illuminating small sections of our past, one speaker said
that the history of Mexico could not yet be written because we
lacked the knowledge of a multitude of facts, while another,
during the first session, expressed himself in a more hopeful
tone, which later turned into reproach because of what he considered the sterility of his labors.

This last speaker began by saying to the members of the
Congress—I don't recall his exact words, but their sense was
this: Mexico is in good shape because, thanks to the studies
about to be developed at Morelia, the country will gain an
exact knowledge of the laws of its past evolution and in that
knowledge will be able to map out its future conduct. This
person, naturally, was disappointed, feeling that the labors of
the members of the Congress did not enlighten him sufficiently
about the evolutionary laws of his country's past, and hence he
was unable to draw any conclusions about its future.

Between these two poles—the attitude of the person who
thinks that the history of a country cannot yet be written because we do not command enough facts, and that of the person
who believes that history can establish laws allowing one to
forecast the future, much as one can predict the eclipses of the

sun—between these two poles may be found all the theories that today are struggling for control in the field of historical studies and striving to lay down the directions that such studies should take.

I shall not attempt to resolve the dispute here, but shall only submit my grain of sand, my experience gained in other countries, where an eagerness for renovation and knowledge led me to study, too enthusiastically perhaps, what had been produced in Europe these past years, in the hope that it might serve as a guide in my own studies, which for a long time had been suffering from the lethargy that infected Spanish life.

I should like to speak to you, then, of what history should be but is not. In a word, I should like to point out the limits within which historical studies must move, and to add certain reflections, partly my own, partly influenced by the recent trends in historical studies which we so enthusiastically adopted in Spain. In each case I shall indicate the authors and works I have consulted in the preparation of these remarks. They are not many, but even these few are not easy to come by in Mexico. Furthermore, I shall endeavor to keep my remarks within the simplest possible framework, in the belief that those who will most profit by them will be the youngest and least advanced academically of my listeners.

When I spoke of the conflicting opinions expressed at the Morelia Congress you may have gathered that the points of view regarding what history can and should be are quite at variance with one another. This insecurity, this uncertainty, will be brought out in the course of these lectures, and I must add that I consider such a condition essential when we embark upon a theme like this one, which has nothing to do with what are called, more or less accurately, the exact sciences.

Our uncertainty begins with the very definition of the word "history." We are perplexed and frightened when we see the enormous variations among the proposed definitions. One and the same person, namely, the German historian Bernheim, author of a treatise on historical methodology, which by and large has not been surpassed, gives in each of the editions of his book a different notion of what history is. I haven't Bernheim's book at hand, but I recently had the opportunity of reviewing his definitions in the analysis of them made by Professor Huizinga, in his study entitled *A Definition of the Concept of History.*

Setting to one side for the moment the definitions made by the specialists, I learn that the word "history," in current acceptance, has different meanings. For example, history is an event that happened in the past, as when we say "That has passed into history." Or it is an account of that event, the value of which is indicated by the attitude of the man in the street, who very sensibly shows his lack of confidence in its trustworthiness, as when he says "That's what passes for history!" Or "Tell it to the marines!"

Well, then, these common notions of the word "history" are pregnant with meaning. When we designate by the same word the events of the past and the narration of them we can see the close connection between history, that is, narration, and life, which *is* history, as I shall bring out. History, therefore, will the better achieve its purpose the more closely it approaches the narration of living events.

The other notions of it I mentioned indicate that the good sense of the man in the street makes him fully aware of the difficulties that beset history and its eminent lack of exactitude. If this is so, and if the knowledge of the past is so very uncertain, how can we accept the idea that history (in its current usage) encompasses an aggregate of knowledge and studies of a scientific kind, such as are approved at the centers of higher learning, and that there are persons and institutions devoting all their energies to it?

Whether history is or is not scientific knowledge is a question that has caused rivers of ink to flow. The question was not, in fact, squarely faced until the past century, when historical studies were highly developed, particularly in Germany, which set the standards for this kind of investigation. And the rivers of ink flowed because the concept of history as a science derived from the sciences best developed and best established at that time, namely, the physical and mathematical sciences, and the biological.

I shall not undertake an analysis of what science and scientific knowledge are. All of us more or less remember from our studies—many of you better than I, since yours are more recent—that we were told there is no science other than the measurable, the general, and the experimental; that the characteristic of scientific knowledge is that it should lead to the establishment of laws, that is to say, universally valid truths, which determine beforehand and for all time what will happen, given a determined set of circumstances.

The French philosopher Bergson said very aptly that science, in this generalizing sense, manufactures ready-made clothing to fit all possible realities. In the past century all disciplines shopped in this great scientific emporium of ready-made clothing, and attempted to establish their immutable and eternally valid laws, and do their measuring and experimenting. There occurred, as you know, a kind of run on the sciences, and people had to stand in line, as happens whenever there is an excessive demand for an article, and it turned out that the most sought-for articles were the purely mathematical sciences. Next came the physical and chemical sciences, then the biological, and finally, but with considerable strain, the psychological.

When poor little History, trembling, approached the counter of this emporium of ready-made clothing, she was scornfully greeted with: "Have your 'facts' any general application? No, madam! Can you measure them? No, madam, no! Can you establish some sort of law with them? I don't think so, madam! Well, then, what are you doing here? Get out! We have no garments that will fit you. How can you deck yourself out in scientific clothing if you can neither measure, nor experiment, nor establish laws? Out you go!"

So poor History, in her rags, bent under the weight of centuries, poor History, one of the first activities that man had engaged in since he began to make use of reason, discovered to her confusion that the great bazaars of science had nothing that would fit her.

And then all those who had devoted themselves to her study acquired a terrible inferiority complex and set out to imitate their colleagues in the other sciences, to see whether they might not find some garment to fit them. They consoled themselves for the disaster they had suffered by saying that if history had not achieved the degree of perfection attained by other scientific disciplines, it was because the field of their studies was the most complex of all, but that, with a little patience, history would also achieve the longed-for precision and establish its laws and don the spanking new clothing of science that had so cruelly been denied her.

Then the historians plunged headlong into a vain effort to organize their discipline according to the system of the natural sciences, and made use of every kind of expedient. It is certain, said some, that if we gather enough data and compare them we shall be able to establish our laws. If we wish to uncover facts on a grand scale we must study statistics. But the catch here is that statistics is a recent science and we shall not find in it data on past epochs. What then? Well, man has always had to face the basic problem of subsistence. Surely, then, economics will provide a key for the interpretation of history. But here also we are up against the fact that, while economics makes it easy to interpret the present, it turns out to be extremely difficult to make it do the same for the past. Let's see, let's see. Well, by seeking out the manifestations of human life which are the most constant, the most eternal, so to speak, namely, language, art, and jurisprudence, can we not discover more solid elements in our quest for laws? It would seem that language lends itself especially to this kind of thing. So let's go in for philology and study the evolution of languages. And also, if the human past is what history is concerned with, why not go back to origins and see what kind of life was lived by the most primitive and rudimentary societies? Let's take up anthropology, then, and see what it has to offer.

In her eagerness to put herself in tune with the respectable and well-established sciences, History then found herself with a whole family of proud little sisters, all aching to supplant her. "I am History," said Economics. "I am History," said Philosophy. "Not so fast!" said Anthropology. "You will see that I too am History. It's only a matter of completing the study of primitive societies and applying the results to the more complex and civilized societies." And, to top it all, History found she had a stepsister in Sociology, who impertinently ordered her to collect materials so that Sociology might classify them and establish her own grand laws of human evolution.

In spite of it all, History-Cinderella kept on working, putting up with the insolence of the others, until in that very nineteenth century, which had so blackened her name by refusing to recognize her scientific character, she came up with some of her most significant contributions. It was the Germans themselves who, in the second half of that century and the beginning of this one, offered a solution, which was, simply, that if History had worked so hard and so well, and if the results of her labor did not measure up to those achieved by the natural sciences, could it not be that History was a different kind of discipline and should we not try to discover what it is?

This apparently simple answer was submitted by a professor at the University of Heidelberg, one Heinrich Rickert, who in 1898 delivered a series of lectures at Freiburg which contained the germ of his book *Cultural Science and Natural Science.* This is a book that every historian should know, although many evidently do not, for the question is continually brought up as to whether history is or is not a science within the now-abandoned concept of natural science.

Professor Rickert begins by stating that the individual sciences are divided into two large groups; that the theologians, jurists, and historians are united by common interests, just as, on the other hand, the physicists, chemists, anatomists, and physiologists are so united. There is no doubt whatever about the natural sciences, which are solidly established and proud of the results achieved throughout the intellectual history of Europe since the Renaissance. But what of the others? The fact is that jurisprudence, economics, history, and the rest lack a common name that would cover them all. One that has found considerable acceptance in German terminology is "science of the spirit," because all of them study phenomena of the human

spirit. Rickert observes, however, that this name is not adequate, because the very science that is held to be a specific
science of spiritual life, namely, psychology, is considered today
to be a branch of the natural sciences. He thinks the term
"cultural sciences" is more appropriate for the first group, as
he proposes, and this is the one by which he always designates
them, for in them we study the various aspects of what we call
"culture," a term not easily defined, but one which is sufficiently well understood by all of us. The cultural sciences are
much younger than the natural sciences, and they lack the
marked inclination of the latter for methodical investigation.
This is the gap that Rickert proposes to fill.

The sciences, he tells us, are distinguished, not only by the
subjects they treat, but also by the methods they employ. That
is to say, their classification is made from the formal viewpoint
as well as from the material. Thus, as against the concept of
nature as defined by Kant, that is, the existence of things "as
soon as it is determined by universal laws," he places the concept of history, "that is, the concept of a single event in its
peculiarity and individuality." The naturalistic method gen-
eralizes and the historical method individualizes—two irreconcilable and logically opposed ideas of conception. The natural
sciences extract from the infinite variety of reality what they
have in common with universal concepts in certain kinds of
facts, while the historical sciences worry not at all about for-
mulating universal concepts, but strive to explain reality (which
for them is never general but consistently individual) in its
very individuality.

But then, you will object, history includes everything, as, indeed, is proposed by certain historians, who assume the attitude of the child who tries to pour the ocean into a hole he
has dug in the sand. I shall return to this later on, but limit
myself here, as I explain Rickert's ideas, to pointing out that
the notion of trying to reproduce reality in its individual
phenomena makes no sense, for according to it the best method
would be to hold up a looking glass to human events. As
Rickert says, the work of the historian is impossible without
the criterion of previous selection, for if the historian should

succeed, as some have suggested, in eliminating his personality, "he still would not produce scientific history, but a meaningless whirlpool of unassociated figures, all distinct, all equally significant, and all without any historical interest."

That is to say, the historian selects from among the events in the human past those which strike him as the most important and the most significant. No historian, in the pursuit of his work, will admit that any event is of no interest to him, although theoretically he may allow it. This, as we shall see, is the normal attitude among historians, that is, to sidestep the basic problems of their profession, saying that it is up to the philosophers, for whom, incidentally, they express a sovereign contempt, as if they were abstract speculators lost in the clouds. We shall also see that history, without the help of philosophy, falls into the worst kind of extravagances. The historian will doubtless appeal to common sense if he is asked why he studies certain themes that he considers essential and passes up others that he says are devoid of interest. This, nevertheless, is one of the fundamental problems of his profession.

Rickert attempts to solve it by recourse to a theory of values, one of the most fruitful of contemporary philosophy. Values are certain entities which the human being holds to be among the good things of culture: nationality, for example, or learning, or justice. History—and this is very important—does not establish values and makes no value judgments, but does indeed refer to values. The historian, consciously or not, always stands on his belief in certain values, and writes his history in fulfillment of that belief. Who can doubt that the histories of Spanish America have been written, up to the present, as a function of one of two opposing ideas: one, that the conquest was a good thing, or, two, conversely, that it was harmful to the native races, even when the historians disguise or disfigure this aspect?

One of the ideas most disturbing in the study of history should be got rid of, namely, that history must be written without bias. The word "bias" has acquired a pejorative context, in that it vitiates and deforms all our judgments. On the contrary, bias is only a previously formed judgment, a point of view within which we approach all the problems of learning, and one which we can never get rid of, because in that case we should be unable to make a selection of our materials and they would all be of equal importance to us.

These things are pretty complicated, and I wish simply to suggest them to you, to put you on your guard against certain ideas now very much in vogue, but patently false. Not long ago I was obliged to read a book on the commerce and navigation between Spain and her American colonies. The book seemed to satisfy the most rigorous demands of so-called scientific objectivity and impartiality. The author apparently does not intrude his own views at all, but only narrates, in the coldest and most impersonal way possible, all the aspects of the Spanish administration of commerce with the Indies. And yet, upon reading the book more carefully, one notes that from the first page to the last it is filled with a running censure of what the author (who, incidentally, is a North American) considers the incapacity of the Spaniards, and a kind of muffled lament, as if the author were always thinking: "What a pity that we were not running it! What marvels we should have accomplished!"

That is to say, the author, perhaps unconsciously, states his whole case in terms of certain values which for him are essential: the efficiency and capacity of his own country for commercial organization. This, it should be well noted, is what always happens. The historian, whatever his claims to impartiality, writes from a certain point of view. And, just as the physician who plans to go into psychoanalysis must begin by submitting himself to analysis, so the historian will have to discover what his own biases are, to appreciate those of other historians, either his contemporaries or those of the past, because otherwise he would understand nothing about them. So the first thing he has to do is carefully to assess what has been called the personal equation of each author, that is, the complex of ideas and sentiments which condition his way of looking at things.

This supports once more what I have said of the singularity and individuality of historical studies. I shall surely be told that the value of such studies must be pretty thin if they are limited to isolated facts interpreted according to individual criteria. Evidently. But history has a way out, because these isolated facts, which the historian interprets by his own standards of judgment, and which change with the changing epochs, countries, and cultures, have a special importance in each case for the person who studies them. Perhaps, if they could be viewed from another planet or from a perspective of thousands of years, according to Rickert, "the few thousands of years of human evolution as we know it, which after all consists of a relatively small number of changes in a more or less constant human nature, such changes will seem to us as inconsequential as the differences in the cobblestones of the street, or the blades of wheat in a field." But, since men, that is, we ourselves, are to all intents and purposes those same cobblestones or blades of wheat, that is the reason why we are so concerned with the modifications that have taken place in our brief past, and that is why its study is one of the most useful and challenging to which we can dedicate ourselves.

If this concept of history is valid, it will include the study of the great personalities, whom we wouldn't know what to do with if we started off by generalizing. It is a curious thing that reality always ends by imposing itself upon us. In certain branches of history, the history of art, for example, we used to speak of painting before Goya, or in music, before or after Beethoven. But in the field of history proper we set up a whole series of equilibriums in order to diminish the importance of outstanding personages. There would be no reason for so doing if we focussed our historical studies as Rickert suggests.

He warns us, to be sure, that he carries his categories to this extreme in order to establish concepts clearly, for the concepts of the universal and the particular are relative. Thus, the concept of "Mexican" is universal if we consider it in relation to Hidalgo or Morelos, but particular in relation to the concept of "Spanish American." History, which is based on the concept of the individual, operates also in numerous *concepts of the group*. A study of the Mexican War of Independence would be perfectly valid, not only for certain regions of the country, or for the study of some personages who played an outstanding part in that war; but the study of the independence movement in all the former Spanish dominions would be no less valid, as would a comparative study of what occurred in those countries during the War of Independence in the English colonies, out of which sprang the United States.

The problem of the great historical syntheses has also been very much discussed. From time to time vigorous minds emerge who manifest their disgust at the narrowness of the fields of study in which historians move, and they undertake wide syntheses. This is a valuable and productive activity, and the books that face the problem have usually an extraordinary success. We have all taken pleasure in reading them, full as they are of suggestions and vast perspectives. And doubtless we have all experienced the disillusionment of seeing that what they have to say about subjects in which we have some competence is woefully insufficient, and is almost always violently distorted in order to fit it into predetermined patterns.

Such books demand of their authors really exceptional qualities, and one should not look upon them with one's mind made up beforehand that they are worthless, nor yet should one cast them aside. Neither should one expect too much of them, or believe that they are necessarily superior to those dealing with more limited subjects. Excellence in historical works does not lie in the amplitude of the theme treated, but in the manner of treating it. The history of a given city, or of a given personage, or of a given aspect of his life, can be much more valuable than many rough and badly thought-out attempts at universal history.

That Rickert was not far off the track is evident in the fact that the social sciences deriving from the universalist ideas of the past century—economics and sociology, for example, which, as I have indicated, began by despising history and attempting to base their studies on great syntheses and universally valid laws—have had to take a step backward, so that their studies today are much more detailed than they were at the beginning, and more historically oriented. This view is supported in a fine study by Postan, Professor of Economic History at Cambridge

University, entitled *Historical Method in the Social Sciences,* in which we can see how far they have retreated from the utopian and generalizing ideas of the past century, and how far they have advanced in modesty after the wild and ingenuous pretensions of the men who considered themselves demigods, and who felt themselves capable of an impossible breadth of vision, given the limitations of the human mind.

"We are hopeful," writes Postan, "because we are modest; we are modest because we are historians and because the experience of a century of historical writing has made us more circumspect than we should have been a hundred years ago, with respect to what history can or cannot do. Our science, like charity, begins at home."

Readings of this kind would have been salutary for that member of the Morelia Congress, to cure him of the notion that the labors of the Congress might produce great laws to enlighten him about the future of his country. Is not this element of uncertainty and mystery perhaps essential for human life itself, this ignorance of the future? What would become of us if we could consult a crystal ball and learn what would happen in the year 1950 or 2000? History is action, it is a human creation, in short, and its function is not to forecast what has not yet been lived, what has not yet been done. History is concerned with the past, and of course the present, and it studies the concrete and individual. It should not become discouraged when it learns that its field is limited, and that its most weighty consideration is that history, which cannot predict the future, cannot at the same time achieve a full and absolute knowledge of the past, and this will be the subject of my second discourse.

2

Yesterday I discussed the efforts of certain historians to establish what history is (and what history cannot be), that is, a generalizing science, a discoverer of laws valid for the greatest possible number of phenomena. I said that the very sciences which have reproached history for its excessive individuality have taken a step backward and applied the historical method to their own problems, thus gaining in precision and efficiency. And I closed by remarking that disillusionment was inevitable for those of the Morelia Congress who believed they could, in their historical studies, arrive at definite conclusions about the evolution of their country.

I also pointed out that theirs is an extreme attitude concerning the potentialities of historical studies, and their attitude has no validity. Let us now have a glance at the opposite attitude held by others of the Congress, namely, that the history of Mexico could not yet be written because we lack the knowledge of a vast quantity of facts. This second attitude is widely held, but, like the first, which demands of history general laws and formulas applicable to phenomena of immense amplitude, is usually advanced by persons who have not especially devoted themselves to historical studies. Just the same, this attitude is general today among professional historians, not only in Mexico, but everywhere. It is the attitude, as I suggested yesterday, of the child who would pour the ocean into a hole in the beach.

It should be added that this point of view, like everything else in the world, can be defended. I suggested furthermore that history is an eminently uncertain discipline. Historians, as one might expect, are quite aware of this, for when they study the works of their predecessors on some subject or other, they are always able to detect errors in them, or deficiencies arising from a faulty knowledge of the facts, or a hasty synthesis based upon incomplete documentation. These errors and deficiencies are the more glaring, the more ambitious and broad the scope of the historical work. This occurred, for example, with the publications of the great French encyclopedists of the eighteenth century, who, saturated with universalist ideas, rushed into vast historical syntheses without adequate preparation.

The undeniable fact is that historical works of great breadth, including some of the most excellent quality, were found to suffer from deficiencies and errors of detail. When this was pointed out, many historians were led to subscribe to the notion that, in principle, the more limited their field of research was, and the more data they gathered for the greater knowledge of minute subjects, the more solid their conclusions would be, and the fewer errors in their works would be detected by those who should study the same subjects after them. Their ideal turned out to be what has been called exhaustive research, which aims to leave no loose ends untied, and which aspires, when it attacks a theme, to exhaust it completely and leave nothing further to be done about it.

Naturally, this attitude can be defended only if one limits one's investigations to very reduced subjects, studied from what might be called a microscopic point of view. By following this road we have come to an excessive specialization in historical studies, to such an extreme that each historian knows only a very small area of his subject and entirely lacks a grasp of great historical problems, in the belief that the only thing of interest to him is the field of his tiny specialty.

This phenomenon of excessive specialization is by no means limited to history, but is typical of all the sciences of our time. We have all known, for example, cases of medical specialists who insist on treating all the diseases of their patients in terms of their own specialty. In history also we have gone to grotesque extremes in the atomization of knowledge. I remember that a few years ago a German specialist in the history of art visited Madrid. His field was early Christian sarcophagi. The investigators of the History of Art Section of the Centro de Estudios Históricos suggested to this gentleman that they would be glad to show him the Prado Museum. "Does it contain any early Christian sarcophagi?" asked the learned German. "No, sir," answered my colleagues of the Centro. "Well," said the German, "in that case I have no interest in seeing it."

A great deal has been written about the danger of excessive specialization, which changes investigators into barbarians totally ignorant outside of their specialty. In history it has caused even greater damage. It has not only caused historians to fix their attention upon matters of slight importance, but also, in their anxiety to avoid the changes that all affirmations and all more or less daring hypotheses suffer in the passage of time, has led historians to take pride in having no opinions whatever, and to believe that their mission is to gather the greatest possible number of data, without making any selection among them, all this in order not to involve themselves or to be accused of partiality or bias.

The result is that history has been reduced exclusively to its earlier phase of accumulating materials, and that the historians have made of their profession a fenced preserve, in which they feverishly chase new data and unedited documents on insignificant subjects, the finding of which interests, in the majority of cases, only half a dozen persons who have been attacked by the same mania.

Their terror of being caught out in a bold thesis resting upon an insecure base has caused historians to fall into the opposite extreme and has converted them into collectors of quite useless data. They might bear in mind an anecdote told about Darwin. Replying to one who reproached him for employing hypotheses in his studies, Darwin said that not to have done so would be like analyzing a heap of stone as to their density, color, and so on, and giving them no further thought.

In the face of this attitude of the historians I must insist, over and over again, that there is no historical study worthy of the name which has been made without a previous criterion of selection. Without such a criterion we find ourselves in today's situation, that is, that the majority of historians pour into their publications the entire contents of the archives, unaware that the archives themselves contain only a small fraction of the real facts of the past.

This exclusive dedication to research in the archives, to which such importance is given, has value only as entertainment. No one, of course, can work in history without making an exhaustive investigation of some minute theme, but to believe that this is the only possible approach to history is to attack things wrong-end-to. The proper work of the historian begins only when, faced with a certain amount of materials and documents of the past, which are necessarily limited and always incomplete, he undertakes the task of elaboration and synthesis.

He is wrong, therefore, who says that the history of Mexico

cannot yet be written because sufficient materials have not been gathered for it. What the historian of today is suffering from is the fear of involving himself, but that is a risk he has to face. It is a curious attitude, this, of those who study human events, which after all are compromises, decisions, and taking a stand, but who refuse to venture an opinion about them.

As a result of such an attitude we are faced with the undigested historical production of today, which has descended, in most cases, to the pure and simple publication of documents, without the slightest attempt to interpret them or derive anything from them. The fact is, we are told, that our age is witnessing stupendous things accomplished in the name of scientific progress and the critical spirit.

In this connection it will be well to recall the words of José Ortega y Gasset, in his somewhat exaggerated but basically sound study entitled *The Hegelian Philosophy of History and Historiography*. In it he makes an extremely cogent criticism of the ingenuous attitude of today's historians, who believe that, beginning approximately with the year 1800, their profession entered upon an era of great scientific seriousness, because it carried out with greater detail than before, the collection of documents and the criticism of sources.

As Ortega properly observes, all historians, ever since history was first written, have collected data for their books and have criticized such data. In the fifth century B.C., Herodotus made journeys to all parts of the known world to gather the materials he needed for his history of the war between Greeks and Persians.

The gathering of materials and their critical appraisal are not, therefore, anything new. What is new, and seriously so, is to suppress the human element in history. Since events, when they occur, are not recorded by some automatic apparatus, but in the minds of those who witness or take part in them (and each witness or participant has his own point of view about the same event), the "scientific" historians have endeavored to eliminate this margin of uncertainty and, as far as possible, to get along without the accounts of contemporaries, which indeed are the only materials upon which a narrative beyond the facts can be based. When historians put aside the accounts of contemporaries, whom they accuse of being "partial," they dash off in search of their famous "documents," which they consider to be more impersonal, that is, diplomatic correspondence, collections of laws, notarial acts, and the like. But historians are in a fine mess if they think that such documents are free from the subjective element which so frightens them in contemporary accounts—chronicles, for instance. All of us are familiar with the credibility, say, of apparently the most objective documents, such as military communiqués, not to speak of judicial decisions. I know of no document more loaded with passion and resentment than the *residencia* of Cortés, which objective historians as a matter of course prefix to the *Letters* of the conqueror.

It is high time for such persons to realize that historical "impartiality," in the absolute sense in which they conceive it, does not exist. The very concept of impartiality is a myth. A man cannot face human events with the same attitude that the chemist takes before his test tubes. Each man, moreover, sees only a part of reality, which is to say that his vision is always partial. Professional historians, for the most part, seem to be unaware of a long-established truth, but one which has only lately been developed with some precision—I refer to the idea of perspective. In this connection it is again worth our while to consult Ortega y Gasset who, in his study, *The Problems of Our Time*, has very clearly stated his points of view regarding the problems of philosophy, which apply equally to history.

We all know, he says, what is meant by perspective when we view an object or a landscape. Two persons looking at a stretch of countryside from different vantage points do not see it in the same way. What for one of them appears nearer, for the other appears to be in the background. Would it make sense if one of the observers describing what he sees, should say that what the other sees is false? Would it make sense for the two of them to agree that, since their observations do not coincide, it is the landscape that is distorted? Evidently not. There is no such thing as an archetype landscape which would look the same to all observers. And what can be said of the landscape can be said of everything observed by the human mind. "Cosmic reality," says Ortega, "is such that it can be seen only within a certain perspective. Perspective is, therefore, one of the components of reality. A reality that would look the same from any viewpoint is an absurd concept."

"This ancient error arises from supposing that reality has, in itself, independently from the point of view from which it is seen, a physiognomy of its own. If we think in this way, every reality, of course, which did not coincide with this absolute concept would be false. The fact is, however, that reality, like a landscape, has an infinite number of perspectives, all equally true and all equally authentic. The only false perspective is the one that claims to be unique."

You can readily see the fundamental importance that these concepts of Ortega have for the work of the historian. For the historian of today, in his observation of historical events, this factor of perspective is essential to every representation of reality. The historian refuses to take a stand and, naturally, he fails to do his job, since what he calls presenting us with the facts is not a presentation of the facts at all, but a presentation of depositions and documents which, in spite of the historian, implicitly reflect the personality of those who observed them.

The scientific historian of today is caught in a blind alley. His attitude, which at first was reasonable enough, suffered from a tendency toward rhetoric, from scanty documentary preparation and a capricious and hasty elaboration of a synthesis, and so reached an intolerable degree of ankylosis, because history, which is the study of human life, attempted to ignore all the essential ingredients of that life.

The historian wishes to be neutral, regardless, and never to involve himself. To this end he has had recourse to every kind of expedient. He has striven to divert attention from the great moments and crises of history, which formerly had been his justly preferred themes, and has concentrated his interest on the most sluggish movements of daily life and the leisurely evolution of certain customs or institutions which seemed to him the most solidly established, existing independently of change and abrupt upheavals.

In this, as in everything, the historian did no more than impose upon the past an idea prevailing in the present, that of a slow and peaceable evolution, corresponding to the notion of what democratic theory and liberalism had formed of the future evolution of humanity. So now, when it is impossible to teach geography to youngsters because frontiers are shifting from day to day, we can see what is left of the illusion of a slow and uneventful evolution. We must not banish from history the study of epochs of crisis, of great shocks and changes of direction in the life of people and cultures, and the lives of great personalities.

It is in this field of institutional history, in this study of the slowest and most continued development of humanity, that history has scored its greatest achievements these past few years. If we compare the results obtained by the history of languages, arts, and juridical or economic institutions with history proper, we shall see that this group is decidedly superior in accomplishment; but it is these very fields that the historian finds it easier not to get involved. He is happy to be able to remove himself from everything that denotes change, insecurity, and risk. He directs his attention into the most remote epochs in order to achieve his longed-for impartiality. Whether he does in fact achieve it is another matter. But the truth is that he does not face, or wish to face, problems that are vital to the very life of his own time, problems that we should like to see formulated somehow, even if they are not resolved.

Naturally, I do not believe that the historian can play a decisive part in the life of his country, but at least he can play a more important one than he has been playing since history became dehumanized. I recall quite clearly what happened in Spain, where in recent years some extremely useful studies had been produced concerning certain medieval institutions, or the language of some lyric poet, or the paintings of some Catalan artist of the fifteenth century. Mind you, that was in *Spain*, where during that time not a single work was published essential to the life of the country—in a field, that is, which should have been taken over by the professional historian. We Spaniards did not recognize, or we scorned, any subject this side of the

French invasion, and today we are paying the price of that neglect. Our great figures in the field of historical studies did not wish to get involved; they refused to take a stand, and the [Civil] War took them by surprise. . . . But why go on?

This is one of the saddest effects of the dehumanization of history. The professional thinks he has nothing to do with the living problems of his country and his time; he thinks that only by ignoring them can he acquire a better knowledge of the past. Thus we reach the point where, as Nietzsche tells us in his marvelous essay, *Of the Utility of History to Life, or its Disadvantage*, only those who are incapable of making history devote themselves to writing it.

I should add in all seriousness that the three years I spent fighting in the Civil War taught me more history than all the textbooks I had ever read. It is for this reason that the contribution to history made by those who have actively participated in the life of their people is so important. Mexico is fortunate in having had a number of first-class historians who not only wrote history, but made it: Lucas Alamán, José Luis Mora, and Justo Sierra, to mention only the most eminent. The works of these men overflow with what the dehumanized professionals lack, that is, life and passion. They chose their themes deliberately, and treated them with warmth and sympathy.

The historian should abandon the notion that he is writing for half a dozen colleagues. He must write for a wider public, whose interest he must capture. In former times, in the prescientific phase of history so scorned today, the historian knew very well that he was writing for a wider public, which he had to interest. "To please the reader" is a phrase that continually occurs in the pages of our chroniclers. None of them would have dreamed of devoting himself to history if he had not felt capable of setting down on paper his personal vision of the facts and sharing it with his readers. But that, of course, happened in the days when history was clothed in what the scientific historians of today would call its most primitive dress, that is, the narrative.

There have been, to be sure, epochs when an excessive preoccupation with form was harmful to historical writing. On the other hand, today we have gone to the opposite extreme, and many are the historians for whom it is a sin to write moderately well, who consider their works to be the more serious and scientific the fewer readers they have, and who take pride in the fact that their writing is boring and indigestible. Their pages are stuffed with footnotes, regardless of pertinence, and their bibliographies are swollen to infinity with works and more works, which in the majority of cases they are acquainted with only by title, or in other bibliographies.

A good defense of what it is the fashion to call the artistic approach to history is to be found in the delightful essay by George Macaulay Trevelyan entitled *Clio, a Muse*, first published in 1913 and reprinted in 1930. Although the author later seems to be frightened by his own audacity, I think the essay can be subscribed to in its entirety. Trevelyan begins by examining the ravages committed by the application of the methods of the physical and mathematical sciences to historical studies. Unlike the analysis of Rickert, his is not in the historical vein, but is a simple expression of ordinary common sense. "What laws," he asks, "have been discovered by scientific history?" He charges the scientific historians with accumulating an enormous quantity of minute facts, and with a scanty or non-existent knowledge of what man is. The dryness or indifference, he says, which they claim for their work deprives it of all human sympathy, and without human sympathy history cannot exist, but becomes archaeology.

For Trevelyan, who is himself a great writer, history is essentially a work of art. Its fundamental purpose is narrative, that is, to bring to life personages and situations, and to make the reader share the historian's feelings. "The writings of today's historians," he adds, "lack fluidity. They do not move like streams, but are stagnant, like water in puddles. The narrative should remind us that the past was once as real as the present is to us, and was as uncertain as the future."

Nothing is more diverting than the attitude of those historians who assume a scornful pose toward the great personages of great moments of history because they can (now) see that certain events were unhappy or fatal in their consequences.

And these same historians, who could have prevented the ruin of the Roman Empire, or the Spanish, for that matter, are incapable of taking the simplest decisions in the affairs of their own time.

Trevelyan is perfectly aware, as are all of us who devote ourselves to such studies, how difficult the task of the historian is. The historian must possess the knowledge of a number of complicated subjects in order to gather and coordinate his materials, and, in addition, he must have the ability to discriminate among them and present them to the reader in such wise that they will instruct him, without having recourse to the inventions of the historical novelist.

When we consider the difficulties that beset the historian, we can fully appreciate why there are so few historians worthy of being read. But this recognition of the difficulty of the task only makes more glaring the paltriness of those who, themselves unable to write history, think they are superior to the great masters if they succeed in uncovering a few errors of detail in their works. It is a poor attitude, that of despising what one would not be capable of doing oneself. We can see clearly today that the great masters of history are not easily surpassed merely because some of their details can be rectified or amplified.

Trevelyan's essay concludes with a summary of English historiography, in which he carefully points out the defects and virtues of its great figures, and calls the attention of students and readers to them. This is the good approach to its study, if we would rescue history from its sickness by bringing the great historians of the past out of the footnotes and making them a prime object of investigation. Only by combining the study of historiography with that of methods of research can we extract history from the mire in which it is stuck.

We must attract to historical studies the interest of the excellent young men who today go into other literary or artistic fields because they are repelled by the heaviness and aridity of the initial phases of historical investigation. And we must contrive to induce historians to feel less proud of being inaccessible. An historical work is not a treatise in higher mathematics, nor is it a preserve forbidden to the uninitiated. Its mission must be to reach the largest possible number of readers. The epoch of "pure" activities is past, when poets wrote for poets and painters painted for painters. History should aspire to take a respected place in the cultural horizon of the man of today. If it refuses to do so, the results will be fatal to it. Only by recognizing the limitations of history and attempting to overcome them shall we be able to prevent its falling into the excesses of the historical novel, or, as in the totalitarian states, into just another weapon in the service of propaganda. The scientific historians should not think that in the critical times in which we live, they are going to be the unique exceptions, for their works are being regarded from the perspective of relativity, and perhaps they will not emerge from the examination as well as they think. A good proof of it is in the words of the English historian Toynbee, who begins his monumental *A Study of History* with a chapter entitled "Relativity of Historical Thought." In all the prodigious output of present-day historians Toynbee sees only an extension of the industrial system, with its division of labor and its fabrication of prime materials on a grand scale. For him the great historians of the present day, when they are studied in the future, will find their works stacked beside the vast constructions of the engineers— which is not excessive praise when we are speaking of historical works.

To conclude this hasty and awkward exposition of the present state of historical studies, I should like to affirm once more that the person who at the Morelia Congress stated that it is not yet possible to write the history of Mexico because we lack many materials for it, was not right. "With the hundredth part of the data which for some time past have been gathered and elaborated," says Ortega y Gasset in the essay already mentioned, "we have enough to establish something of scientific validity, something much more authentic and substantial than is to be found in the history books."

This is the truth. Every work of research, every publication of documents, will be sterile unless it is accompanied by meditation and interpretation, as always can and should be done.

We cannot allow ourselves to be guided in our studies by obsolete norms. Nor can we stand today on the naïve progressive notion that we can make stupendous discoveries at every step. It could happen that in the papers of the archives we shall still unearth a few unknowns, but the majority of those that await discovery are to be found precisely in what it seems we already know, but what, nevertheless, always lends itself to further thought.

On the Present State of
Historical Studies

The editors of *Cultura y Educación* have done me a doubtful service in asking me to make a few remarks on the present state of historical studies. There would seem to be no more innocent or legitimate question, nor one more easily answered than this, put by a non-specialist to one who works in some particular field: "Tell me, what is the present state of the object of your study?" Perhaps in other branches of learning the answer would be easier; but when it comes to historical studies, the theme is so complicated that many historians would long reflect before venturing a reply. If I venture to do so, it is with the stipulation that the following notes are to be interpreted only as the answer to an inquiry, simple personal observations, and not as an attempt to draw the complete picture of such an extremely broad and complex subject.

The first thing we must bear in mind is that the historian devotes himself to the study of certain aspects of the human past, and that these aspects, and not history itself, are the aims of his thought. If he pauses for a moment and casts his eye over the whole field of his study, he will discover that he is not able, all by himself, to give an answer to the problems thus brought up.

He will have to call to his assistance the students of related sciences: the anthropologists, economists, sociologists, and, above everything else, the philosophers, merely to outline the essential problems of his discipline, for he cannot get along without them if he is to talk about its present state.

Well, let's not make any more excuses, but plunge alone into this dangerous examination of conscience. The mere title of my theme suggests a whole string of delicate problems. If, for example, without going further, we speak of the present state of historical studies, we admit that such studies are susceptible of a purely temporal development, independently of the place in which they are pursued; that history is written in England or the Soviet Union, in Germany or Mexico, in obedience to the same scientific principles, as if it were a matter of bacteriological analysis, or a calculation of the resistance of materials.

I confess I have my doubts that this is the case. If, in order not to complicate things, we limit ourselves to the entity we call the West—Europe and America—an entity with a common cultural base, even so the problem continues to be pretty thorny. The western historian of today dwells in an ivory tower and tries to withdraw himself from, and pay no attention to, the world that surrounds him, so that he may devote himself entirely to his studies and his investigations of the past. But all he has to do is to read an occasional newspaper, or listen to an occasional broadcast, or view current events presented on the screen, to realize perfectly that this world in which he lives is being shaken by tremendous struggles of ideas and interests, by gigantic conflicts between the most opposed concepts of life, culture, politics, and religion. The historian [if he should do so] will no longer doubt that he is living in an epoch of profound crisis, even though he may be lucky enough not to be drawn into it personally in a very direct way.

Could it be that the object of his study, the science of history itself, is pursued without an awareness of that crisis? Many historians of today will say they are not concerned. Secure in the isolation they have claimed for themselves, faithful to the scientific optimism of the past century, they are still unconcerned.

They will say that history, after passing through a series of pre-scientific phases, became a science a century and more ago. Like the other sciences, history has entered upon a period of prosperity, and is interested only in knowing more and more, in piling up data, and in collecting materials for the greater understanding of an epoch, an institution, or personages of the past. It feels tranquil and confident within the great scientific torrent.

I should like very much to share in that optimism, but I should be false to myself if I did so. This is not an easy thing to admit, for historical science is, among all humane studies, the one most intimately concerned with the very life of peoples, the one most subject also to variations and influences. This, to be sure, is denied by the scientific-positivist historians, who believe, as always, that their point of view, which is partial and limited, the product of the cultural postulates of a certain epoch, is nevertheless universally valid and immutable.

Here is an example by way of clarification: Germany is assuredly the country that has put the greatest effort into making history a science in the sense I have just alluded to. The histories published in Germany since the beginning of the past century—books, reviews, pamphlets, doctoral dissertations of all kinds—would fill whole libraries. Well, go today to a German university and see what has been produced in the field of history since National Socialism came into power. You will find that a large part of the above-mentioned work has been wholly repudiated, on the pretext that the search for impartial and disinterested truth, under which it was undertaken, is a false and wicked principle. [Note: this was written in 1940. Ed.] There you will surely find Alfred Rosenberg's book entitled *The Myth of the Twentieth Century*, the historical Bible of National Socialism—which I have had the patience to read entirely—a book in which universal history is considered to be the history of the Aryan race, a book in which are discussed, in the German fashion, with footnotes and bibliographical references, such erudite problems as the color of Cleopatra's hair, and which ends with the triumphant conclusion that she was a blonde. In it universal history is conceived of as a melodramatic struggle, in which the good people are Aryan blonds, and the bad people the dark-skinned of other races.

I shall be told that this is a typical example of the National Socialist delirium. So it is, but at the same time it is a grave problem, the implication of which cannot escape the historian whose eyes are open, that is, that Germany, the country to which all of us have gone to school, has fallen so low as to produce books like that of Rosenberg's.

In this example, which I have deliberately exaggerated, there is an insistent lesson, however painful and disturbing it may be to the scientific-positivist historian, and it is that history cannot slough off the environment in which it is written, and that historical impartiality does not exist. To achieve such impartiality the historian would have to be a god, not a man, and would have to be situated beyond time and space, free from the ties of his environment. It is not possible to reduce history to archeology. Perhaps impartiality could be achieved if we should study peoples, cultures, men, or ideas far removed from us, which have ceased to operate as ingredients in our own history. Perhaps impartiality could be achieved if we devoted ourselves to a history of the Egypt of the Pharoahs. Could the same thing be said of pre-conquest Mexico?

The scientific historian has sensed the danger and has taken refuge in the study of problems in which neutrality is most easily maintained: the history of language, of literature, of the plastic arts, of the most deep-rooted and durable institutions; the history of anything that does not imply political or social change, while he carefully skirts the living problems that might have repercussions in the present and might oblige him to take a stand. It is in these fields that history has produced the most valuable achievements these past years. In Spain, for example, the Centro de Estudios Históricos of Madrid was fundamentally an Institute of Philology, turning out basic works for understanding the history of our language, our literature, our art, but not a single one on the period of the House of Austria, or a work of even moderate value on the great political and religious problems of our sixteenth and seventeenth centuries, so crucial for the comprehension of our history. Let us not speak now of the absolute ignorance of the majority of Spaniards, including those of us who were devoting themselves to history, with respect to our nineteenth century, which we ought to have known. This interest in some subjects, and this neglect of others, was not accidental, but was owing to the self-consciousness of the modern Spaniard, who looked with scorn upon the part his country had played in the history of Europe, and who seemed to be apologizing to the historians of other countries for what he considered the errors and stupidities of his own ancestors.

What would have been the historians' attitude if Spain had triumphed in the great struggles of the sixteenth and seventeenth centuries? How vast would have been the heap of scientific and objective monographs on Philip II and the victory of the Invincible Armada! But the fact is that history is thought of always in terms of the present, of the present of the particular country to which the writer belongs. The historian approaches the past with a cargo of ideas necessarily conditioned by his view of the facts. He has to treat problems of enormous complexity, using insufficient, distorted, and contradictory data. And don't believe that this happens only when it is a question of the past. The great pile of facts of the present period serves rather to disorient than to guide the historian of the future. To make an analysis of any question whatever he will have to depend upon the testimony of those who have taken part in it. And here the positivist historians have fallen into another error, for they have tried to eliminate the personal element in the account of events, that is, the distortion, deliberate or not, of those who have been actors in, or witnesses of those events. The order of the day has been to take refuge in documents assumed to be impersonal.

That is to say, we face the fact that history, a study that embraces the most complicated problems, is also the one that must use as its instruments the most fragile, slippery, and uncertain materials. Is it, then, impossible to acquire historical knowledge? By no means. That there exist great difficulties in its acquisition can never be a reason for abandoning the effort. History has always been written, and always will be. It should not surprise the positivists—so proud of their own methods, so proud, among other things, of their skepticism—that we in our turn have our doubts of them; that we do not share their ingenuous pride in thinking that they have gone far beyond everything in their field written before the nineteenth century. All historians have had to use documents to write history, and all, including the positivists, have employed certain partial criteria when they wrote it—they, perhaps, more than anybody else.

This is why historical studies today have acquired so much importance, studies that are not limited to the appraisal of the heap of data they have gathered, but analyze and evaluate them as an integral human production, in which the historian is present with his ideas, his passions, and his prejudices, reflecting the place and the epoch in which he wrote it.

We recognize today that the works of the great historians of the past are not out of date in any event, and that the re-reading and study of them will yield results in no way less valuable than the quest for new documents, a quest that has been insisted upon lately with perilous exclusiveness.

In the field of the teaching of history this order of the day "to return to the classics" is of the utmost importance. The scientific and mechanical progressivism that assumes that a book published in 1940 necessarily renders obsolete—as if it were the model of an automobile—the book published in 1925, has had a lamentable effect. History, however scientific its point of departure, will always be under the patronage of Clio. It will always be a work which in its essential aspect—selection, synthesis—will be closer to the arts or to philosophy, with its eternal ups and downs, its continuous re-workings, than to a positivist science in constant progress, that is, if such progress really exists in the positivist sciences.

This conclusion should not by any means discourage us—assuming that others share it. The painter of today does not stop painting because Michelangelo or Goya preceded him; nor does the composer stop composing because Beethoven once wrote his symphonies; nor does the philosopher stop philosophizing because he is crushed by Aristotle's *Metaphysics* or

Kant's *Critique of Pure Reason.* Indeed, the artist and the philosopher stand to gain lessons of high value from studying the masterpieces of their predecessors. The historian must never be more proud than they; if he should be, he is taking the wrong road.

Educación y Cultura. Mexico, June, 1940.

Right and Left in the
Morelia Historical Congress

Morelia, the city that might well consider itself Castilian, whose warm stones remind one of Seville, Salamanca, and Alcalá de Henares, made a proper framework for the Fourth Mexican Historical Congress, held there during the last week of the past January [1940], coincident with the celebration of the [fourth] centenary of the founding of the Colegio de San Nicolás.

The writer had not attended the previous Mexican Historical Congresses, which are held every two years, and hence felt like an intruder in a little-known field. Nevertheless, he would like to set down his impressions of it.

What first strikes the eye of the spectator is the deep rift, the radical difference in points of view, among the participants. It is apparent in their manner of interpreting the history of opposing ideas which is agitating the country, and the Mexican, being a passionate man, brandishes these ideas so vehemently that perhaps they interfere with that sober reflection which we are told is the characteristic of scientific studies.

In the Congress there were, speaking in general terms, partisans of the past and the enemies of the past—the old struggle between ancient and modern—the traditionalists and the revolutionaries, the apologists for Spain and the *indigenistas*. It is evidently very difficult for those who are born here to break out of this pattern. It is well known that the inhuman impartiality which historians are supposed to have does not exist, and in a land like this one, in which not only cultures and ideas are crossed, but also races and blood, no one should be surprised if there should be a conflict. What we need to do is to make that conflict fertile—hence the great usefulness of these Congresses, in which opposing ideas are confronted and persons with divergent points of view are brought face to face.

At first glance the traditionalists seem to have the best of the argument. To insist upon talking [as their opponents do] about ignorance, oppression, and obscurantism, in a city where one sees nothing but colleges and where the establishment of cultural institutions four centuries ago is being commemorated, is a little hard to take—although it would be a different matter to inquire who is admitted to these colleges. The traditionalist historian has time on his side, and that is a solid foundation which it would be dangerous to destroy by denunciation.

The revolutionary should bear in mind that his point of view is more recent, that it is useless to deny the existence of a culture, different from his, to be sure, but a culture none the less, and that the only way to defeat it is by surpassing it. If a theory is excellent, for that very reason its application imposes a greater duty. Faith without work does not suffice. The Marxist historian, resting upon his doctrine of enormous political force, has shaken the world from one end to the other, has stirred up revolutions and changes of all kinds, and has brandished his doctrine as a magic wand, in the possession of which he takes his ease, exempted from making any other effort whatever. And in this he is mistaken. Historical materialism presupposes controversy, a conflict of ideas, and it has its enemies in the field of investigation no less than in politics. It is precisely in the field of investigation that the Marxist historian is in a weaker position vis-à-vis his opponent, for the Marxist must frequently engage in activities in the social or political field which have nothing to do with investigation, to say nothing of the simple necessity of making a living. His opponent, on the contrary, whatever his standing, is today in Mexico a person who is free of political duties and who can spend his time—and his money also—in study. He is not on that account an enemy to be despised, and nothing is gained by shouting him down or by trying to crush him with violence.

I say all this because I have noted in the Congress an excessive confidence on the part of leftist historians, who display a dangerous tendency to rush blindly to the defense of a feeble paper, as did the member [of the other side] who in the last plenary session started the furious discussion, his only reason being that the authors professed leftist ideas. In the scholarly field works are judged, not by their ideology, but by their intrinsic merit. For this very reason Marxism as a method of investigation and historical interpretation should be employed with extreme care and extraordinary competence, lest one arm one's opponent with it. It is childish, for example, to believe that by applying the terminology of the present conflicts to the events of the past we are being Marxists. When it is said, as somebody in the Congress said, that Hidalgo was the first leader of the labor party and the originator of the present [revolutionary] party, carefully failing to mention that he was a priest, we get nowhere. Hidalgo has enough to his credit without our having to saddle him with the notions of today's fighters.

Things are considerably more complicated than that. The Marxist historian must never forget that he is confronted with a very delicate task, and that his focus upon social and collective problems of great breadth requires a mass of data more minute and much more ample than those collected by a historian of the traditionalist school, who sticks to local problems and even perhaps to limited aspects of a single individual.

Nor should he forget that if his interest is essentially in economic problems, neither Marx nor anybody else has said that these are the only problems that exist. A person who undertakes a study of industrial arts is not necessarily a reactionary. In this regard you may recall what happened in the Soviet Union to the historian Pokrovski, author of *The Economic Causes of the Russian Revolution,* much criticized today because of his em-

phasis on economics and his attempt to reduce history to figures, statistics, and price lists, while he ignored the fact that a
whole series of complex human problems rested upon the accepted economic base, which the historian must not lose sight
of. If the historian did so, it would amount to getting angry
with a poet who, while describing his feelings upon viewing a
landscape, fails to tell us of the geological structure underly-
ing it.

The proper approach to the matter was indicated by the
Rector of the University of Morelia, who urged that this should
be the basic theme for discussion at the next meeting of the
Congress, . . . and that its title should be "Scientific methods
of investigation and the interpretation of history"—a truly magnificent subject, for which the Marxist historians, as well as the
anti-Marxists, should sharpen their dialectical weapons, each
demonstrating by the solidity of his study, the solidity of his
convictions.

Romance. Mexico, February 15, 1940.

Two Notes on Medieval Castilian Historiography

1. A Short Anthology of Four Chronicles*

The present piece was published in Madrid just before the outbreak of the [Civil] War, in the spring of 1936. It was meant as a diversion, in the military sense of the term. Since 1932 I had been working on a critical edition of Bernal Díaz del Castillo's *True History of the Conquest of New Spain,* which was interrupted by the war. At odd moments I collected notes on passages in the first royal chronicles that struck me as being particularly interesting, and I gathered them together in this anthology, which has no claim to being either erudite or philosophical, but aims only to present to the reader, in understandable language, texts that are usually held to be arid, and are certainly hard to come by.

These chronicles have suffered the same oblivion as all our [early] historical works, victims of the present obligatory "sci-

---

* [*Crónica del Rey Don Alfonso Décimo* (1252–1284). *Crónica del Rey Don Sancho el Bravo* (1284–1295). *Crónica del Rey Don Fernando Cuarto* (1295–1312). *Crónica del Rey Don Alfonso el Onceno* (1312–1350).—*Tr.*]

entific" fad, which holds that the chronicles are unreliable and prejudiced witnesses, not compatible with the dehumanization of history which has lately prevailed (and still prevails), with its irritating and foolish quest for impartiality. The cult of science, which attempted to convert the historical into the mathematical sciences, brought the chonicles into disrepute because they are "partial," as if partiality, or point of view, were not an unavoidable factor in the appraisal of human events, and hence in their narration, which is what history is.

Luckily, things have changed. The Hollander Huizinga has wisely brought to our attention the value of the chronicles as historical evidence, and has beautifully demonstrated in his *The Autumn of the Middle Ages* what they can yield when a genuine historian uses them properly.

Today the chronicles, if we accept the relativity of historical knowledge, have regained their lost prestige. They can give us a spiritual approach to the past; they have the value of an immediate datum, the freshness of a life that has not been tampered with, which cannot be surpassed. They are keys of a forgotten past, but they were not well enough known in 1936. And so it happened that I began a task that might have had a more ample development if it had been based upon anthropological works—a vulgarization, if that is the word, aimed at recovering for history the attention of a public alienated by excessive scholarly apparatus, a public which had sought nourishment in such hybrid substitutes as the historical novel.

Limiting ourselves to the four chronicles here mentioned, we may say that those who have studied them have stopped with attempts to establish dates and authors, with unhappy results. It is believed that they were written about the middle of the fourteenth century. We do not know whether they are all the work of one hand, nor do we know who wrote them. They have been hurt by their anonymity, and especially by their being followed by the historical work of the Chancellor Pero López de Ayala (1332–1407). Despite all this, the judgment of Menéndez y Pelayo has been accepted as if nothing had happened; that is, he speaks of the abyss that lies between these chronicles and those of the Chancellor. But Ayala is only the highest point reached by a very full flood, which had begun with the publication of the *Crónica General*, a work of the thirteenth century which gave to the Castilian tongue the capacity to write history. Later, the royal chronicles that we are concerned with here were painfully opening the way for a completion of the *Crónica General*.

The writing of history in our fourteenth century is a splendid thing, and Ayala represents only its culmination. The Chancellor's work is not conceivable without the previous chronicles, especially the *Crónica de Alfonso XI*, in which there is a richness of content, a breadth of narration, and a consciousness of the importance of historical writing, which are evidence of a full maturity. Above all, it has *life* in it. This is the essential quality of historical writing, and my selection has been made on that basis.

What we must look for in historical works is the heartbeat of life they offer us and evaluate them by their capacity to bring us nearer the period they treat of. This, to be sure, is not easy, for a chronicle may be very vivid and very inaccurate at the same time. What's to be done about it? Quite a number of scholars have gone no farther than to verify dates, and, although some may take off in the opposite direction, perhaps the time so spent has not been altogether wasted. At any rate I have got together the texts of our ancient chronicles as they appear in the *Biblioteca de Autores Españoles* and have made this selection of them, with brief connecting commentaries. In the first edition I used the term *trailer*, which I have now discarded because of its ambiguity. There is no Spanish word that I know which translates this bit of movie jargon, and I should have liked to keep it because the chronicles have a good deal of the movie in them.

The *trailer* accomplishes its purpose if it stimulates in the public a desire to see the film thus advertised. In the same fashion I wanted this brief anthology to awaken the interest of the layman in the complete works. Their reading is worth our while.

Preface to *Baraja de Crónicas castellanas del Siglo XIV*. Mexico, Editorial Séneca, 1940.

2. *El Victorial* [*Crónica de Don Pero Niño*]

On October 4, 1379, a son was born to Juan I of Castile who was to reign some years later as Enrique III. Count Pero Niño, whose deeds are narrated in the *Victorial*, was a little older than Don Enrique, having been born probably in 1378. Gutierre Díez de Games was of about the same age as his lord, the Count. He was possibly a Galician, for his references to places in Galicia are very precise. Pero Niño traversed the lands of Pontevedra [Galicia] before the age of twenty-three, and could easily have made the acquaintance there of the man who was to become his standard-bearer and biographer. Also, the language of Díez de Games has some traces of Galician.

The *Victorial* does not span the whole life of Don Pero Niño, but stops in the year 1446. The Count died in 1453, and most likely Gutierre died before him. We know that in 1435 Díez de Games was busy writing the chronicle of the exploits of his lord. For this date we have Don Pero's will, in which he says: "And I order that the book of my history, which Gutierre Díez de Games is writing, be given to the Countess during her life, and that after her death it be securely kept in the treasure chest of the church of my *villa* of Cigales and not removed elsewhere; but that if anyone desire to read it he be permitted."

The heart of the chronicle, the part in which the narrative is continuous and full, covers the years 1403 to 1410, from the time Don Pero attacked the Mediterranean pirates down to his marriage with Doña Beatriz.

The reigns of Enrique III and Juan II were the period of the Marqués de Santillana, Pérez de Guzmán, Juan de Mena, and the *Cancioneros*—a period of interest in everything human, of an overflowing lyricism, and also of the pen-picture, biography.

These early years of our fifteenth century have not been sufficiently studied; rather, their spiritual aspects have not been given the attention they deserve. Thus, while the more or less trivial compositions of the *Cancioneros* have been minutely sifted, no one has interested himself especially in the historical flowering of the days of Juan II. The reason for it is that in this historically minded age history has been a weak sister, concerning herself not at all with the evolution of historical writing; nor has she considered as worthy of record the subjects preferred or rejected by each period.

Nevertheless, the gesture of Don Pero Niño in ordering that the book of his life be guarded in the treasure chest is pregnant with meaning. The men of the late Middle Ages have transferred their preoccupation with the divine to a preoccupation with the human. If they feel an urge to attain immortality, it is a terrestrial immortality, in which their bodies and their souls, their *proporciones y virtudes*, are not condemned to oblivion. This urge, this longing for fame, which led to a historical flowering, especially in biography, produced the chronicles called personal or domestic, as opposed to the royal.

In biography, as in everything else in the late Middle Ages, we can trace the shift of interest in the divine toward the human. The hero of our first romance of chivalry was Cifar, "The Knight of God." The Portuguese page boy, Nuno Alvares Pereira, is vastly disturbed when his father speaks to him of matrimony, because he has read many books of stories, particularly those of the Knights of the Round Table and, seeing that one of the Knights, Sir Galahad, had performed great and noble deeds because he was a virgin, Nuno had often thought of preserving his virginity, with the help of God. In France, Marshal Jean le Maingre of Boucicault, gives many [similar] proofs of piety.

In the lives of these knights there is still an echo of the first centuries of the Middle Ages, when saints were the only beings whose deeds merited recording, but within a few years the change has become absolute. Woman now occupies the seat of divinity. Thus, in the advice of the Sieur de Lalaing to his son, he has all the virtues of love derive from woman. The knight has moved up a step, but his mission has lost its transcendency and he ends by becoming a sportsman, spectacular and useless, roaming about in foreign parts, jousting in tournaments and suffering hardships for love of his lady. The knight of the late Middle Ages is to the primitive hero of the *chanson de geste* what the Gothic is to the Romanesque: he is graceful, delicate, conventional, and decadent.

The *Victorial* has a greater interest for us than the French books I have alluded to, which have been considered as models of chivalrous biographies. Its hero is less affected. His exploits make sense; they meet the needs of Castile, and there is nothing of the purely spectacular in them. Also for that reason their narration is more varied and lively.

The *Victorial* has another great virtue, in that it does not indulge in persistent and distorting adulation, which is the great danger in made-to-order biographies. The stature of the hero is displayed in the importance of his deeds. In the pages of the *Victorial* there is none of the heavy emphasis on the virtues of the protagonist, none of the constant calling of the reader's attention to them, which stultifies and renders insipid the chronicle of Don Alvaro de Luna, otherwise so beautiful. Nor is there in it the plebeian admiration of pomp and ostentation one sees in the chronicle of the Constable Miguel Lucas de Iranzo. Moreover, Pero Niño displays in his actions a civility and an elegance totally at variance with the crudity and violence of Don Alonso de Monroy, Treasurer of Alcántara.

Díez de Games was able to place his hero among the myths without taking from him his human qualities. The knight rises to the greatest heights by the strength of his arm. He is the son of his own works. And that is why the life of Don Pero Niño is modern, like all the biographies of chivalry, despite its medieval profile.

Preface to *El Victorial, Crónica de don Pero Niño*. Mexico, Editorial Séneca, 1940.

Hernán Cortés

We have abundant proof that Cortés was much given to writing letters. Many have already been published, and it is to be hoped that many more will be.[1] It is not my intention, however, to examine the whole of Cortés' correspondence, but to stick almost exclusively to his longer letters, called *Cartas de Relación,* in which he informs the Emperor Charles V of his actions in the lands he has discovered. Five of his letters belong to this category, of which the first has not been found.[2] They were written in 1519, 1520, 1522, 1524, and 1526, when Cortés was fully mature—he was born in 1485—at the

---

[1] The most useful collections for the study of Cortés' correspondence are: *Cartas y relaciones de Hernán Cortés,* collected and published by Don Pascual de Gayangos (Paris, 1866); *Escritos sueltos de Hernán Cortés,* in the *Biblioteca Histórica de la Iberia* (Mexico, 1871), vol. XII; Mariano Cuevas, *Cartas y otros documentos de Hernán Cortés . . .* (Seville, 1915). A good English edition is that of F. A. MacNutt, *Letters of Cortés* (2 vols., New York, 1908).

[2] For the *Cartas de Relación,* see the introduction to Gayangos' edition and MacNutt's bibliographical note (vol. I, pp. 101–107). The lost first letter is replaced by that of the town council of Veracruz, of July 10, 1919. More complete details will be found in Henry Harrisse, *Bibliotheca Americana Vetustissima* (New York, 1866), and in J. T. Medina, *Biblioteca Hispano-Americana* (Santiago, Chile, 1898), vol. I.

time of the events there described. These five letters, along with various shorter ones, of unequal importance, are in the Gayangos collection, although the edition is plagued with errors.[3] The foregoing observations are made to remind the reader that when we work with the *Letters* of Cortés we are working with badly edited documents.

The first thing that surprises all who read the *Letters* of Cortés is their moderate, equable, and impassive tone. Although they describe events that have stupefied whole generations, we do not find in his pages any sign of the overflowing emotion, exaltation, passion, and impetuosity that would seem to be perfectly understandable, or even unavoidable, given the nature of the events described.[4]

The narrative style of Cortés is sober, calm, and uncluttered, as, for example, in his description of the high moments of his adventure, such as the destruction of his ships.[5] "And since, besides those henchmen and friends of Diego Velázquez who wished to leave this country, there were also others who, seeing how vast it was and how heavily populated, and how few we Spaniards were, had the same opinion. And I thought that if I should leave the ships there they would seize them, and all who felt the same way would make off, and I should be left alone—which would interfere with the great service which I

---

[3] The page numbers following the citations made below refer to the Gayangos edition. References to the *Escritos sueltos* and to the collection of Father Cuevas are indicated separately.

[4] MacNutt, the English editor of the *Letters*, remarks very justly: "The restraint and self-control of which he was master appear in the equal and passionless style of his writings; for he seems neither exalted by success nor cast down by misfortunes, both of which he describes with calm simplicity in language which is both natural and fluent" (*op. cit.*, vol. I, p. 105).

[5] The purpose of this essay not being to make a study of the conquest but of its historians, I am proceeding on the assumption that the reader is familiar with the events I allude to. The most readable book on the conquest of Mexico is that of the North American historian, William H. Prescott, which I have used in the Spanish translation of Don José María González de la Vega (2 vols., Mexico, 1844). Volume IV of Don Manuel Orozco y Berra's *Historia antigua y de la conquista de México* (4 vols., Mexico, 1880) is extraordinarily solid and well documented, although it is not as pleasant to read as that of Prescott. For a briefer account, Carlos Pereyra's *Hernán Cortés* (Madrid, 1931), and Salvador Madariaga's *Hernán Cortés* (Buenos Aires, 1941) will be adequate.

was performing in that country for Your Majesty and God. So I, on the pretext that the ships were not seaworthy, arranged to beach them. By this device all those who had hoped to leave the country lost that hope, and I began my march inland more confidently, no longer fearing that the men I was leaving in the *villa* [of Veracruz]* would desert me" (p. 54).

When he realizes that there are profound divisions, bitter enmities, and continual wars among the Indians: "I was well pleased to see how divided they were, for it suited my purpose very much and would provide the means to subjugate them more quickly, as the common proverb has it: *Del monte sale quien el monte quema* ['From the wood emerges he who will burn it'], and I even recalled the Biblical text that goes: 'Every kingdom divided against itself is brought to desolation.'[6] So I played them against each other, and secretly thanked each in turn for the tidings they brought me, and I persuaded each faction to think I held it in greater esteem than the other" (p. 70).

Then he reaches Tenochtitlán, the Aztec capital, and meets Moctezuma. This is the very summit and culmination of his aspirations in the first stage of his explorations. A trait stands out in his reporting of the interview which we shall always find in him: great precision and detail, satisfaction in describing what he sees, and the conciseness and slight importance he gives to his plans and actions, or how they can influence him: "Once we had crossed the bridge, the Lord Moctezuma came out to receive us, with a company of perhaps 200 nobles, all barefoot and dressed in a kind of livery very different from the garments the others were wearing, this also according to custom. And they approached us in two files, hugging the walls of the street, which is very wide, and very beautiful and straight,

---

* [The *villa* was the traditional municipal corporation of Castile ranking just below the city (*ciudad*) in importance. Its members (*vecinos*) enjoyed very considerable privileges, and the *villa* itself was recognized as an original source of political power. All the Spanish municipalities of New Spain were organized as *villas* and built along the lines ordered by Cortés. For a more extended treatment, see L. B. Simpson, *Many Mexicos* (4th ed., Berkeley and Los Angeles, 1966), chap. 9.—*Tr.*]

[6] The Gospel according to St. Matthew 12: 25.

and the same from one end to the other, two-thirds of a league long, having on either side handsome big houses, dwellings or temples. And the said Moctezuma came walking down the middle of it, supported by two nobles, one to his right and one to his left, one of whom was the great lord who I said had come out in a litter to speak to me, the other a brother of the said Moctezuma, lord of the city of Ixtapalapa, which I had left that same day. All three were dressed alike, save that Moctezuma was shod and the others were barefoot. . . . And when we met I dismounted and advanced to embrace him, but the two lords who accompanied him held me back and prevented my touching him. And they and he also went through the ceremony of kissing the earth; which done, he ordered his brother to stay with me and take me by the arm, while he and the other [noble] went before me a little way. And after I had spoken with him, all the other nobles in the two files came up likewise to speak to me, in line, one behind the other, and then returned to their procession.

"And at the time I came up to speak to the said Moctezuma, I took off a necklace of glass pearls and diamonds I was wearing and threw it about his neck. And after we had gone a little way along the street, a servant of his approached carrying wrapped in a cloth two necklaces of shrimps made of the shells of red snails, which they esteem highly. And from each necklace there hung eight golden shrimps, very perfectly wrought, almost a span long. And when they were brought to him, he turned to me and threw them about my neck.

"And he continued along the street in the manner described until he came to a very large and beautiful house, which he had prepared for us. And he took me by the hand and led me to a great room that gave upon the courtyard by which we had entered. And there he seated me on a very rich dais that he had ordered erected, and told me to wait for him there. And he left, and a little later, when all the men of my company had been assigned quarters, he returned, with many kinds of ornaments of gold and silver and featherwork, and with as many as 5,000 or 6,000 pieces of cotton cloth, very rich, woven and worked in many ways. And after he had presented them to me, he took his seat on another dais, next to the one I occupied, and, having taken his seat, spoke to me as follows:

'Many days ago we learned from writings left by our ancestors that I and all those of us who inhabit this land are not natives of it, but are strangers who came here from very distant parts; and we also learned that our ancestors brought with them a lord whose vassals they were. He returned to his own country and long afterward came here again, so long afterward that those who had remained here had taken wives from among the natives of the country and had multiplied greatly, and had founded towns where they were living. And when he tried to take them away with him, they refused to go; still less would they accept him as their lord; so he left. And we have always believed that his descendants would return and conquer this land and reduce us all to vassalage. And, in view of the direction from which you say you have come, that is, from the rising sun, and in view of the things you say about the great lord or king who sent you here, we believe and hold it to be certain that he is our natural lord, especially since you say he has long had tidings of us. Be assured, therefore, that we shall obey you and consider you as acting for the great lord you mention, and in this there will be no fault or deceit whatever; and in all this country, I mean, wherever I rule, you can command as you please, because you will be obeyed and recognized, and everything we possess shall be at your disposal.

'And now that you are in your own country and your own house, enjoy yourselves and rest from the hardships of the journey and the wars you have been in, for I am well informed about what you have been through between Potonchán and this place, and I know well enough that the people of Cempoala and Tlaxcala have spoken much evil of me, and that some of them who were my vassals have rebelled against me since you came, and they say these things to curry favor with you. And I know also they have told you I have houses with walls of gold, and that the mats on my daises and the other things of my service are likewise of gold, and that I was a god and considered myself as such, and many other things besides. But my houses, as you can see, are of stone and lime and earth.'

"Then he lifted up his robe and exposed his body, saying: 'Here you can see that I am of flesh and blood like yourself and everybody else, and am mortal and palpable.' Here he touched his arms and body. 'So you see how you have been lied to. It is true that I have a few pieces of gold that my ancestors left me. Everything that I have here is yours whenever you wish. I shall now retire to some other houses where I live. Here you will be provided with everything necessary for yourself and your men; and take no thought of it, for you are in your own house and country.'

"And I made answer to everything he had said, satisfying him as much as seemed proper, especially with regard to having him believe that Your Majesty was the one they had been expecting, whereupon he took his leave. And we were very well provided for, with many chickens [turkeys], and bread, and fruit, and other necessities for the service of our quarters. And in this fashion we were very well supplied with everything we needed, and were visited by many of those lords" (pp. 84–87).

Cortés makes no further comment on one of the most astonishing scenes in the history of the world. Moctezuma's account of Quetzalcoatl's prophecy strikes him as something to be expected, as does his identifying Charles V with God.[7] He merely assures the Aztec monarch that he is right. He adds nothing that implies the least surprise at what had happened, or the pleasure he must have experienced when he realized that this amazing episode made it entirely possible for him to carry out his plans. On the contrary, he devotes long paragraphs to the formalities of his meeting with Moctezuma, to the dress of the latter and his companions, to their movements and the presents that were exchanged—in short, to everything visible and external. And today we are the ones who are stupefied when we see how naturally Cortés accepts the marvelous and the unusual as guides to his conduct.

It should not surprise us at all that a man who decides to

[7] On the vacillations and fears produced in Moctezuma by the news of the landing of the Spaniards and their advance upon Tenochtitlán, the most complete account is that of Orozco y Berra, who bases it on the texts of native chroniclers (*op. cit.*).

take Moctezuma prisoner does not abandon his usual tone when he tells us why and how he did it:[8]

"Six days after I entered the great city of Tenochtitlán, Most Unconquered Prince, and had seen certain aspects of it, although few in comparison with those yet to be seen and described—judging by these few and by what I had seen of the country, it seemed to me that it would be necessary for your service and our safety to have this lord in my power and not allow him his entire freedom, lest he have second thoughts and abandon the good will he had shown to serve Your Highness. More especially [I resolved to do so] because we Spaniards are somewhat restless and importunate, and because if Moctezuma should become angry he could do us much mischief, so much so that there would be no memory of us, such is his great power; also, if I had him with me, all the lords his subjects would the more readily accept the service of Your Majesty, as afterward happened" (pp. 88–89).

So he suggests that Moctezuma come and live with him until the attack on a certain Spanish garrison, apparently made by vassals of the Aztec lord, should be cleared up. "We had long conferences and arguments about this matter, too long to describe to Your Highness. Besides it would not be germane to the subject, so I shall say only what he finally said, that he would be pleased to go with me" (p. 90).

These paragraphs make it clear that we cannot speak of the unawareness of Cortés, for he was fully cognizant of the faults of his men and of how dangerous they might be in their situation. It was quite possible that the natives would attack them and wipe them out so thoroughly that not a trace or a memory of their coming to those lands would remain. Indeed, the situation is such that it is tempting to stress the danger that threatened them and give Cortés credit for having met it. He appraises the situation in his own fashion, according to which the

---

[8] Cortés himself tells us that he had this idea when he first learned of the existence of Moctezuma. At the beginning of his second *Carta de Relación*, referring to the first, he says: "I recollect that in my quest for this lord I undertook to do more than I could possibly do, for I certified to your Highness that I would have him either a prisoner, or dead, or subject to the royal crown of Your Majesty" (p. 52).

boldest and most incredible enterprises turn out to be entirely normal.

I could multiply the examples of this spirit of Cortés as reflected in his letters. In this first stage of the conquest, in the fullness of his success, he attaches not the least importance to what he is doing. Many years will have to pass, he will have to feel himself shunted to one side and neglected by the Emperor, before he will insist over and over again, with tiresome and justifiable monotony, upon the unique and extraordinary value of the deeds he had done in the lands of Mexico.

I have suggested above that Cortés, although he attaches no importance to what he does, does give very great importance to what he sees. He has an immense admiration for the grandeur and beauty of the lands he discovers, and for the power and diversity of the native social organization, which is much superior to anything the Spaniards had found thus far in the islands. It is then that the conqueror becomes the conquered, and it is then that Cortés, so sober and spare in his accounts of his exploits, so exact in his descriptions, confesses that admiration blunts his pen and makes it impossible for him to say all he would like to say. "On the subject of Moctezuma's service and the many things in it that are admirable in their grandeur and circumstance, there is so much to say that I don't know where to begin, or even to describe a small part of them. For, as I have already said, could there be a greater wonder than that a barbarous lord like this one should possess, imitated in gold and silver and featherwork, everything under the sun that is found in his domains? Or wrought in gold and silver in so lifelike a fashion that no workman in the world could surpass it? And as for precious stones, can one imagine with what tools they are cut so perfectly? And their featherwork, how could it be equalled in wax or embroidery, so marvelous is it?" (p. 109).

"Because, Most Puissant Lord, to give your Royal Excellency some notion of the grandeur and the strange and wonderful things of this great city of Tenochtitlán, and of the domain and service of Moctezuma its lord, and of the rites and customs of the people, and their manner of government, not only of this city, but of the others once subject to this lord, would take a long time and many expert reporters. I cannot relate the hundredth part of the things that could be said of them; but, as best I can, I shall tell of a few of them which, though badly expressed, will, I know, be so astonishing that they will not be believed, for even those of us who see them with our own eyes have not the wit to understand them" (pp. 101–102).

In other words, for Cortés Mexico is a fantasy, such a stupendous illusion that, even though he sees it with his own eyes, his brain cannot take it in. And he falls in love with his illusion and ardently wishes to make it his own. He is not possessed by a rage to destroy it, as has been so often repeated, but by a desire to own it and enjoy it.

Cortés is astonished by everything; everything about the lands he has discovered pleases him. Evidence of his wish to assimilate them is the name he gives them: "From what I have seen and learned of the similarity between this country and Spain, in its fertility, its size, its climate, and in many other features of it, I thought that the most suitable name for it would be New Spain of the Ocean Sea, and thus in the name of Your Majesty I have christened it" (p. 156).

Cortés admires nature and the landscape in the new lands. "Eight leagues from this city of Cholula are two high and very marvelous mountains, which even at the end of August are so covered with snow that nothing else can be seen on their summits. The taller one often emits, day or night, a puff of smoke as big as a house, and it rises to the clouds straight as an arrow, with such force, it seems, that even the strong wind that is always blowing cannot deflect it.

"And because I have always desired to give Your Highness a very exact account of all the things of this land, I wished to discover the secret of this mountain, which seemed very marvelous to me, so I sent ten of my men, such as were fitted for such an undertaking, with a few natives of the country to guide them, and I urged them strongly to attempt the ascent of the said mountain and learn the reason for that smoke, and whence it came and how it emerged. And they went and tried their best to climb it, but were unable to do so because of the great amount of snow on the mountain and the many whirlwinds of

ashes from the mountain which wander about over it, and also
because they could not endure the sharp cold up there on the
summit. But they did come close to it, so close indeed that
while they were up there the cloud of smoke began to pour
out, and they say it came with such a rush and noise that it
seemed the whole earth was falling down. So they descended,
and brought along a deal of snow and icicles to show us, which
seemed a strange thing for these torrid parts, according to the
opinion that pilots have held up to this time" (pp. 77–78).

What most strikes the conqueror, however, is the level of
culture attained by the natives. His amazement is most evident
in his descriptions of the cities.

Tlaxcala. "It is so large and so astonishing that, although I
shall relate little of what I could say of it, that little is almost
incredible, for it is much bigger than Granada and very much
stronger, and its buildings are as good, and it has many more
inhabitants than Granada had at the time of its fall, and it is
better provided with native foodstuffs, such as bread, fowl,
game, fish from the rivers, and garden products and good
things to eat.

"There is in this city a marketplace to which some 30,000
souls come every day to buy and sell, not to mention many
small markets in other parts of the city. In this marketplace
they trade in everything imaginable, food and clothing and
footgear; it has jewelry shops stocked with gold and silver and
precious stones, and other ornaments of featherwork, as well
displayed as in any market of the world; crockery of all kinds as
good as the best of Spain; a great deal of firewood and charcoal, and herbs, edible and medicinal. There are hairdressing
shops and barber shops and bathhouses. In short, these people
enjoy every kind of good order and government; they are of
great intelligence and industry, so much so that the best of
Africa does not equal them.

"This province has many level and beautiful valleys, all of
them cultivated and planted, not a vacant spot in them. It
measures ninety leagues around and more. The political system in use up to the present is that its people govern themselves, more or less like the seigneuries of Venice and Genoa,

or Pisa, for there is no general lord of all; but there are many lords, and all of them reside in this city. The people of the country are farmers, vassals of these lords, and each one owns his own land, although some have more than others. In time of war they must all assemble, and all together they arrange and plan it.

"It is believed that they must have some kind of justice for the punishment of evil-doers, because one of the natives of this province stole some gold from a Spaniard, and I spoke of it to that Maxixcatzin, who is the greatest of all the lords. An investigation was made and the thief was followed to a nearby city called Cholula, and he was captured and brought to me, with the gold, and they told me to have him punished; but I said that since he was in his own country they should deal with him according to their custom, for I would not interfere in the punishment of their people while I was in their country. They thanked me for this, and they seized him; his crime was announced by the public crier, and he was brought to the great marketplace and placed upon a kind of stage in the middle of it, and the crier climbed up on it and in a loud voice recited the crime the fellow had committed, whereupon in the sight of all they struck him upon the head until he died. And we have seen many others in fetters who wore them, it was said, because of their thefts and crimes" (pp. 67–69).

Cholula. "This city is very rich in farms, because it has much land, most of it irrigated. It is a more beautiful city seen from without than any city in Spain, for it is very level and has many towers. And I assure Your Highness that from a temple I counted 400-odd towers in the said city, all of them belonging to temples. It is the city most fitting for the residence of Spaniards that I have seen between the port [Veracruz] and here, because it has water and vacant land for raising cattle, which none of the cities have that we have seen, because such is the multitude of people who dwell in these parts that there is not a palm of uncultivated land. Even so, there is a scarcity of bread in many places, and there are many poor who beg from the rich in the streets and houses and marketplaces, as the poor do in Spain. The respectable people (*gente de razón*) live elsewhere" (p. 75).

Ixtapalapa. "This city of Ixtapalapa has 12 to 15,000 inhabitants. It stands upon the shore of a great salt lake, built half
over the water, half on land. Its lord has some new houses, not
yet completed, which are as good as the best of Spain—I mean,
in their size and construction, in their stonework as well as in
their carpentry and floors, with every kind of decoration except
the carving and other fine things common in Spanish houses.
Many of the houses, high or low, have very cool gardens with
many trees and fragrant flowers; also, ponds of sweet water
very well built, with stairs leading down to the bottom. Next
to the house is a large orchard, and looking over it a gallery of
very beautiful corridors and rooms. In the orchard is another
large pond of sweet water, very square, with walls of fine stonework, and around it a good brick walk, wide enough for four to
stroll along it abreast. The pond is 400 paces square [about
2,000 feet], which makes it 1,600 paces in circumference. Beyond the walk toward the orchard everything is sheltered by
[a fence of] canes and posts, and beyond that are all kinds of
groves and fragrant herbs. In the pond are many fish and birds,
such as ducks and widgeons and other kinds of water fowl, so
many of these that frequently they almost cover the water"
(p. 83).

Cortés moves from astonishment to astonishment, as he explores this civilization, from the barber shops, bathhouses, and
jails of Tlaxcala to the beggars of Cholula and the refinements
of the mansion of the lord of Ixtapalapa. Note that when he
makes comparisons it is always to Mexico's advantage, not
Spain's. Note also that Cortés, after sincerely excusing himself
and telling us that he is unable to describe what he sees, cannot
resist the temptation to make the attempt, and succeeds perfectly. But his admiration and enthusiasm reach their peak
when he explores the capital city and describes its squares and
marketplaces. "This great city of Tenochtitlán is built upon a
salt lake, and from whatever direction one approaches it, it is
two leagues from the mainland. It is entered by four gates, all
on causeways built by hand, two lance-lengths wide. The city
is as large as Seville and Córdoba [combined?]. Its streets, I
mean the principal ones, are very wide and very straight, and
some of the latter, and all the rest, are half on land and half on

water, in which they circulate by canoe. And all the streets are cut at intervals to allow the water to flow from one to the other. All these cuts are crossed by bridges made of very thick timbers, so strong and well built that ten horsemen can ride abreast on many of them. And since it could happen that the people of the city might treacherously rise against us, and since they had ample means to do so, what with the city's being situated as I have described, by removing the bridges at its gates and leaving us to starve to death before we could escape to the mainland—I, therefore, as soon as I had entered the city, hastily set about constructing two brigantines, big enough to carry 300 men and our horses in case of need, and had them finished very quickly.

"This city has many squares, where markets are continually held, with much commerce of buying and selling. One of these squares is about twice the size of the city of Salamanca, where more than 60,000 souls gather every day to do their buying and selling, and where one may find all the different kinds of merchandise produced in the whole country: provisions and foodstuffs, gold and silver jewelry, and ornaments of brass [bronze], copper, tin, precious stones, bones, conch shells, snails, and featherwork. They sell lime, cut and uncut stone, adobes, bricks, and finished and unfinished lumber of various kinds.

"One street is restricted to game; in it they sell all the different kinds of birds to be found in the country, such as chickens [turkeys], partridges, quail, wild ducks, flycatchers, widgeons, doves, pigeons, little birds in cages, parrots, owls, eagles, falcons, sparrow hawks, and kestrels; and they sell the skins of some of these birds of prey, complete with feathers, heads, beaks, and claws; and rabbits, hares, deer, and little dogs which they castrate and raise for eating.

"Another street is restricted to herbalists, where they sell all the roots and medicinal herbs produced in the country. It has shops like our pharmacies, in which prepared medicines are sold, in liquid form as well as in ointments and plasters. It has barber shops where hair is cut and washed. It has men like those we call *ganapanes* [porters] in Castile, for carrying burdens. It has a great stock of firewood, charcoal, earthenware, braziers, and every kind of mat for beds, and finer ones for covering seats and halls and bedrooms.

"There one finds every variety of greenstuff, especially onions, leeks, garlics, cress, nasturtiums, borage, sorrel, thistles, and golden thistles; also, many kinds of fruits such as cherries and plums like those of Castile. They sell bee-honey and wax and a syrup made from the stalks of maize, which are as sweet and tasty as sugar cane, and the sweet sap of a plant called *maguey* in the islands, which is very much better than [our] syrup. From this same plant they make sugar and wine [*pulque*], which they also sell.

"They sell many kinds of cotton yarn of all colors, in skeins, very like the silk market of Granada, although this one is more abundant. They sell pigments for painters, as many as one can find in Spain, and of as excellent colors. They sell deer skins, with or without the hair, dyed or white or of several colors. They sell a great deal of pottery in bulk and very good: many jars, large and small, pitchers, pots, bricks, and an infinite amount of other clay vessels, all of excellent quality, all or most of them glazed and painted.

"They sell maize, shelled or in the form of bread, which is superior in grain and in flavor to anything produced in the other islands and Tierra Firme. They sell pies made of fowl and fish wrapped in dough; a great deal of fresh and salt fish, raw or cooked. They sell chicken [turkey] eggs, and those of geese and all the birds I have mentioned, in great quantity, and ready-cooked omelets.

"In short, in the said markets they sell all the things produced in the whole country which, besides those I have spoken of, are so many and various that I can't remember them all, and since I don't even know their names, I omit them. Each kind of merchandise has its own street, in which nothing else is allowed, and in this they are very orderly. They sell everything by quantity and measure, but up to the present I have not observed their selling anything by weight. In the great square there is a fine building like a courthouse, in which ten or twelve men, the judges, are always sitting, and they preside over all the disputes and quarrels that occur in the said

market, and order the punishment of delinquents. There are
other men in the square who walk about continually among
the people, keeping an eye on what is sold and the measures
used in the sales, and they have been observed to smash false
measures" (pp. 103–105).

Here follows a description of the temples, the idols, the
palaces of the nobles, and the system of conducting and dis-
tributing water, and Cortés gives us his impression of the
whole in the following words: "The people of this city are more
elegant and exquisite in their dress than those of the other
provinces and cities. The reason for this is that the lord
Moctezuma resided there, and all the lords and their vassals
always came to the city, so in it there was more elegance and
care in everything. And so as not to be prolix in my account of
this great city and spin it out beyond need, I shall only add
that in the service and intercourse of its people, it much resembles life in Spain, and with as much good order and dignity;
and, in view of the fact that these people are barbarous and so
remote from the knowledge of God and communication with
civilized nations, it is astonishing to see how intelligently they
manage all their affairs" (p. 109).[9]

The admiration and love that Cortés feels for the lands he
has discovered determine his whole policy. At the very beginning of his march he has already decided not to continue trad-
ing, that is, simply exchanging trifles for native gold, but to
colonize the country and incorporate it into the crown of Spain.
For this purpose he is interested, above all else, in capturing

---

[9] In order not to prolong these quotations beyond need, although quotations are the essential part of my study, I shall not repeat the description
Cortés makes of Moctezuma's palace and the life there. All of it fills him
with as much admiration as does his view of the city. Indeed, the
appearance of the Aztec Tenochtitlán must have been marvelous, and it is
hard to understand the urge to belittle its grandeur manifested in certain
comments of Carlos Pereyra (*op. cit.*, p. 217), who, carried away by his
exaggerated prejudice for all things Spanish, writes a description of it
that does not agree with that of the conquistadores themselves. On the
other hand, the reconstruction of it that Alfonso Reyes undertakes in his
Visión de Anáhuac is very beautiful (Madrid, 1923). [For an English
translation of this essay, by Charles Ramsdell, see *Mexico in a Nutshell*
(Berkeley and Los Angeles: University of California Press, 1964), pp.
80–98.–*Tr.*]

the good will of the Indians and putting into practice his policy of conciliating them, reassuring them, as he says; and he always speaks to them and acts with this purpose in mind, whether the natives flee from the presence of the Spaniards, or oppose them and refuse them admission. "The Captain [Cortés] spoke to him [the cacique of Cozumel] and told him that he did not wish to do them any harm whatever, nor was such the object of his coming, but it was to bring them to the knowledge of our Holy Faith, and to inform them that our rulers were the greatest princes in the world, who obeyed its highest Prince, and that what the said Captain Hernán Cortés desired of them was only that the caciques and Indians of that island should also obey Your Highnesses, and that if they did so they would benefit greatly thereby, for no one could then vex them. And the said cacique answered and said that he would be very glad to do so, and he at once summoned all the caciques of the said island, who came, and when they arrived were much pleased by all the said Captain Hernán Cortés had told the said cacique, lord of the island. And so he dismissed them and they departed very contented. And the towns were so reassured of their safety that within a few days they were as full of people and as populous as before, and all the Indians moved about among us with as little fear as if they had known us for a long, long time" (p. 10).

If Cortés' policy of concilation goes astray in this first stage, it is because of his excessive impatience. For him, the fundamental difference between Spaniard and native, the gap that must be bridged, is their difference of religion. He tells us quite clearly, after he completes his description of the Aztec capital, that the natives' way of life is almost that of Spain, "and with as much good order and dignity," which he finds hard to imagine in people removed from the knowledge of the divine truth. That is to say, once the natives should be brought to that knowledge, their identification with the Spaniards would be perfect and without friction, more especially since, as his first letter indicates, their evangelization would seem to be easy, given the natives' superior intelligence and capacity.

"It may be believed that not without cause was Our Lord

pleased to have these parts discovered in the names of your Royal Highnesses, to the end that Your Majesties reap the harvest and gain God's thanks by commanding that these barbarous people be instructed and led by the hand to the Faith, for, according to what we have learned of them, we believe that if interpreters were available and men to make them understand the truth of the Faith and the error of their ways, many of them, perhaps all, would quickly abandon that mistaken religion of theirs and accept knowledge of the truth, because they live more politically and reasonably than any of the people thus far seen in these parts" (p. 25).

Hence the impatience of Cortés, and hence such impolitic acts—impolitic because premature—as his destruction of the idols when he first enters the capital. It is difficult for us today to believe that Moctezuma himself, with smiling face, helped Cortés to clear the temple and make way for the new gods. But it is evident that Cortés believed it. And this assurance of his in the success of his enterprise, this eagerness to see it completed, is what led him also to react violently when the Indians displayed any resistance to his plans for immediate assimilation. A good example of this violence is his conduct with the emissaries of Tlaxcala, whom he suspected of being spies.

"The next day there appeared about 50 Indians who seemed to be men of consequence, saying they were bringing us provisions; and they began to examine the entrances and exits of the camp, and the few huts where we were quartered. And the Cempoalans came to me and told me to beware, because those were bad men who had come to spy and find out where they could attack us; I might be sure they had no other purpose. And I had one of them seized secretly, unseen by the others, and I took him aside with the interpreters, and threatened him to make him tell me the truth, and he confessed that Xicontécatl, the captain general of the province, was hidden behind some hills near the camp, with a large number of men ready to fall upon us that night, because they said their daylight attacks had failed and they wanted to try it by night, when their men would not be terrified by the horses, cannon, and swords. And [they said] those who had sent them wanted to learn where they might enter our camp, and how to burn our straw huts. And then I had another of the Indians seized, and I interrogated him, and he confirmed what the first one had said, in the same words. In view of this I had all fifty seized and their hands cut off, and I sent them back to tell their lord that by night or by day, or whenever he should come, he would find out what manner of men we were" (pp. 63–66).

His ferocity at Cholula is even worse when he hears that the Indians are preparing an ambush. "And so for this reason, as well as for the signals they were making, I made shift to forestall them, and I had several of the lords of the city brought before me, and I told them I wished to speak with them, and I put them in a room. Meanwhile, I told our men that upon their hearing a musket shot they should fall upon the large number of Indians in that room and outside. And so it was done, for after I had the lords in the room I had them tied up, and mounted my horse, and had the musket fired, and we struck them so hard that within two hours more than 3,000 of them died. And so that Your Majesty may know how well prepared they were, I shall say that before I left our quarters they had blocked off all the streets, and all their men were fully armed, although, since we took them by surprise, they were easily routed, especially since they were without their chiefs whom I had seized" (p. 73).

But even in cases like this, as soon as the action was over, what interested him most was to continue his policy of conciliation, to erase quickly the marks of the occurrence, and reestablish the normal course of things. "As soon as I returned to my quarters I spoke with the lords I held captive and asked them why they had tried to kill me thus treacherously. And they answered and said they were not to blame, for the Culhuans, who were vassals of Moctezuma, had put them up to it, and that the said Moctezuma had posted a force of 50,000 men in a spot, as was later confirmed, about a league and a half distant, to attack us. But now they knew they had been deceived, and they begged me to release one or two of them, who would gather up all the people of the city and bring back the women and children and clothing that had been sent away.

And they begged me to forgive them their error and assured me that thenceforth no one would deceive them, and that they would be true and loyal vassals of Your Highness, and my friends. And after I had scolded them thoroughly for their mistake, I released two of them. And the next day the whole city was full of women and children, as carefree as if nothing had happened. Then I released all the other lords I had seized, whereupon they promised me they would very loyally serve Your Majesty. So within a matter of fifteen or twenty days the city and country were so peaceful and full of people that it looked as if no one was missing, and its merchants and commerce were as active as they had formerly been" (p. 74).

This is a good example of the working of Cortés' mind—how in his imagination he advances toward his goal in forced marches. It is not possible that after slaying 3,000 Cholulans —or possibly even fewer—the next day the city should be as peaceful and well populated as if nothing had happened. Cortés distorts the facts in his desire to promote his policy of conciliation. And, indeed, his policy yields excellent results, the best proof of which is that when he marches upon Mexico City his small army of Spaniards is accompanied by thousands of Indian friends, who serve him loyally, even to the point of making the maximum sacrifices for him. The undoubted fact is that Cortés possessed to a high degree the character of a man born to command, and enjoyed a prestige that appears in his first letter, in which we are told that Governor Velázquez of Cuba intends to make him leader of the new expedition, "because at that time Cortés had a larger following than any other man in the island, and he believed that with him as chief many more men would go than under any other" (p. 8).

His ascendancy over his countrymen he soon achieves also over the Indians. "And I left behind the whole province of Cempoala, and all the mountain country bordering upon the said *villa* [of Veracruz], where there must have been some 50,000 warriors and 50 towns and fortresses, and all very secure and peaceful, and true and loyal vassals of Your Majesty, which up to the present they have been, and are, for, as I was informed, they had been subjects of the Lord Moctezuma, but had been forced to be so not long ago. And as I had told them of your very royal and great power, they indicated that they wished to become vassals of Your Majesty and my friends, and they begged me to protect them from that great lord who held them by force and tyranny, and who seized their sons to kill and sacrifice to his idols; and they made many other charges against him. And with this [assurance] they have been and are very true and loyal to the service of Your Highness, and I think they will remain so to free themselves from his tyranny, and also because I have always treated them well and favored them" (p. 53).

Along with this ascendancy of Cortés goes a total exclusiveness, a conviction that he is the only promoter of the enterprise, regardless of the will of his companions, of destiny, of everything. "And after hearing of the victory that God had given us, and how he [Cortés] had pacified those cities [Tlaxcala and Cholula], there was much rejoicing, for I assure Your Majesty there was not a single one of us who was not filled with dread at finding ourselves so far inland, among so many and such [warlike] people, and so without the expectation of help from any direction. And so true is this that I have heard it said in private and almost in public that I had acted like a Pedro Carbonero* and brought them to a pass from which they could not escape. Even more, I overheard some of my companions, in a hut whence they could not see me, say that if I was crazy enough to get them into spots I could not get them out of, they were not [crazy], and would return to the coast, and if I wanted to go with them, well and good; otherwise, they would leave me behind. And they often demanded that I do so, but I rallied them by reminding them they were vassals of Your Highness, and that Spaniards had never failed anywhere, and

* [Pedro Carbonero was a more or less legendary hero of the wars against Granada in the fifteenth century. His romantic exploit, in which he was said to have faced an army of Moors with twelve knights and defended his honor to the death, was celebrated in popular ballads and was made the theme of a play by Lope de Vega, *El Cordobés valeroso Pedro Carbonero*, ed. José F. Montesinos (Madrid, 1929). See note in Francisco López de Gómara, *Cortés, the Life of the Conqueror*, p. 112. English translation by L. B. Simpson (Berkeley and Los Angeles: University of California Press, 1966).–*Tr.*]

that we had the opportunity to win for Your Majesty the greatest kingdoms and seigneuries in the world. And besides [I told them] that we had the duty as Christians to oppose the enemies of our Faith, and in so doing we should win glory in the next world, while in this one we should achieve a greater renown and honor than any former generation had achieved; that we had God on our side, to whom nothing was impossible, as they could see by the victories we had won, in which so many of our opponents had died, but none of our own men. And I spoke to them of other things that occurred to me, by which and by the royal favor of Your Majesty they recovered their spirits, and I persuaded them to accept my plan, which was to carry through the quest we had begun" (p. 65).

"And after having rested a bit, I went out one night, after the first watch had made its rounds, with 100 foot and horse and our Indian friends, and a league from the camp five of the horses and mares collapsed, and I was entirely unable to make them proceed, so I sent them back. And, although all the men in my company told me to retreat, for that was a bad sign, I went ahead, in the belief that God is superior to nature" (p. 64).

In the foregoing paragraphs we note the motives that Cortés considered the basis and justification for his enterprise. (I shall return to this later on.) What we are concerned with here is to bring out to what extent he considered it his exclusive task. Out of his blind faith in himself and his success arises the excessive self-confidence that leads him to believe, from the moment of his recent arrival at Mexico City, that his work of conciliation has been solidly established. We see him occupied in exploring the land, looking for good ports, and especially the location of gold mines, so that he will be able to remit some to the Emperor. All these activities show him to be totally sure and convinced that he has the natives in hand.

"I also begged the said Moctezuma to tell me whether there was on the seacoast some river or roadstead in which ships might enter and be safe. He answered that he did not know, but would have a map painted of the whole coast, with its rivers and roadsteads, and he told me I should send Spaniards to see them, and would give me someone to guide them and go with them, as he did. And the next day they brought me a cloth on which the whole coast was represented.

"After I had learned from him very completely how great was his desire to serve Your Highness, I begged him to show me the mines from which gold was extracted, so that I might more fully give Your Majesty an account of the things of this land, and with great good will he said he would be pleased to do so. And he at once summoned several of his servants, and two by two he assigned them to the four provinces where he said gold was mined, and he asked me to give him Spaniards to go with them and see it mined. So I gave him two Spaniards to go with each pair of them" (p. 92).

"I remained in this great city seeing to things necessary to the service of Your Sacred Majesty, attracting to it and pacifying many provinces and territories containing many large cities and *villas* and fortresses, and exploring mines, and learning and seeking out many secrets of the domains of this Moctezuma, and many others adjacent to them of which he had information, and which are so many and so marvelous as to be almost unbelievable. And the said Moctezuma did all this with so much good will, as did the natives of the said territories, that it seemed from the beginning as though they had recognized Your Sacred Majesty as their king and natural lord. And with no less willingness they did all the things I commanded them to do in your royal name" (p. 113).

Cortés was soon to learn that things were not so simple as he had imagined, for it was impossible, merely by appealing to the good will and consent of the vanquished, to take over their government and establish a new order. If it should ever be pleasant to entertain hypotheses, it would be at this moment: a Cortés who in his own mind had succeeded peacefully in incorporating the dominions of Moctezuma into those of Charles V. But this, quite simply, could not be. From the letters of Cortés we learn nothing of the true feeling of the Aztecs. The conqueror gives us only a completely optimistic view, one that is in accord with his purposes. This lover's blindness of Cortés is curious—Cortés, who was anything but a visionary, and who, as a good military commander, was extremely foresighted. For example, when he entered the city and saw how it was laid out, the first thing he arranged for was the construction of brigantines for navigating the lake. There are many instances to show that he never neglected the most minute precautions. What he did neglect was the essential business of learning the true feeling of the Aztecs vis-à-vis the Spaniards. It cannot be doubted that a dominant and warlike people would not long suffer foreign subjection without putting up a vigorous resistance. But the deadly thing about it was that it was the Spaniards themselves who completely ruined the work so handsomely begun, one which apparently was already concluded.[10]

Diego Velázquez, Governor of Cuba, will not accept what Cortés and his men have done in Veracruz. He considers that their change of the expedition's purpose is a violation of their instructions, and he sends Pánfilo de Narváez against them. The latter adopts the most stupid and dangerous tactic possible at that moment: to discredit Cortés with the Indians, telling them he would restore their liberty and leave the country as soon as Cortés should be beaten. He announced to Moctezuma "that he was coming to seize me [Cortés] and all those of my company, after which he would at once leave the country; that he was not looking for gold, but that, as soon as I and my men were captured, he would leave the country and its inhabitants in full liberty" (p. 121).

Cortés, blindly confident in himself, and in his prestige and success, leaves the capital to confront Narváez. "And when I saw the great mischief that was brewing, and how the land was rising because of the said Narváez, it seemed to me that things would calm down if I went to him, because the Indians would not dare revolt if they saw me there" (p. 119). He is aware of the danger that his leaving the city might entail. "And I did not dare abandon it, for fear that as soon as I should leave the city the people would rise and I should lose such a great quantity of gold and such a city, for once it was lost, all the country would also be lost" (p. 118).

---

[10] There are other factors in the change of attitude of the Indians. What should be kept in mind is that here we are trying to see the enterprise as Cortés saw it.

Despite all his fears he resolves to move against Narváez, "in view of the fact that if I should die in the service of my king, in the defense and protection of his lands, and not allow them to be usurped, I and my companions would win sufficient renown" (p. 123).

He defeats Narváez easily and takes him prisoner, but the damage has been done. When the Indians see the division among the Spaniards they no longer venerate Cortés and his men or consider them supernatural beings, and prepare to get rid of them. "And according to what I learned from the Indians, they had resolved that if the said Narváez should capture me as he had told them he would do, his victory would not be so cheap that many of his men would not die, along with many of their own and those of my company. Meanwhile they would kill the men I had left in the city—as they attempted to do—and afterward they would assemble and attack those who were left, so vigorously that they and their country would be free, and of the Spaniards there would hardly be a memory" (p. 125).

Cortés fears upon leaving the city are confirmed. During his absence there is a collision between Spaniards and Indians.[11] He has to return by forced marches. His only anxiety was not to lose the city. "In view of the danger the Spaniards in the city faced if I should not come to their rescue, that is, they would be killed by the Indians and we should lose all the gold and silver and jewels we had taken in the country, those of

---

[11] It may surprise the reader that I seem to be walking on eggs when I touch upon a subject that has caused such torrents of ink to flow; but I must repeat that my purpose here is to trace a silhouette of Cortés and his works based on his writings, to see things from his point of view. This is why I have not taken the time to find out whether the slaughter that occurred in Mexico City during the absence of Hernán Cortés was or was not owing to the savagery of Pedro de Alvarado. The curious reader will find the subject well documented in Orozco y Berra (*op. cit.*, pp. 410–418). For me the most interesting and important thing about it is that Cortés blames the failure of his policy of conciliation, not on Pedro de Alvarado, but on Pánfilo de Narváez, as he tells us years later (1526) in his fifth *Carta de Relación*: "Although it was lost [the gold of Charles V and that of the conquistadores] because it was seized when we were driven out of the city during the uprising that occurred when Narváez came to this country, it may be charged to my sins, but not to my negligence" (pp. 485–486).

Your Highness as well as those of the Spaniards and mine, the best and most noble city of all the newly discovered world would be lost, and this would mean the loss of everything we had won, because it was the head that all obeyed" (p. 126).

The scales had fallen from the eyes of the Indians, but it is very difficult for Cortés to tear off his own. Up to the last moment he thinks that the situation can be saved, that his power and prestige will continue, and that the Mexicans will remain at peace, as they have been until then. Returning to the capital, he finds it calm. "Then I went to the fortress, in which and in the great temple next to it my men were stationed, and they welcomed us with as much joy as if we had just saved their lives, which they had given up for lost. And we passed that day and night very pleasantly, thinking that everything was peaceful. And the next day after Mass I sent a messenger off to the *villa* of Veracruz to give them the good news that the Christians were still alive, that I had entered the city and it was safe. But this messenger returned within the half hour, all beaten and wounded, shouting that all the Indians in the city were on their way to attack us and had removed all the bridges. And just behind him came such a multitude of men from all directions that you couldn't see the streets or the windows for the crowd, which came with the greatest howling and shouting imaginable, and they shot so many stones into the fortress with their slings that it seemed to be raining stones, and they shot so many arrows and darts that the walls and courtyards were covered with them and we could hardly move" (p. 128).

The situation is hopeless. Moctezuma makes a final appeal for conciliation, which will cost him his life.[12] "The said Moc-

---

[12] The death of Moctezuma is another hotly debated subject. It is well known that the Spaniards have been accused of murdering him. Genaro García, in his *Carácter de la conquista española en América y en México.* . . . (Mexico, 1901), a book as heavily documented as it is tendentious, adduces a great deal of testimony and argument to demonstrate that Moctezuma was already dead when he was exposed to his vassals on the roof of the building they surrounded (pp. 213–219). MacNutt himself, although favorable to Cortés, believes him guilty in this instance (*op. cit.*, vol. I, p. 107). The conqueror, to be sure, was not a man to balk at cruelty if he considered it necessary for the furtherance of his designs; but to kill Moctezuma at such a moment would have been the greatest piece

tezuma, who was still a prisoner, and a son of his and many other nobles who had been seized with him, told them [the Spaniards] to bring him out upon the roof of the fortress, where he would talk to the leaders of his men and make them stop fighting. And I had him brought out, and as soon as he appeared on the battlement one of his men threw a stone at his head with such force that he died three days later. And I had two Indian prisoners pick up his body, and they carried it out to the people on their backs, and I don't know what they did with it; but the fighting did not stop on that account and became heavier and more bloody every day.

"And that day I was summoned to the place where the said Moctezuma had been wounded, for certain captains wished to talk with me; and this I did, and we had a long conversation, I begging them not to fight with me, for they had no reason to do so, and to consider the favors they had received from me, and how well I had treated them. Their reply was to tell me to go away and leave their country, and that they would [in that event] stop fighting, but that, if I did not, I could be sure that they would all die, or kill us. Apparently they said this to get me out of the fortress so they could capture me between the gates. And I answered them saying that they should not think I was begging for peace because I was afraid of them, but because I was sorry about the harm I was doing them, and would do, and because I did not wish to destroy their beautiful city. And still they answered that they would not stop fighting until I should leave the city" (pp. 129–130).

The Indians' purpose is very clear. The work of Cortés is tumbling to the ground. Now that Moctezuma is dead, the Aztecs redouble their efforts in besieging the Spaniards. And now, and only now, does that Cortés appear whom many Mexicans

---

of stupidity he could have committed. It should be borne in mind that in all the atrocities committed by Cortés—the massacre at Cholula, the torture and execution of Cuauhtémoc—he is the first to reveal them to us, and there is no reason to think that in this case he would have acted differently. Indeed, if any subject proves that there is no such thing as impartial history, it is that of the conquest of Mexico, in which events that occurred more than four centuries ago still inflame passions and are as hotly argued as any piece of recent news.

have not yet forgiven, a Cortés who speaks of extermination and war without quarter, a Cortés made mad by the loss of everything that, in his ingenuous love for his work, he had considered already his. After the attack on the great temple he again addresses the Indians: "And then I went out upon the roof again and spoke to the captains who had spoken to me before, and who were aghast at what they had seen. They approached at once, and I told them to consider that they could not be helped, and that we were doing them greater harm every day, that many of them were dying and we were burning and destroying their city, and this was not going to stop until nothing was left of it or of them. They replied that they could see well enough we were hurting them badly and many of them were dying, but that they were all resolved to die if by so doing they could put an end to us. And [they told me] to consider how full of men the streets and squares and rooftops were, and how they had calculated that if 25,000 of them died for every one of us, we should be destroyed first, because we were few and they many. And they told me they had cut all the causeways at the entrances of the city—as in fact they had, all except one—and that we had no way to escape but by water, and they knew we had few provisions and little fresh water, and could not hold out very long without dying of hunger, even though they should not kill us. And in truth they were quite right, for even if we had had no enemy other than hunger and lack of provisions, that would be enough to finish us all in a short time. And so we argued back and forth, each favoring his own side" (p. 132).

Unhappy Cortés! Of the beautiful idea of unity that he had conceived, the possibility of a rapid and bloodless assimilation of the Aztec empire within the universal and Christian empire of Charles V, nothing was left. His was the simple notion of all peoples and all men who believe themselves superior, the elect; and he could not consider the legitimate reaction of the Aztecs to be anything but treason.[13] The conflict was inevitable and

---

[13] This notion of Cortés was strengthened during his fleeting friendship with Moctezuma when the latter had made his vassals swear fidelity to Charles V (Gayangos, *op. cit.*, p. 98).

had to be without quarter. Cortés is as vehement in his policy of extermination and as single-minded as he had formerly been in his attempt at conciliation. He is infuriated by the magnificent heroism of the natives and thinks to crush them more rapidly by terrorism, and thus he works his own ruin. Attacked from all sides, he has no recourse now but to abandon the city. He clearly shows his melancholy and despair in his description of the preparations for withdrawal. "And, seeing the great peril we were in, and the losses they were daily inflicting on us, and also fearing they would cut that [last] causeway as they had the others, for if it were destroyed we should all die inevitably, and because the men of my company had many times demanded that I leave, and because all, or almost all were wounded, so badly that they could not fight, I agreed to do so that night. And I took all the gold and jewels of Your Majesty that could be carried out, and I put them in a room, and there I turned them over to Your Highness's officers whom I had appointed in your royal name; and I begged the *alcaldes* and *regidores* and all the other men to help me get it out and save it, and I gave them a mare of mine for the purpose, and they loaded upon her all she could carry; and I ordered several of my Spanish servants and those of others to accompany the said mare and her burden; and the other officials and *alcaldes* and *regidores* and I distributed the rest among the Spaniards for them to bring out. Then we abandoned the fortress carrying the rich booty, that of Your Majesty and mine, and I left as quietly as I could" (pp. 134–135).

Cortés conceals nothing in his letters. He openly exposes his great cupidity and describes in meticulous detail his efforts to save the treasure. In this regard it should be remembered that he was writing for the Emperor and that his saving, or his attempt to save, the Emperor's treasure was proof of zeal and merit. The ambition of Cortés was great, but riches did not occupy first place in it, although he was far from scorning them.[14]

---

[14] The historian Don Lucas Alamán, in the sixth of his *Disertaciones sobre la historia de la República Megicana* (3 vols., Mexico, 1844–1849), clearly points out this trait in the character of Cortés: "The ambition of

I was saying that Cortés conceals nothing when he describes the frightful disaster of his retreat from Mexico [the Noche Triste]. His reporting has all the sobriety of a military communiqué. "In this defeat I learned by count that 150 Spaniards had died, and 45 mares and horses, and more than 2,000 Indians who were in the service of the Spaniards, among whom the son and daughters of Moctezuma were killed, as well as all the nobles we were taking with us as prisoners" (p. 137).

He does nothing to minimize the disaster, not even hiding the fact that the Spaniards were a prey to the despair common to defeated troops, thinking they were being attacked from all sides, even when the enemy was not pursuing them. "Night was coming on, and it was God's will to show us a tower and a good place on a hill, where we fortified ourselves. And during the night [the Indians] left us, although just about dawn we had another alarm, which was caused by the fear we all had of the multitude of men who were still pursuing us" (p. 137).

This military sobriety of Cortés is a fine quality, for if he does not conceal his reverses, neither does he boast when his luck is in, as at Otumba. Witness the space he devotes to the famous episode of the death of the Indian standard-bearer: "And we marched for most of the day in the greatest trouble, until by the grace of God one of their men, who must have been a noble, died, and at his death the whole action ceased" (p. 139).

Cortés is not one to let himself despair. He has hardly en-

Cortes changed with the field in which it operated. The same man who had gone to Española in quest of gold, in New Spain thought of it only as a means of achieving higher purposes, and what in the beginning had merely been cupidity became ambition for glory and power. It was for this reason, in his distribution of the rich treasure of Moctezuma, that he gave the soldiers his own share of it, this to quiet the grumbling that followed the [former] unequal distribution. [His ambition was] to found in Mexico a great empire for his sovereign and establish the Christian religion in it—ideas common in the minds of the conquistadores and the dominant ones of that century—to expand that empire even more by explorations in the South Sea and bring under the crown of Castile China and the Spice Islands, thus realizing the original plan of Columbus. Such were the aims of Cortés' ambitions, and the consequence of his efforts was to have been his own aggrandizement and fortune" (vol. II, pp. 14–15).

tered the friendly territory of Tlaxcala when he shows his resolve to return to Mexico and recover what he has lost. Once
again we see him overcoming the resistance of his companions.
"When the men of my company saw that many of them had
died and that the survivors were tired and wounded, and they
themselves were frightened by the perils and hardships they
had been through, and by those yet to come, which at that time
were near at hand, they many times demanded of me that I fall
back on the *villa* of Veracruz, where we might fortify ourselves
before the natives of that country, whom we thought to be our
friends, seeing us defeated and weak, should make an alliance
with the enemy and seize the passes we had to negotiate, and
fall upon us from one direction, and upon the garrison of Veracruz from the other. For [they said], with all of us there together, and our ships, we should be stronger and better able to
defend ourselves should they attack us, until we could send to
the islands for help. But I, in view of the fact that if we should
expose our weakness to the natives, especially to our friends, it
would cause them the more quickly to abandon us and go over
to the enemy; and I remembered that Fortune always favors
the bold, and that we were Christians and trusted to the infinite mercy of God, who would not allow us all to perish and
lose so great and noble a land as the one we had pacified for
Your Majesty, or had almost pacified; nor would He fail to do
Himself the great service in continuing the war, in which the
pacification of the country would be completed, and it would
be as it was before. So I decided not to go down to the seaport
in any event, and I told them that despite all the hardships and
dangers we might face I would not abandon this land, because
in so doing it seemed to me that this would be a shameful thing
to do and very dangerous for everybody, besides which we
should be committing an act of very grave treason toward
Your Majesty. Therefore, I was determined to attack the enemy from every possible direction and in every possible way"
(pp. 142–143).

He now completely abandons the language of conciliation
and peace, in the belief that the only way to recover what

he has lost is by subjugating the natives by terror and force.[15] "And I also purposed to enslave the Mexicans in order to intimidate them, for there are so many of them that, if I should not punish them severely and cruelly, they would never mend their ways" (p. 144).

Severely and cruelly. Under the banner of vengeance and retaliation Cortés bends all his feverish energy to the rehabilitation of his army, to his renewed policy of making alliances with the Indian enemies of the Aztecs, and to the minute and thorough preparations for dealing the city its death blow, the city he had once believed his, which had humiliated and defeated him. But he has met with enemies of his stature who do not rest on their laurels either. "From those I had captured in the city of Huaquechula, and especially from the wounded men, I learned in great detail what had transpired in the great city of Tenochtitlán, and how, after the death of Moctezuma, he had been succeeded by his brother, Cuitláhuac, lord of the city of Ixtapalapa, who had taken over because Moctezuma's son and heir had died on the bridges, and of his two living sons, it is said that one is mad and the other a paralytic, because of which his brother had been named, and also because this brother had fought with us and was held to be a brave and very wise man. I also learned that the people of the city were fortifying themselves, as they were doing in all the other cities

---

[15] It is interesting to find in a Mexican historian as serene as Don José María Luis Mora the same explanation of the radical change in Cortés which I have been stressing in his correspondence. "The second phase of Cortés' expedition, which we may think of as the military or warlike phase, begins after his retreat from Mexico City. Just as in the first phase his principal means of action were seduction, persuasion, and everything that constitutes a delicate negotiation deliberately carried out, with recourse to battles as force only in extreme cases, in the second, military operations occupy the principal place, with peaceful negotiations merely auxiliary [to them]. In the first phase he was only trying to win friends and allies by flattery, gifts, and persuasion; in the second he suggested to the towns openly and clearly that they should submit to the crown of Castile, and threatened them with force if they should refuse. In a word, in the first phase he was seeking friends, whom he sought to interest in helping his weak colony; in the second, he was seeking subjects, who were ordered to obey without question a general who had a conquering army under his command, one who knew he had the strength to carry the law on the point of his sword" *Méjico y sus revoluciones*. . . . (3 vols., Paris, 1836), vol. I, pp. 90–91.

of his domain, and were erecting many barricades and digging shelters and ditches, and making arms of all kinds. And especially did I learn that they were making lances as long as pikes, to be used against the horses; and we have even seen some of them in this province of Tepeaca, where they have been used in battle; and in the camps and shelters of the Mexicans in Huaquechula many of them were also found. And I learned many other things which I shall omit lest I weary Your Highness.

"I am dispatching four vessels to Española to bring back immediately horses and men to help us. I am also arranging to buy four more [vessels] to bring us horses and arms and crossbows and powder from the said island of Española and the city of Santo Domingo, because these are the things most needed here, for foot soldiers armed only with shields can do very little against such a mass of men in possession of cities and fortresses as strong and great as those. And I am writing to the Licenciado Rodrigo de Figueroa and to Your Highness's officers residing in the said island, to give us all the support and help possible, because it is very necessary to the service of Your Highness and the security of our persons. And if this help and support comes, it is my intention to attack that great city and its territory. And I believe, as I have already told Your Majesty, that in a very short time it will be in the state in which I held it before, and our past losses will be recovered. Meanwhile, I am having twelve brigantines built, to be launched upon the lake, and the timbers and parts of them are being fashioned, because, since they are to be transported by land, when they arrive they may be assembled very quickly. Also, the fittings are being wrought, and pitch and tow and sails and oars are being prepared, and all the other things necessary. And I assure Your Majesty that until I achieve this purpose I do not intend to rest or desist in any way whatever, regardless of all the trouble and danger and expense I may have to face" (pp. 153–154).

Cortés' second letter ends on this note, and the third begins where the other leaves off, as he stresses once again the reasons for his resentment against the natives and his resolution to destroy them. "And at the end of the said account I told Your

Majesty that, after the Indians of the city of Tenochtitlán had driven us out, I had marched against the province of Tepeaca, which was subject to it and had rebelled [against us], and that with the remaining Spaniards and Indian friends we had made war upon them and reduced them to Your Majesty's service. And [I also told you] that since the late treachery and the great harm and the killing of Spaniards was so fresh in our hearts, my firm decision was to attack the people of that city, which was the cause of it all, and for that purpose I had begun the construction of thirteen brigantines to do them as much damage on the lake as I could, that is, if the people of the city should persevere in their evil designs" (pp. 161–162).

Where one sees very clearly the trend of Cortés' thinking is in the speech he makes to his troops at Tlaxcala, when he musters them before beginning his advance on Mexico. "On the second day of the said Christmas season,[16] I mustered the troops in the said city of Tlaxcala, and I counted 40 horse and 550 foot, 80 of the latter being crossbowmen and arquebusiers, and eight or nine field guns, but very little powder for them. And I divided the horse into four squadrons, ten men in each, and the foot into nine companies of sixty men each.

"And when all were gathered at the said muster, I spoke to them and said they all knew how they and I had colonized this land in the service of Your Majesty, and how all the natives had accepted the vassalage of Your Majesty, and had continued in that state for some time, they receiving our favors, and we theirs; and how, without any excuse whatever, all the inhabitants of the great city of Tenochtitlán, as well as those of all the provinces subject to it, had not only rebelled against Your Majesty, but had even slain many of their kindred and our friends, and had driven us entirely out of their country. And [I told them] to remember all the perils and hardships we had gone through together, and to see how necessary it was for the service of God and Your Caesarian Majesty to recover what we had lost, for which we had on our side just causes and reasons: one, to fight for the increase of our Faith; two, to serve Your

---

[16] Wednesday, December 26, 1520.

Majesty against these barbarous people; another, to protect our lives; another, because we had helping us many native friends —all of which were potent reasons to raise our spirits. I begged them, therefore, to be of good cheer and strength, and since I, in the name of Your Majesty had issued certain ordinances for the proper conduct of the war—which I then had the public crier read to them—I begged them to obey and observe them, for it would redound greatly to the service of God and Your Majesty. And they all promised to obey and observe them, and said that very willingly they would die for our Faith and the service of Your Majesty if they might go back and recover what they had lost and avenge the great treachery committed against us by the people of Tenochtitlán and their allies. And I thanked them in the name of Your Majesty, and so we returned to our quarters quite happily on that muster day" (pp. 165–166).

The ordinances to which Cortés refers are of the greatest interest. In them the conversion of the infidels is stressed as a justification for the conquest. "With all the force at my command I exhort and beg all the Spaniards of my company who engage in the war to which we are now going, or in all the other wars and conquests to which by command in the name of Your Majesty they may engage in, that their principal motive and intent be to banish and uproot the said idolatries from among all the natives of these parts, and to bring them salvation, or at least to desire it, and to the knowledge of God and His Holy Catholic Faith; because if the said war should be waged with any other purpose it would be an unjust war, and everything that we should do would be offensive and subject to restitution, and His Majesty would have no reason to reward those who had served in it" (*Escritos sueltos*, p. 15).

As skeptics, we may wonder today whether this desire to convert the natives would have been so ardent if gold had not been discovered in the new lands; but such reflections are idle. One doesn't have to be a lynx to see the thirst for gold and wealth by which the conquistadores were consumed. They are the first to admit it, being rough and outspoken men, for whom material interests do not have to be disguised under high-sounding ideologies, as happens today. But it would be a prejudiced person who did not recognize in them, at least in the best of them, an equally strong desire to bring about the salvation of the Indians.

The ordinances, which deserve to be read entire, have other very interesting aspects;[17] for example, they forbid the companies to mock at each other; they forbid the soldiers to hide in the baggage; they forbid the looting of the enemies' houses, "until they are completely driven out and victory is assured." Especially picturesque is the ordinance in which Cortés forbids gambling except in his own quarters, which shows how fond he was of it, for which we have other testimony.[18] "But since during a war it is well to allow the men some amusement to keep them out of mischief, it is allowed that in my quarters cards and other games may be played for moderate stakes, but not dice, and cursing will not be permitted; at least those who indulge in it will be punished" (*Escritos sueltos*, p. 17).

We find in the ordinances not only the greatest liveliness and animation, but the most complete picture of life among the men of Cortés. His account of the second march on Mexico is more detailed and intimate than that of the first. In it there are frequent notes on the conquistadores' state of mind: "And after marching half a league it was God's pleasure to let us descend to level ground, and there I halted to wait for the men, and when they came up I told them all to give thanks to Our Lord for having brought them safely to that point, from which we could see all the provinces of Mexico and Tenochtitlán in the lakes and around them. And, although we were glad enough to see them, at the same time we were sad, remembering the hurt we had received there, and we all swore never to leave without victory, or to die there. And with this resolution we were all as merry as if were on a pleasure excursion" (pp. 168–169).

In spite of their desire for vengeance and their confidence

---

[17] This is a very well-known document. It has been published in the edition of Prescott already cited (vol. II, p. 387); in the *Colección de documentos para la historia de México*, of Joaquín García Icazbalceta (2 vols., Mexico, 1858–1866), vol. I, p. 445; and in the *Escritos sueltos*, p. 13.
[18] This is one of the charges in which all the witnesses called to testify in the *residencia* of Cortes are in agreement (*Residencia de Cortés*, published by Ignacio López Rayón, 2 vols., Mexico, 1852–1853).

in victory, we can sense in the Spaniards a feeling of unease and fear, which Cortés does not conceal. "The next day, a Monday, the last of December, we continued our march in our usual order, and a quarter of a league from this city of Coatepec, all of us uneasy and wondering whether the inhabitants would meet us in war or in peace, four Indian nobles received us carrying a gold emblem on a staff weighing four marks [two pounds] of gold, by which sign they indicated they were coming in peace. And God knows how we welcomed it and how we needed it, being so few and so remote from any help and surrounded by the forces of our enemies!" (pp. 169–170).

Indecision and uneasiness, and the fear that precedes every battle, are very evident in Cortés' bids for peace. "After three days in this city without any encounter with the Indians, because at that time they did not dare attack us and we were not anxious to seek them out, for my ultimate aim, whenever they should come in peace, was to receive them and always beg them so to come" (p. 172). . . . "And since I wished to win over to our friendship those of the city, for upon it depended peace or war in the other rebellious provinces, I had the messengers untied, and I told them not to be afraid, for I wished to send them back to Tenochtitlán, and I begged them to tell the lords there that I had no desire to make war upon them, although I had reason to do so, but wished for us to be friends as we had been before. And the better to reassure them and attract them to Your Majesty's service, I sent them word that I was well aware that the nobles who had opposed me in the late war were now dead, so we should let bygones be bygones, for I did not want them to give me cause to destroy their lands and cities, which I should regret to do" (p. 173).

Operations proceed slowly until the brigantines are finished. Then Cortés takes heart, his confidence increases, and once again he employs the language of vengeance and retribution. "The said Alguacil Mayor[19] advanced five or six leagues to a town of Tlaxcala, the one nearest the border of Culhúa, and there came upon the Spaniards and the men carrying the brig-

---

[19] Gonzalo de Sandoval.

antines. The day after he arrived they set out with the planking and timbers, on the backs of more than 8,000 men, well organized, so well organized indeed that it was wonderful to see, and it seems to me to be something worth the telling, to carry thirteen *fustas* eighteen leagues overland. And I assure Your Majesty that they stretched out more than two leagues from the van to the rear. At the beginning of their journey they were led by eight horse and 100 Spanish foot; at either side marched Yutecad and Teuhtlipil, two of the noblest lords of Tlaxcala; in the rear a hundred-odd Spaniards and eight more horse, with 10,000 more warriors under the command of Chicamecatecle, one of the noble lords of that province, with other captains in his company. He, at the time they left, led the van with the planking, and the rear, with the rigging, was led by two other captains. And when they entered the territory of Culhúa the masters of the brigantines ordered the rigging sent on ahead and the planking sent to the rear, for it would be the most troublesome if anything should occur. But Chichimecatecle, who was escorting the said planking, and who up to this point had led the van with his warriors, took it as an insult, and it was very difficult to persuade him to stay with the rear, because he wanted to be in on any action; and, even though he [finally] agreed, he did not want any Spaniards to stay with him in the rear, for he was a very valiant man and wanted that honor for himself. And these [two] captains led 2,000 Indians with the provisions. So in this order they set off on their journey, which took them three days, and on the fourth they entered this city [of Texcoco] with great rejoicing and beating of drums, and I went out to receive them. And as I have said above, the men were stretched out so much that from the time the first began to enter until the last had done so, more than six hours elapsed without a break in the line. And after they had arrived and I had thanked those lords for the good things they were doing for us, I had them lodged and provided for as best I could. And they told me they wanted to meet the Culhúans, and for me to consider what I wanted them to do, for they and their men wanted to avenge themselves, or die with us. And I thanked them and told them to

rest, for we should soon give them all the work they wanted"
(pp. 184–185).

And this would be soon enough. His language is quite different from that of his earlier letters. Now the warrior in Cortés has come to the surface, the man who thirsts for revenge
and takes pleasure in destroying the enemy without mercy, as
he tells us on the occasion of the brigantines' first engagement
on the lake: "And as I greatly desired that their first encounter
should be very successful and so conducted that the enemy
would conceive a great fear of the brigantines, because these
were the key to the whole war and could do the greatest harm
to the natives on the water, where we could also be hurt. And
it pleased God that while we were watching each other a land
breeze came up, very favorable to our attack. So I at once ordered the captains to dash through the fleet of canoes and pursue them until they had them sealed up in the city of Tenochtitlán. And, the wind being very good, we dashed through the
middle of them, although they fled as fast as they could, and
wrecked an infinite number of canoes and drowned many of
the enemy, a most amazing thing to see" (pp. 211–212).

This is only one example of Cortés' satisfaction as he relates
the defeat and annihilation of the Aztecs. Expressions like the
following are very numerous: "In this fashion we did them a
great deal of harm, because many of our Indian friends joined
us and, as they were fresh and their opponents almost dead of
fatigue, they killed many of them. So within a short time the
field was empty of the living and filled with the dead" (p. 149).

"And when the time was ripe we sallied forth and began to
ply our lances among them, and we kept up the pursuit for
about two leagues, all as level as the palm of one's hand, and
it was a very handsome thing to see, for many of them died at
our hands and at the hands of our Indian friends" (p. 188).
"And we attacked them so vigorously that none of them escaped
except the women and children. In this action twenty-five of my
Spaniards were wounded, but for all that it was a glorious victory" (p. 211).

Even the women and children do not escape on this occa-

sion, as Cortés tells us. The conqueror, now convinced of the
failure of his policy of conciliation, sets out to achieve by terror the submission of the Aztecs, employing methods that only
in these days of total war have come to seem normal. "We
knew now that the Indians of the city were very frightened, as
we learned from one of them of little importance who had
slipped out of the city by night and come to our encampment,
for [he said] they were dying of hunger, that they went out
after dark to fish among the houses of the city, in that part
which we had taken, and to look for wood and weeds and roots
to eat. And, since we had cut many of the canals and smoothed
many bad spots [in the causeways] I resolved to make an entry in the early morning watch and do all the damage possible.
So the brigantines sailed before dawn, and I, with ten or fifteen
horse and some foot and Indian friends, dashed in. But first I
posted scouts who as soon as day broke, we being in ambush,
gave us the signal, and we fell upon an infinite number of men
who, since they were the same kind of poor wretches who were
out looking for something to eat, were most of them unarmed
women and children. And we did so much damage among them
in all that part of the city in which we could move, that between
prisoners and killed they numbered more than 800 persons, and
the brigantines took many men and women and canoes that
were out fishing and wrought great havoc among them. And
when the captains and nobles of the city saw us moving about
in it at that unusual hour, they were as frightened as they had
been at the recent ambush, and none dared to come out and
fight with us, so we returned to our camp with many captives
and food for our friends" (pp. 245–246).

This is another fearful aspect of the war, that there should
be food for the friends, that Cortés should tolerate cannibalism
among the Indians who accompanied him. There is no doubt
about it, as he makes clear in another passage: "In this ambush
more than 500 were killed, most of them noble, daring, and
valiant men, and that night our friends dined well, taking
pieces of the dead to eat" (p. 244).

We are now in the presence of a Cortés who we could wish
had never existed, of a Cortés in whose spirit had occurred the

inevitable polarization of all wars, a division into *ours* and *theirs*. And he who so calmly describes the atrocities we have just witnessed is deeply moved by the death of a simple mare. "And that day those of our camp were in no danger, except that when we sallied forth from our ambush some of the horse collided, and a man fell off a mare, and she ran away straight to the enemy, who shot her full of arrows, and when she saw the trouble she was in she came back to us, and that night she died. And although we felt very badly about it, because our lives depended on horses and mares, yet our grief was not as bad as if she had died in the hands of the enemy, as we thought had actually happened, for if she had, they would have had greater pleasure out of it than any grief they felt for the men we had killed" (p. 245).

On many occasions Cortés blames the Indian friends for the cruelties they practiced, as in the attack on Ixtapalapa: "It was God's will to inspire His own with such strength that we drove them into the water, at times up to their breast, at times swimming, and we took many of the houses that were built over the water, and more than 6,000 souls died, men, women, and children, because our Indian friends, seeing the victory that God had given us, did nothing but kill right and left" (p. 174). And in the attack on Tacuba: "And at daylight our Indian friends began to sack and burn the whole city, except that part where we were quartered, and they worked at it so hard that they even burned one of our rooms" (p. 187).

Examples could be multiplied. It is a useful expedient to charge the cruelties of the war to the account of the Indian allies, but one notes that the tone of Cortés is as indulgent as that of a grandfather toward a mischievous little grandson, whom he does not judge with great severity. It is also true that the Spaniards were swamped by the vast number of their Indian friends and were quite unable to control them, even if they had wished to do so. Cortés himself complains of his helplessness: "That day more than 40,000 souls were killed or captured, and such was the grief and wailing of the children and women that it would have wrung the heart of anyone. And now we had more trouble in restraining our friends from killing and committing such atrocities than we had in fighting the Indians. And never at any time was such cruelty seen, so beyond nature, as among the natives of these parts. Our friends took a great deal of booty that day, and we could by no means restrain them, because we Spaniards numbered only about 900, and we could not keep the Indians from looting, although we did everything possible to prevent it" (p. 254).

In the preceding paragraph, which refers to scenes during the last days of the siege of the capital, we see that Cortés' attitude has changed from the one that I have been pointing out. It is not the only example of it, and I should be unjust if I did not indicate in the conqueror, even when he is at his most violent, an urge other than that of destruction. It would be impossible for Cortés not to feel some compunction as he destroys all the places which he has described with such affection and admiration when he first saw them. He seems to be expressing this compunction when he tells of the razing of Xochimilco: "And we were in this city for three days, in none of which did we cease fighting, until at last we left it burned and desolated. And truly it was something to see, because it had had many houses and temples of its idols built of stone and mortar; but not to be prolix I refrain from mentioning the other notable things about it" (p. 201).

This feeling of Cortés grows in proportion as the destruction of the Aztec capital increases: "On that day from one end to the other and on both sides of the principal street, we did nothing but burn and demolish houses, truly a sad sight; but, as we could do nothing else, we were obliged to continue with it. Seeing so much ruin, the people of the city, to whip up their courage, told our friends to keep on with the burning and destruction, for they knew they would have to rebuild the houses in case they should win; if not, they would have to rebuild them for us. And in this last statement it pleased God that they should be telling the truth, although [actually] it was the others who rebuilt them" (pp. 246–247). "Seeing that those of the city were in rebellion and were showing such determination to die in its defense, I gathered two things from it: one, that we should recover little or none of the treasure they had taken from us; and,

two, that they were forcing us to destroy them totally. And I
was most regretful of the latter, and I was hurt in my soul, and
I wondered what I might do to terrorize them so thoroughly
that they would recognize their error and the harm we might
do them, and I did nothing but burn and raze the towers of
their idols and their houses. And to pain them still further, that
day I set fire to the great houses on the square, where the Spaniards and I had our quarters before they drove us from the city.
These houses were so large that a prince with more than 600
persons in his service could be lodged in [one of] them. And
the other houses next to them, although somewhat smaller,
were much cooler and more pleasant, and in them Moctezuma
kept every kind of bird to be found in those parts. So much to
my regret I resolved to burn them, because it would greatly
pain the enemy, and they showed it, as also did their allies
around the lake, because none of them thought us strong enough
to penetrate so far into their city, so they were much discouraged" (p. 222).

Cortés regrets the destruction of a city that had captivated
him and filled him with astonishment. Now in the fighting he
had further cause for astonishment: the mettle of the natives,
their courage and their admirable tenacity in the defense of
their liberty. Cortés recognizes that he has met with enemies
worthy of him, and he frequently mentions their valor: "They
were so brave that many of them were bold enough to attack
the horse with their swords and shields" (p. 199). "And, although the enemy saw they were being hurt, they were such
mad dogs that we could by no means prevent their pursuing
us" (p. 219). "And so, as we were retreating and they were
pursuing us so delightedly, at times we pretended to fly and
then turned the horse upon them, and we always took twelve
or thirteen of the boldest. And with this [stratagem] and the
ambushes we always set for them, they always got the worst
of it. And truly it was an astonishing thing to see, for, however
notorious was the harm and damage they received from us as
we retreated, they did not desist from the pursuit until they
saw us leave the city" (p. 224).

If on the one hand the stubbornness of the defenders exasperates Cortés, on the other it increases his desire to make peace, which he offers them repeatedly. "I always sought, Most Puissant Lord, in all the forms and ways I could, to persuade the people of Tenochtitlán to be our friends; for one reason, to prevent their bringing about their own destruction; for another, to give [us] rest from all our past conflicts; and especially because it would benefit the service of Your Majesty. And whenever I captured a man from the city I sent him to admonish them again and beg them to surrender in peace" (p. 191). "And as my motive is always to make these people understand that we do not wish to harm them, however guilty they may be, especially if they will become vassals of Your Majesty; and, since they are people of such intelligence that they recognize all this, I ordered that they were not to be further harmed, and when they came to talk to me I received them very well" (p. 195).

"And from that tower I surveyed all that we had won in the city, which was doubtless seven-eighths of it, and I saw that it was impossible for that mass of enemies to survive in such close quarters, especially since the remaining houses were small, all of them built over the water; and since there was a very great hunger among them—in the streets we had found gnawed roots and the bark of trees—I decided to cease fighting for a day or so, and try to persuade them to come to some arrangement and prevent the death of such a multitude of people, for truly I was saddened by the pain and harm that were being inflicted on them, so I continually urged them to accept peace. But they said they would not surrender, regardless, and that if only one of them should survive he would die fighting, and that we would have nothing left of all we had won, for they would burn it all or cast it into the water, from which it could never be recovered. And I, not to return evil for evil, pretended that I would not fight them" (pp. 248–249).

All the efforts of Cortés come to nothing in the face of the firm decision of the natives not to surrender, and they come to beg him to kill them all and get it over with, to put an end to their sufferings. "The next day we returned to the city, and I ordered [our men] not to fight with or harm the enemy. And when they [the enemy] saw such a multitude of men coming to attack them, and recognized them for the vassals they had once commanded, and realized their own extreme necessity, for they had no place to stand except on the dead bodies of their men, such was their desire to be quit of so much ill fortune that they asked us why we didn't kill them at once. And with great haste they begged me to be summoned, for they wished to speak with me. And, since all the Spaniards wanted the war to stop, and were sorry to see all the harm they were causing, they were very glad, thinking that the Indians were suing for peace. So they came to me quite joyfully and urged me to approach a barricade where certain nobles wished to speak with me. And, although I knew that my going would be of little profit, nevertheless I went, knowing that the decision to surrender would be up to the lord [Cuauhtémoc] and three or four nobles of the city, because the rest of the people only wanted to get out, dead or alive. So I went to the barricade, and they said that since they believed me to be the child of the sun, and since in the short space of a day and a night the sun makes the circuit of the earth, why did I not with the same speed finish killing them and release them from their pain, because they wished only to die and join Huitzilopochtli, who was waiting for them to give them rest? This idol is the one they most venerate. And I answered saying many things to persuade them to surrender, but none of it did any good, even though we offered them more signs and promises of peace than were ever made to a vanquished people, we being, by the grace of God, the victors" (pp. 250–251).

The Aztecs stupefy Cortés with their tenacity, as they had once stupefied him with their splendor. Not knowing how to overcome their resistance, he decides to level the whole city, house by house. "And for this purpose I summoned all the lords and nobles of our friends and told them what I had decided, asking them therefore to bring in many men from among their farmers, with their *coas*, which are the sticks they use in digging, as spades are used in Spain. And they answered that they would be very glad to do so, and that it was a very good decision, at which they were very pleased because they thought

this was a way to destroy the city, whose destruction they desired above anything else in the world" (p. 241).

"On the morning of the next day we again entered the city,
and when our friends saw how methodically we were going
about its destruction, such a multitude of them came every day
that they could not be counted" (p. 246). Cortés does not share
in the rejoicing of his allies. "I, in view of the great stubbornness of the people of the city, and how determined they were
to die, more so than any generation in history, did not know
what to do about them, or how to relieve us of so many dangers
and hardships, or how to save them and their city from complete destruction, for it was the most beautiful city in the
world" (p. 240).

Having unsuccessfully resorted to the greatest violence and
atrocities, Cortés tries again to soften his approach, but too
late. "And when more than five hours had been spent in these
parleys, and some of the people of the city were standing on
their dead, and others without water, others swimming,
and still others drowning in the large lake where they had
their canoes, their suffering was so severe that one could not
imagine how they could endure it, so they did nothing; but a
great multitude of men, women, and children approached us,
and they were in such a hurry to get out that they pushed each
other into the water, where they drowned among the mass of
corpses. And it seemed that from drinking the salt water, and
from hunger and the evil smell, so many of them had died that
their number came to 50,000 souls, the bodies of whom, to prevent our learning of their necessity, they did not cast into the
water, lest the brigantines find them; nor did they cast them
out of doors, lest we observe them in the city. And so in the
streets we found the dead heaped up, and no one could avoid
stepping on them. And, since the people of the city were coming out to us, I posted men in all the streets to prevent our
friends from killing the poor wretches, who were countless.
And I also told the captains of our friends not in any circumstances to allow the slaughter of those who came out; but these
were so many that day that the killing of more than 15,000 souls
could not be prevented" (p. 256).

Cortés is unable to stop the slaughter that he himself has initiated. In vain he repeats his orders not to kill the refugees, and to respect the lives of women and children. It is impossible to check the Indian auxiliaries, who are accustomed to war without quarter. "The next day, after the catapult had been placed, we again went into the city, and, since we had not been fighting for three or four days, wherever we went we found the streets filled with women and children and other poor wretches, who were dying of hunger, and were so worn and thin that it was the most pitiable thing in the world to see them. And I ordered our friends to do them no hurt whatever" (pp. 249–250). "And so great was the mortality among our enemies that the dead and prisoners numbered more than 12,000, upon whom our friends practiced such cruelty that they left none alive, however much they were reprehended and admonished by us" (p. 250).

All Cortés' attempts to speak with Cuauhtémoc and propose peace directly to him come to nothing. He succeeds in confronting him only when all resistance has become impossible. The Indian chief ends the epic of his people with an admirable gesture. And Cortés, now that the resistance of the Aztecs has been broken, recovers his natural sobriety, and tells us modestly that he is renewing his policy of conciliation. "And it pleased God that the captain of a brigantine, one Garci Holguín, was pursuing a canoe, in which it appeared that persons of importance were riding, and since he had with him two or three crossbowmen who were facing the men in the canoe, the latter indicated that their lord was there and [begged them] not to shoot. And they advanced quickly and seized him and Cuauhtémoc, and the lord of Tacuba and other nobles who were with him. And the said Captain Garci Holguín brought the lord of the city and the other noble prisoners to the roof where I was, on the shore of the lake. And I, without showing him any severity whatever, had him sit down, and he addressed me in his language to the effect that he had done everything it was his duty to do, to defend himself and his people until they found themselves in the pass in which they now were, and that I might do anything I liked with him. And he put his hand upon a dagger that I was wearing and told me to stab him and kill him. And I comforted him and told him to have no fear whatever. And so, with the capture of this lord the war stopped at once, which it pleased God Our Lord to end on Tuesday, the feast of St. Hippolytus, August 13, 1521.

"So, from the time the city was besieged, May 30th of the said year, to its fall, it took 75 days, in which Your Majesty can see the hardships, perils, and misadventures suffered by your vassals, as proved in their persons and their deeds. And in all these 75 days there was none in which they did not fight with those of the city, little or much. On the day of the capture of Cuauhtémoc and the fall of the city we gathered up the spoils that could be had and went back to our camp, giving thanks to Our Lord for the singular favor and our so-desired victory, which he had given us. I spent three or four days in the said camp, attending to many necessary duties. Afterward we went to the city of Coyoacán, where I have remained up to the present, looking after the order, government, and pacification of these parts" (pp. 256–257).

It would be a fine thing for us if, as Don Antonio de Solís[20] does, we might say farewell to Cortés in the ruins of Tenochtitlán with words of praise for his achievement; but such a spectacular ending would not fit the true character of the conqueror; nor would a final view of ruin correspond to the nature of his work. It is Cortés himself who, in one of the numerous memorials he addresses to the Emperor, tells us of the magnitude of his services and merits. "He only entreats Your Majesty to review and consider the services in which he has distinguished himself in those parts, in the conquests he has carried out there, as well as in the preservation and conversion of the natives, and the peopling and government of the lands, for no one other than he has accomplished these three things, and Your Majesty has nothing in those parts except what he has

---

[20] Solís occupied the post of Chronicler of the Indies from 1681 to 1686. His *Historia de la conquista de México* (Madrid, 1684) is widely renowned for the beauty of its style. The book ends with the fall of Mexico and the following words of the author: "Admirable conquest! And more than illustrious captain, one of those whom the centuries rarely produce, and of whom History seldom offers examples!"

won and governed, and you would have had more if he had not been interfered with" (*Escritos sueltos,* p. 322).

We know well enough how Cortés abused the first person singular, but at bottom his words are perfectly just, for there appears in them, as always, a full consciousness of the achievement he has realized. If the part he played in the conquest was outstanding, no less so was his work as governor and explorer.[21] Cortés did not limit himself to being a great captain, as his panegyrist Solís has it. If he had been nothing more than that, he would have ceased to exist historically with the fall of Mexico and his repression of the rebellions that occurred for some time after that; but the fact is that Cortés is all that a governor should be. His methods are simple. He openly proclaims his pragmatism, the necessity of acting according to the circumstances: "And I shall always take care to add whatever I think is necessary, because, owing to the great size and diversity of the lands that are daily being discovered, there is need to apply new opinions and advice to them, and if in any of these [opinions] that I have expressed to Your Majesty in the past, or shall express hereafter, it seems to Your Majesty that I contradict former ones, Your Excellency may believe that I meet new situations with new opinions" (p. 323).

Nevertheless, as we review the letters and memorials of Cortés to the Emperor, the contradictions in them are not as great as he tells us. Whenever he proposes measures for government, or disagrees with those ordered, as he does openly, we find in him the two basic principles of his whole policy: to achieve at all cost the preservation of the Indians, and to induce the Spaniards to strike root in the new lands. "In New Spain he brought many provinces, *villas,* and towns under the royal crown of Your Majesty, as he believes Your Majesty to be fully aware. As soon as they were pacified, he strove to make it possible for the natives to preserve their lives and estates, to know God, and

---

[21] For the study of Cortés as governor his fourth *Carta de Relación* (Gayangos, *op. cit.,* p. 273) and his numerous memorials to the Emperor are of fundamental interest. There is a good over-all exposition of the activities of Cortés as governor and explorer in the *Disertaciones* of Lucas Alamán, especially in the sixth, "Private enterprises of Cortés" (vol. II, pp. 63 *et seq.*).

to serve Your Majesty, very contrary to what had been done up to that time in those parts, as is evident in the event. He settled them with Spaniards at much cost to himself, giving them a great deal of money, so that some of them might go back [to Spain] for their wives and daughters, and thus strike root in the land, and helping [the latter] to find husbands, paying the passage of others and supporting them, and providing them with provisions and clothing and horses and other things" (*Escritos sueltos*, pp. 313–314).*

Clear-sighted as always, Cortés recognizes perfectly what the native problem is. He has witnessed the disastrous effects of the Spanish rule in the islands and the disappearance of the native population, and will not tolerate their repetition in the lands he has conquered. "For what would it profit me to have conquered these parts and increased the patrimony of Your Majesty, if I should fail to tell you what I can about their preservation?" (*Escritos sueltos*, p. 169).

As always, he trusts his own judgment and fears divided counsels, and he takes upon himself all responsibility for his conduct. "For I know that if this country should be governed by divided counsels, as the other islands were governed, it will end as they have ended, which God forbid!, and let Him also forbid that since He made me His instrument for winning this land, I should be the instrument for its destruction!" (p. 336).

Cortés has behind him his valuable experience in the islands, and knows he must do exactly the contrary of what was being done there. He is well aware that if the natives of the islands have disappeared, it is owing to the violence and ill-treatment to which they have been subjected. "The order that I have established here in the [forced] labor of the Indians is such that I hope it will not result in their diminution, as occurred in the islands under the Spaniards who have now settled in these parts. I resided in the islands for twenty-odd years and

---

* [To initiate his policy of creating a strong Spanish aristocracy permanently rooted in New Spain, very early on (in 1524) Cortés advanced money to pay the passage of the Comendador Leonel de Cervantes and his seven daughters, all of whom he married off to the more prosperous of his conquistadores (Manuel Orozco y Berra, *Historia de la dominación española en México*, 4 vols., Mexico, 1938, vol. I, p. 110).–Tr.]

witnessed the harm done there and its causes, so I shall take great care to avoid that course and steer things in the opposite one, for it seems to me that I should be more culpable that those who first committed such errors if in full knowledge of them I should perpetuate them" (p. 329). "The service that I shall perform will not be small, or of less merit, in advising what should be provided for the preservation of these parts, for converting their inhabitants to our Holy Faith, and insuring that the revenues of Your Majesties shall be very great and shall increase, not decrease, as they did in the islands and Tierra Firme for lack of good government, and because the Catholic Monarchs, the parents and grandparents of Your Majesties, followed the advice of men who looked after their own interests and failed to act out of zeal for the royal service" (p. 487).* "For it is evident that if all the islands and provinces thus far conquered in those parts have been stripped of their native population, and if those that are not entirely stripped have been ruined and diminished, it clearly shows that the latter are going the way of the others, whether the evil is the result of conquest or of the process of government" (p. 563).

Cortés knows well enough where the root of the evil lies. Nothing [he thinks] will be gained by the oppression of the Indians. If they have helped him to conquer Mexico, it is precisely because they wished to free themselves from the oppression against which they were always on the point of rebelling. "Your Caesarian Majesty may well believe that these people are of such a turbulent disposition that they will be stirred to rebellion by any novelty or new device, because they have been in the habit of rising up against their lords and will always find a way to do so" (pp. 302–303).

If the natives, when they are well treated, fear one thing more than another, it is a return to the state in which they were before. "And it has happened, and happens every day, that to frighten certain communities and induce them to serve

---

* [The "parents and grandparents" are, of course, Doña Juana "la Loca" and Philip I, the parents of Charles V, and Ferdinand and Isabella, his grandparents. Until Doña Juana's death, in 1555, Charles V nominally ruled Castile and the Indies jointly with her—hence "Your Majesties."— *Tr.*]

the Spaniards to whom they have been assigned [in encomienda], they are told that if they are unwilling [to serve] they will be sent back to their former lords, which is what they fear above any other threat or punishment" (p. 329).

So the only way to keep the Indians peaceful is to treat them well. This is the first article of Cortés' instructions to those who are going out to found new *villas*: "First, because God Our Lord and His Majesty benefit from the good treatment of the natives of these parts, which makes for the pacification and prosperity of the country, you will exercise particular care to insure that they are well treated, and you will not permit any person to abuse them or do them any violence whatever, and you will severely punish, in the presence of the Indians, anyone who does so, explaining to the Indians why he is so punished, to the end that they may know they will be protected and ruled with justice, they and their estates as well" (*Escritos sueltos*, p. 86).

Cortés thinks the natives are entirely justified in rising against their oppressors. "Because during my absence [in Honduras, 1524–1526] several provinces rebelled because of mistreatment, and more than 100-odd horse and 300 foot, with many guns and a large number of Indian friends marched against them, under the command of the Veedor [Peralmíndez Chirinos], who was acting as governor, and they could not prevail against the rebels; rather, on the contrary, the rebels killed ten or twelve Spaniards and many Indian friends, and the situation remained as it had been. And when I returned, they were apprised of my arrival by a messenger I sent them, and the principal men of the province of Coatlán [Oaxaca] came to me at once and told me why they had risen, and they were completely justified in so doing" (p. 477).

It is not surprising that the stupid and selfish conduct of certain captains should arouse the distrust of the natives and make them difficult to conciliate. "Although they told me that they were afraid that the captains my predecessors had lied to them, and later had carried off the women assigned to them for making bread [tortillas] and bearing their burdens, and this is what they thought I might be doing also" (pp. 455–456).

This distrust has to be overcome, and the task is rendered doubly difficult because the Indians of New Spain are superior, in intelligence, culture, and standard of living, to those of the islands. So at the beginning Cortés advises against the introduction of the encomienda and the forced labor of the Indians. "In one of my letters I informed Your Majesty how much greater was the capacity of the natives of these parts than that of the natives of the other islands, and they seemed to us to have sufficient intelligence and understanding to make them fairly capable, and for this reason I thought it would be a grave mistake to compel them to serve the Spaniards, as was done in the other islands" (p. 271).

He does accept the encomienda later on, but only because it is the lesser evil, because he has no other way to reward the Spaniards for their services. If he should not settle the conquistadores in the new lands and allow them to use the labor of the Indians, it would be necessary to maintain an army of occupation, which would cost a vast amount of money and destroy everything. "And since there [in Spain] it may be urged that Your Majesty should keep a paid army in this country in order to hold it, this should not even be thought of, because, in order to keep what we have won, to say nothing of enlarging it or conquering more territory, it would be necessary to keep at least 1,000 horse and 4,000 foot in it. And no cavalryman would stand for being advanced 1,500,000 *maravedís* [roughly, 3,000 *pesos de oro*], of which he would have to spend more than half for a horse, especially now when the people of Española have prohibited the export of mares from any of the islands, this, so that they may sell their horses at a higher price, and the rest of the money would not be enough to buy horseshoes or clothing, so high are these articles. So such an arrangement would not even feed them, and the 1,500,000 *maravedís* were only to cover the needs of the cavalry. As for the foot soldier, even if he should be paid only the wage of the lowest rank, it would come to 200 *pesos de oro*, which, multiplied by 4,000, makes 800,000 pesos. Your Majesty should consider, therefore, how such a sum could be raised, especially since even at this rate the men could not be found. And even if they could be, such a pestilence in itself would be enough to destroy the country. Besides, and this would be worse, the conversion of the natives would necessarily cease, because each friar going to a village to preach would have to take a guard with him, which would desolate the place in three days, and truly the land would be destroyed in a very short time" (pp. 322–323).

Cortés knows that most of the Spaniards come to the new lands to make their fortune quickly, and that their fierce selfishness, their contempt for the natives, and their unedifying conduct will cause grave difficulties. "And if all the Spaniards now in these parts, or who come here, were friars, or if their main purpose were the conversion of the natives, I well believe that their association with them would be very beneficial; but this is so contrary to what is happening that it would have the opposite effect, because it is a notorious fact that the Spaniards who come here are of a low class, lecherous and steeped in many vices and sins. And if they should be allowed freely to go about among the Indian towns, for our sins they would convert them to their vices instead of attracting them to virtue; and this would be a grave obstacle in the way of their conversion, for the Indians, after listening to the words of the friars and preachers, who in their sermons prohibit vices and counsel the practice of virtues, and seeing that the actions of those who are engaged in their conversion are contrary to what our Holy Faith preaches, will take it all as a joke and think that the words of the religious and the other good people are spoken for selfish ends, and not for the salvation of their souls. Moreover, mistreatment would cause them to rebel, for they would not put up with it, and now that they have learned our skills, they could manufacture many kinds of weapons, offensive and defensive, to use against us, for they have plenty of ability to do so; and, since they are innumerable and we by comparison nothing at all, they would soon finish us off" (pp. 326–327).

For this reason Cortés' whole effort is to interest the Spaniards in the work he has done in the government and to bring about their permanent settlement. "There is no doubt that, in order to induce the natives to obey the commands of Your Majesty and serve you as you wish, it will be necessary to settle a large number of Spaniards permanently in the land, and this cannot be done unless they have something to live on, enough so that their self-interest will oblige them to remain here and forget their native country" (*Escritos sueltos*, p. 270).

If he would have them strike root, the first obstacle he must meet is the resistance of the Spaniards themselves. "I issued certain ordinances and had them read by the public crier, and, since I am sending a copy of them to Your Majesty, I shall only add that the observation of the said ordinances is indispensable, if everything I have been able to foresee here is to be accomplished. The Spaniards who reside in these parts are not happy about some of them, especially those that require them to settle here permanently, because all, or almost all, of them think to do here what they did in the islands where they first settled, that is, to strip and destroy them, and then abandon them" (p. 322).

Cortés has little confidence in the conduct of his countrymen, or even the clergymen [seculars], so for the work of evangelization he asks that friars of an austere life be sent over, not bishops. "For if bishops and other prelates should be sent, they would not abandon the habits which, for our sins, they have today of spending and disposing of the wealth of the Church in wasteful ostentation and other vices, and setting up entails for their sons or relatives. An even greater evil would come of it, for the natives of these parts in their time had monks in charge of their religious ceremonies, and these were so strictly secluded and kept honest and chaste, that if any of them should be discovered violating the rule, the punishment was death. And if the natives should see the affairs of the Church and the service of God in the hands of canons or other dignitaries, and should learn that these were ministers of God, and see them indulging in the vices and profanations now common in those kingdoms [of Spain], it would cause them to despise our Faith and think it a joke, and this would bring so much harm that I don't think any amount of preaching would do any good whatever" (pp. 319–320).

In these ideas of Cortés, the governor, we can clearly see the essential traits that were evident in the [first] stage of the

conquest: love for his work, interest in the natives and in raising their standard of living, desire to incorporate them in his
enterprise, and respect for their institutions, which should not
be interfered with except to improve them. A necessary corol-
lary is his effort to inspire in the Spaniards the same love he
felt for their new country and make them forget their native
land and strike root. These ideas, which are now in vogue and
are thought to be so very modern, can be seen as the inspiration of Cortés.

In this same pattern of thinking he includes the consolidation
of the conquered territories, his work as governor, and the con-
tinuance of his exploration of new lands and seas. The South
Sea—the Pacific—especially attracts him. "A desire to learn is
a universal trait in all men," he tells us at the beginning of one
of his letters. He applies this Aristotelian principle to his own
explorations, and recommends it constantly to his captains: that
they should desire to learn, and omit no detail in the accounts
of their discoveries. One of the worst charges made against
Juan de Grijalva, the predecessor of Cortés, is that he fails in
this minute observation. "And when he had taken on water he
returned to his ships without penetrating the land or exploring
its secrets, and in this he erred, for it was his duty to penetrate
it and learn about it, in order to inform Your Royal Highnesses
what that island [of Cozumel] was like" (p. 5). "The said
Captain Grijalva sailed along the coast with his remaining ships
for 45 leagues without touching land or observing anything at
all except what he could see from the water, and from this
point he began his return to the Isla Fernandina [Cuba] and
never saw anything of the land worth relating. So Your Royal
Highnesses may believe that all the accounts of that land that
have been submitted to you cannot have been accurate, for
[their authors] saw no more of it than they wished to write"
(p. 7).

Cortés does not wish to be guilty of this defect, nor does he
wish his captains to be. So he orders Diego Hurtado de Mendoza, when Mendoza sets out to explore the South Sea: "You
will follow the said coast for 100 or 150 leagues, always enter-
ing its ports and rivers, and taking possession of them as has

been said, and informing yourself most particularly about all
the qualities of the land and its people, and all the customs,
laws, or rites which they may have, so that you will be able to
bring back a very exact and lengthy account of everything"
(*Escritos sueltos*, p. 203).

This curiosity is not wholly disinterested. "You will observe
whether the people who come to speak with you wear ornaments on their persons, and you will observe which are the ones
they most value, so that you may bring back an account of that
also. And you will observe whether on any part of their bodies
they wear gold or pearls or precious stones, and what these
stones are. And do not ask them about anything, or show yourself struck by one thing more than another among their ornaments, so that they may not suspect or take notice of anything,
but very secretly you will note all the things they most esteem"
(*ibid.*, p. 201).

Nor is he to neglect military matters in his examination of the
new lands: "And [find out] what arms and forces they have,
and the kind and disposition of the terrain, and whether it may
be conquered by horsemen" (*ibid.*, p. 137). He is to make every
effort to communicate with the natives and obtain from them
the greatest possible amount of information. "You will present
to the lords of the lands where you arrive or settle, the letters
of mine that you will carry for them, written in Latin, which
is the most universal language in the world; and it may happen
that you will find Jews or other persons who will be able to
read them, for they engage in the spice trade and other commerce with many nations of those parts. And in the event that
you do not encounter such persons, you will have the letters
translated or explained to the Arab interpreter you will have
with you, and from him, I believe, you will get more information because of the extensive trade they have with the
Moors. And in case they haven't any [information], you will
take along a native of Calcutta, and he will certainly find an
interpreter to understand him, and through him you will be
able to tell the natives of the country whatever you please"
(*ibid.*, p. 144).

Cortés never neglects to describe the lands he discovers, not even in the most perilous moments of military operations such as in the frightful hardships of his expedition to Honduras. It is important to emphasize how essential to the work of Cortés is the matter of exploration, and how it fits into his wide vision of a universal empire for Charles V. The South Sea and the vessels he orders built for its exploration are an obsession with him. "I hold these vessels to be more important than I can say, for I am very certain that with them, if God pleases, I shall be the agent by whom Your Caesarian Majesty shall be in these parts the lord of more kingdoms and seigneuries than up to the present our nation is aware of. May it please Him to direct [my expedition] in such wise that it will bring much profit to Your Caesarian Majesty, for I believe that when it is done Your Excellency will have nothing further to do to make yourself monarch of the world" (p. 308).

Cortés' concept of his task is on an immense scale, and he sees it as a necessary and harmonious complement to the Emperor's accomplishment in the Old World. "I beseech Your Majesty please to keep me informed of your wishes, so that I may fulfill them, which is my principal desire, and to instruct those of your Council to do the same, for they are in a better position to [fulfill them]. And also please do me the favor of ordering me to write Your Majesty an account of everything that has happened in these parts, for here we thank God and rejoice in His victories, and I hope that through Your Majesty's holy intentions, you on your side and we on ours, we shall bring to the fold a great part of these lost sheep" (p. 506).

Cortés is intoxicated with his grandiose plans, which he clings to all the more closely the more he is plagued by adversities. He, who is so laconic in his successes, is joyful upon his return from Honduras, when he concludes his letter describing the disastrous expedition with these words: "As I have already told Your Majesty, my South Sea ships are now ready to sail, because as soon as I reached this city [of Mexico] I began to hasten their departure. They would have sailed by this time, except they had to await certain arms and cannon and munitions being sent from those kingdoms [of Spain], to equip the said vessels and put them in better condition. And I trust in

God Our Lord and in the good fortune of Your Majesty that in this voyage I shall be performing a signal service, for, even though I should discover a passage to the South Sea, I expect to find thereabouts [in Panama] a route to the Spice Islands, and I shall inform Your Majesty every year of whatever is done in that land. And if Your Majesty should be pleased to order me granted the privileges I begged for in a certain agreement concerning this voyage I am undertaking, [I shall] explore on this side all the Spice Islands and the others, of the Moluccas and Malacca and China, and even make it possible for Your Majesty to acquire the Spice Islands, not by purchase, but to possess them as your own. And I shall undertake to have the natives of those islands recognize and serve you as their king and natural lord; for I undertake, with the said additional help, to send there such a fleet, or to go there in person, that I shall conquer them and colonize them, and stock them with munitions and artillery in such wise that all the princes of those parts, and even others, may be able to defend themselves [against the Portuguese?]. And if Your Majesty should be pleased to have me undertake this negotiation, granting me what I have asked for, you may believe that you will be greatly served thereby; and I [further] undertake, that if what I have said should not be accomplished Your Majesty may order me to be punished as one who does not tell the truth to his king" (p. 490).

The plans of Cortés are so vast and so out of the ordinary, even for such a period as that of Charles V, that they arouse every kind of suspicion, especially among the bureaucrats who surround the conqueror. So the notary Diego de Ocaña advises Charles V not to authorize the expedition that Cortés is planning. "Hernando Cortés has made a contract with Your Majesty to undertake an exploration in those seas, in exchange for certain privileges that have been promised him; but, since Your Majesty can have [such an expedition made] without granting them, you might well have it determined whether you might not have it made at your own expense, and give it in charge to someone whom you can remove at your pleasure, for some of us here believe, to judge by what we have observed in the past, that if Cortés carries it out he will die with a crown on his head" (p. 360).

In Spain these fears find an echo,[22] and all sorts of stumbling blocks and difficulties are put in Cortés' way. He is unable to carry out his great scheme in the South Sea. All his expeditions end in failure.

Before we contemplate Cortés sunk in disgrace, we should examine another aspect of his work into which he puts all his love and energy: the peopling and founding of *villas*. He was no longer concerned with discovering new lands, drawing maps of them, and then abandoning them, but in establishing himself in the country he had discovered and striking root there. He had to colonize it. Among the preoccupations of Cortés as founder, the reconstruction of Mexico City has first place. Hardly has he occupied the capital when he dictates orders for its rehabilitation. And once again he shows his admiration for the Aztec city. "For the past four or five months the said city of Tenochtitlán is being rebuilt. It is very beautiful, and Your Majesty may believe that it will be rebuilt and so ennobled day by day that it will become what it was before, the noblest

---

[22] I have cited Diego de Ocaña's charge at random from among many like it. They may be found in detail in the *residencia* already referred to. One of the points in the *residencia* that calls for investigation is the real character of Cortés' expedition, for the crown evidently believes that he intends to make off with the ships. "And to the provinces of Zacatula, a port on the South Sea where he keeps the ships he had built to explore the Spice Islands, he sent many [man] loads of gold; and these ships, which he always said were built to discover the strait, had actually a different aim, namely, to sail to a place where his treasure could not be seized. This, they say, seems to be very clear from the conjectures and signs that have been noted, because for more than a year and a half, or two years, he has kept his ships there and has never dispatched them, although he has sent off many armed expeditions by land and sea" (*op. cit.*, vol. I, p. 27).

The question as to whether Cortés was or was not caressing the idea of making himself independent has also been much debated. The best exposition of the subject, to my knowledge, is that of Luis González Obregón, in his *Los precursores de la independencia mexicana en el siglo XVI* (Mexico, 1906). "In spite of his audacity, courage, and political experience, he hesitated to mount the glorious pedestal upon which the founders and liberators of a nation stand" (*op. cit.*, p. 186). I do not believe that this conclusion fits the character of Cortés. It would have cost him nothing to free himself from the crown if he had really meant to do so, given the prestige he enjoyed among the majority of the conquistadores and, above all, among the Indians.

city and mistress of all these provinces" (p. 262). "And because there is a large supply of stone, lime, and lumber, and
the many bricks that the natives make, all of them build such
fine large houses that Your Sacred Majesty may believe that
five years from now [1524], it will be the noblest and most
populous city in the occupied world, with the best edifices"
(p. 310).

Cortés is as painstaking and foresighted in the founding of a
villa as he is in the exploration of new lands. And it is pleasant
to read among his instructions details that illuminate the common daily life of the men whom we imagine always to be
caught up in the whirlwind of their adventures. "You will forth-
with begin very diligently to clear the site of the said *villa* that I
have laid waste; and, after you have done so, following the plan
that I have drawn, you will mark out the public places there
indicated, such as the square, the church, the town house and
the jail, the meat market, the slaughterhouse, the hospital, and
the house of trade, according to the plan and map in the hands
of the council's notary. And you will assign a lot to each of
the *vecinos* of the said *villa*, at the place I have indicated on
the said plan. And to those who come later you will also assign
lots according to the said plan. And you will take particular
pains to see that the streets are very straight, and for this purpose you will seek out persons equipped to do this, and you will
appoint them as *alarifes* [surveyors or engineers, with police
powers], to measure and mark the town lots and streets" (*Escritos sueltos*, p. 92). "And this said officer will indicate one,
two, or three places, or as many as may be necessary, depending on the quality and arrangement of the said *villa*, for the
disposal of the offal and waste from the houses, and in each
of the said places the said officer will erect thick, tall stakes,
and it will be announced by the crier that all the citizens and
dwellers and inhabitants of the said *villa* are to deposit their
offal and waste in the said places and nowhere else, on pain
of half a *real* of silver for each violation" (*ibid.*, pp. 78–79).
"And the said butchers will be obliged to do their slaughtering
on Saturday afternoon, and weigh the meat that is to be eaten
on Sunday, and the butcher shops will not open on Sunday

morning" (*ibid.*, p. 80). "The said bakeries will sell the said
bread thoroughly baked and dried, for they [are in the habit
of leaving it undone] so that it will weigh more" (*ibid.*, p 81).
"On Sundays and obligatory feast days all the citizens and
dwellers and inhabitants of the said *villa* will attend High
Mass at the principal church, and will enter before the reading of the Gospel, remain until the priest pronounces the *Ite
missa est* and gives the benediction, on pain of half a gold peso
for each violation, which will be distributed, half to the constable who denounces it, and half to the fund for the building
of the said church" (*ibid.*, p. 82).

Now indeed we should have liked to take leave of Cortés, in
his task as founder, ordering that the streets be straight and the
villas clean, but we must follow him briefly until his death.

I have already mentioned Cortés' expedition to the Gulf of
Honduras, which interests me particularly because the conqueror devotes the last of his great narrative letters (the fifth)
almost entirely to a description of it. This is an extraordinary
document which should be read completely. The struggles of
his lost and bewildered men as they cut their way through the
virgin forest test their endurance. The expedition is a disaster,
in which men and animals die in large numbers. There are
moments in it when Cortés himself seems to be on the point
of losing his self-confidence. "I passed twenty days in this
village, and in that whole time I did not desist from looking for
a way out of it, but did not find one, large or small; rather, in
whatever direction we took there were such huge and frightful
swamps that it seemed impossible to make our way through
them" (pp. 402–403). "This estuary or bay worried me more
than I can describe, because it didn't seem possible to get
through it, so great was it, since we did not have canoes to get
us across and, although we had a few for our baggage and
the men, the horses could not pass, for at its entrance and exit
there were very great swamps and the roots of trees which,
unless we could fly over, it would be useless to think of getting
the horses across" (pp. 413–414). "In all the time we spent
crossing this pass it never stopped raining, night or day; and
the mountains were so steep that they did not catch enough

rain to allow us to quench our thirst, from which we suffered greatly, and most of the horses died of it. And if it had not been for the camps and huts we built for our shelter, in which we caught the water in pots and other vessels, for it rained so heavily that we caught enough for us and the horses, it would have been impossible for man or beast to escape from those mountains" (p. 433). "For ten days we had nothing to eat but the buds of palms and palmettoes, and not many of them, for we lacked the strength to cut them down" (p. 434). "And so I spent the whole of that night in the heaviest rain that was ever seen, and in the greatest plague of mosquitoes that can be imagined; and such was the forest and the road, and so dark and stormy the night, that, although I tried two or three times to go out and look for a village, I could never find my way, although we must have been very close to one, for we could hear its people talking" (p. 446).

Such is the general tone of his narrative. At the end of this letter, along with grandiose plans for exploring the Pacific, Cortés lets himself go in his complaints to the Emperor and in his defense against the charges he was accused of. Complaints, defenses, demands for the recognition of his merits, and remonstrances against the injustices he has suffered, fill the correspondence of Cortés during the twenty long years following his return from Honduras in 1526, until his death in 1547.

This is the most troubled part of his life, and these are the most monotonous of his writings, in which he stubbornly attempts to defend his work from what seems to him intolerable meddling. Cortés cannot allow himself to be checked, to be deprived of credit, to have *oidores* appointed over his head, and a viceroy later on, to govern the lands whose incorporation in the crown of Castile has been his work, and whose problems he feels that he understands better than anyone else. So in his complaints he strikes every note, from scorn and threats to the most emotion-laden and abject prayers. His attitude is that of a jealous man, frightfully tormented because others possess and enjoy what has been his greatest love, New Spain.

Hence he reproaches in others the vices from which he is not free himself, cupidity, [for example] in the *oidores*. "If

they had proceeded [correctly] they would not have been able
to amass, as they have amassed, each of them, 50,000 gold pesos
a year, not counting an equal amount that they have spent in
paying their debts, and in sending to those kingdoms [of
Spain], as they have sent, in the names of third parties, a great
sum in gold and jewels, and spending it on banquets and fes-
tivities and women, and other dishonest things; but, since there
are many reporters of this business who have sent accounts to
Your Majesty and your Council, I shall not dwell upon it"
(pp. 503–504).

He [accuses] Nuño de Guzmán, President of the Audiencia,
of having cruelly tortured the lord of Michoacán, he, who
had done the same thing to Cuauhtémoc! "It is well known
that he tortured the said Cazonci most cruelly with fire and
water, burning, as he did, his feet and hands and belly, and
when the Cazonci lay dying he had him dragged [through the
streets] and quartered, on the pretext that the Cazonci intended
to rebel against the said Nuño de Guzmán" (p. 509).

The main target, however, of the wrath and scorn of Cortés
is the Viceroy, Don Antonio de Mendoza. He demands a *residencia* to investigate Mendoza's conduct, which he thinks is
deplorable. He cannot forgive Mendoza for engaging in conquests and expeditions on his own account. "Your Highness
must know that Don Antonio de Mendoza, your Viceroy in the
said land, neglecting the duties of Viceroy and Governor for
which you appointed him, has undertaken, and is undertaking,
explorations and conquests of new lands,* because of which he
has not only been, but is, remiss in looking to the good government of the country, which is his principal duty and the one
for which Your Highness sent him here, and also, in order to
pursue the said explorations and conquests, he has committed
many extortions, wrongs, and abuses against the said natives,
as well as against the Spanish settlers" (Cuevas, *Documentos*,
p. 202). "The Viceroy was the cause of all this [trouble], meddling in the said conquests and explorations, and neglecting
his duties, and interfering in other people's affairs; because the

---

* [The Coronado expedition to the "Seven Cities of Cíbola."—*Tr.*]

said Viceroy had no authorization from Your Highness to make [conquests in] or explore new lands. On the contrary, Your Highness has declared that when the Governor and Audiencia and Captain General [Cortés] of the said New Spain should think it necessary for the good of your royal service to undertake some war or conquest, and it should be agreed upon, the execution of it was to be entrusted to the Captain General. And doubtless the rebellion, war, and explorations of the said Viceroy have cost more lives of the natives of the land, and more destruction of their property, than did the whole conquest of Mexico" (*ibid.*, p. 204).

Cortés does not stop with these censures. He is even shocked by the conduct of the Viceroy's servants. "His servants and hangers-on have committed many evil and harmful acts in the houses of married women and maidens which, out of regard for their reputations, I shall not describe. The Viceroy has been informed of some or all of them, and the remedy he suggests is that everyone should look out for his own house" (*Escritos sueltos*, p. 333).

Cortés the Puritan! Cortés, of whom López de Gómara, his chaplain and biographer (who can hardly be accused of denigrating him) says: "He was jealous in his own house, but free in his neighbor's!" Gómara has women in mind, but Cortés feels the same way about the conquest. He is jealous in his own house, and his house, the home of his love and his desires, is New Spain—hence his irritation at seeing it in the hands of others. He refuses to give it up and, when he is removed from his command, his love is manifest in his avowal to defend it, even as a common soldier.

He replies in this vein to the Licenciado Marcos de Aguilar, when the latter suggests that he retire as Captain General. "If the said Señor Licenciado, disregarding what the said Señor Governor [Cortés] has asserted, should, acting in his capacity as justice, order him to give up the said command, he [Cortés], not willingly, but in obedience to the justice of His Majesty, will do so. He protests, however, that if because of his removal an uprising should occur among the natives or the Spaniards of this New Spain, or some tumult or villainy which might result in the ruin of the country, or in a diminution in the revenues of Your Majesty owing to the cessation of gold mining and the pacification of new provinces and lands, or for any cause or reason Your Majesty should suffer disservice, the blame will fall upon the said Licenciado and not upon the said Señor Governor" (Cuevas, *Documentos*, p. 19). "And he likewise declared that if a rising of the natives should occur for this reason, he would not march against them as Captain General, but as a citizen, that is, if the said Señor Licenciado, acting as justice, should command him to do so, but not otherwise" (*ibid.*, pp. 19–20).

He repeats the same thing, but in humbler terms, to the Emperor. "Your Majesty will provide as you please. What I pray for myself is that Your Majesty, since I am held in such small esteem that I cannot serve in this office, will do me the honor of entrusting it to someone who will fill it better, because, although up to the present I have not erred, I should like not to err in the future. As a citizen I shall do whatever I am commanded to do" (*Escritos sueltos*, p. 193). "And if in Your Majesty's opinion others will serve better, you should charge them and give them authority to do so, because in whatever Your Majesty should be pleased to command him [Cortés], he will consider it a privilege, and whenever those in command order him to serve with his lance, he will do so to the best of his ability" (*ibid.*, p. 238).

There is haughtiness and pride in these words, but there is love also. Cortés, it should be noted, does not for a single moment think of abandoning New Spain, but his tone becomes depressed and more and more embittered. "If this seems to Your Highness and worships a very long letter for a report, please accept it in place of a petition, for if I were to write an account of all the wrongs I am suffering here, and the slight relief provided for me there [in Spain], even though it should cover as many pages as it has leagues to travel, they would be too few [written in 1533]" (*Escritos sueltos*, p. 515). "I am hard put to it to support my wife and myself in this village [of Coyoacán] and I do not dare reside in this city [of Mexico] or go there, because I have nothing to eat in it; and, if I go there once in a while, it is because I cannot avoid it, for if I spend a day in it I must fast for a year [written in 1538]" (*ibid.*, p. 285). "I am poor, old, and in debt [he writes in 1543]" (*ibid.*, p. 345).[23]

He sounds the depth of his bitterness in the memorial he addresses to the Emperor in February, 1544, which opens with the famous words: "I had thought that the labors of my youth would bring me rest in my old age, but for the past forty years I have spent my life in sleepless nights, eating badly and at times not eating at all, wearing my armor, endangering my person, spending my estate and my years, all in the service of God, to bring the most distant sheep of our hemisphere into His fold—which is not noted or described in our chronicles—and increasing and magnifying the name and patrimony of my king, winning for him and bringing under his royal yoke and scepter many and very great kingdoms and seigneuries of many barbarous nations and peoples, won in my own person and at my expense, without any help whatever, but on the contrary very much interfered with by envious competitors, who, like leeches, have swelled to bursting with my blood" (p. 567).

Three years later Cortés dies in Spain and, faithful to the love of his lifetime, in the first article of his testament he begs that his remains be brought to Mexico. "First, I order that if I should die in these kingdoms of Spain, my body be placed and deposited in the church of the parish where I shall die, and be kept there until it shall seem proper to my successor to transport my bones to New Spain, as I charge and order him to do within ten years, or sooner if possible, and take them to my *villa* of Coyoacán and inter them in the convent of nuns

---

[23] It is hardly necessary to indicate that Cortés is exaggerating, but in view of the magnitude of his services to the crown his complaints are justified. [That Cortés could not have been flat broke may be inferred from the inventory made of the Marquesado del Valle in 1569, after its sequestration during the trial of Martín Cortés for conspiracy. At that time it still had 60,903 tributaries, that is, heads of families, who were paying about 86,000 pesos a year to the Cortés estate, and this after the catastrophic decline in the native population, estimated at 50 per cent since the conquest. See L. B. Simpson, *The Encomienda in New Spain* (rev. ed., Berkeley and Los Angeles, 1966), pp. 165–167.—*Tr.*]

that I order to be erected in the said *villa* of mine, which shall be named the Convent of the Conception of the Order of St. Francis . . . , and I designate it and constitute it the burial place for me and my successors" (*Escritos sueltos*, p. 353).

But not even his bones were to enjoy the tranquillity he had never known during his life.[24] It seems that the destiny of this extraordinary man was to wander, in life or in death, arousing fear and hatred among those he had tried to serve. His contemporaries lost no time in cataloguing his faults, a task that has been pursued down to the present day. Even so, we should not forget a very essential factor in our appraisal of Cortés: the love and esteem he enjoyed among the Indians. There are abundant proofs of it, but I shall mention only one, a very characteristic one, the testimony of Dr. Cristóbal de Ojeda in the *residencia* of the conqueror: "Also, this witness knows of, and saw, that the said Don Fernando Cortés enjoyed the great confidence of this Indians of this country, and he observed that the said Indians loved well the said Don Fernando Cortés and obeyed his commands very willingly."[25]

In Ojeda's view this is a charge against Cortés. In mine it is the highest honor to which he could have aspired, that of having won the love and confidence of the Indians. He could hardly have done so if he had been merely a tyrant bent on enriching himself.*

---

[24] A brief summary of the wanderings of Cortés' remains may be found in Pereyra (*op. cit.*, pp. 426–433). For more detailed information consult the *Postrera voluntad y testamento de Hernán Cortés, Marqués del Valle*, introduction and notes by G. R. G. Conway (Mexico, 1940), Appendix I. [An account of the final wanderings and burial of the bones of Cortés in the Hospital de Jesús of Mexico City is in L. B. Simpson, *Many Mexicos* (4th ed., Berkeley and Los Angeles, 1966), pp. 22–24.—*Tr.*]

[25] *Residencia de Cortés*, vol. I, p. 123.

* [This last is the burden of the accusations made against Cortés in his *residencia*, many times repeated down to the present.—*Tr.*]

Peter Martyr

Peter Martyr (Pietro Martire d'Anghiera) was
a secular priest and humanist. He was born in Italy in 1447.[1]
He lived in Spain from 1487 onward, filling important posts
and much involved in the life of the court. He was an eyewitness of many of the great events that transpired during the
turn of the fifteenth and sixteenth centuries. He had an unsur-
passed place from which to hear news of the recent conquests
and discoveries, for he was a member of the Council of the
Indies [established in 1524]; but his many duties and his
curious and impressionable mind make him a slave to novel-
ties, which he writes of in great haste and then sends them
off in all directions while they are still fresh—hence his use
of the epistolary form. His letters are a kind of newspaper of

---

[1] For Peter Martyr and his work consult Henry Harrisse, *Bibliotheca
Americana Vetustissima* (New York, 1866), p. 123, and the introduction
to the Spanish translation of the *Décadas*, published by Don Joaquín
Torres Asensio for the celebration of the fourth centennial of the discovery
of America, under the title, *Fuentes históricas sobre Colón y América:
Pedro Mártir de Anglería* (4 vols., Madrid, 1892), vol. I, pp. xxviii *et seq.*
See also F. A. MacNutt's introduction to his translation of *De Orbe Novo,
The Eight Decades of Peter Martyr d'Anghera* (2 vols., New York, 1912).

the time, written helter-skelter and disconnected like all news letters.

His *Décadas* (*De Orbe Novo*) are of the same kind, lengthy epistles in which he strives to limit himself to the discoveries and conquests in the New World. The *Décadas* are eight in number, and were first published in their entirety in Alcalá de Henares in 1530. They are written in a confused Latin. "Some of us would have preferred him to write in Romance, or better or more clearly," the chronicler López de Gómara was to say some years later.[2]

Peter Martyr tells us that he finished his *Décadas* in 1526, and also tells us that he was sixty-nine on the second of February of that same year.[3] But as he also tells us that his memory was very faulty, even to the point of his forgetting everything that he had just written, scholars have had the pleasure of disputing the date of his birth. All that I am interested in at the moment is that Peter Martyr is old and forgetful when he takes up the narrative of Cortés and the conquest of New Spain.

Naturally, the source of his account of the conqueror is the latter's *Cartas de Relación*. "Letters have been received from Hernán Cortés, prefect of the Emperor's army, written from the lands he was trying to bring under the power of Spain, and in them he relates strange and unheard-of things, astonishing beyond belief," he says at the beginning of the fifth *Década*. But the strange and unheard-of things he writes down hastily, and his account is hardly more than an extract of that of Cortés. When the latter writes of Ixtapalapa, Peter Martyr comments: "He includes so many trifling matters that I am already fatigued by his prolixity" (vol. II, p. 180). And when he describes the arrival of Pánfilo de Narváez in New Spain, he tells us that he will omit "many things of slight importance,

---

[2] I have used the *Décadas* in the Spanish translation of Don Joaquín Torres Asensio. The volume and page numbers in my citations of Peter Martyr refer to that edition.

[3] "My seventieth year, upon which I shall enter on the second of next February, 1526, has wiped my memory as with a sponge, so thoroughly that when my pen has hardly finished an episode, if anyone should ask me what I have written, I shall answer that I do not know, especially since things have come to my hand which I have noted at different times and taken from various persons" (vol. IV, pp. 377–378).

such as those the Jews and Greeks (who always saw themselves bound within narrow limits) would have included in
their histories as if they had occurred to their countrymen; but
we, in the midst of such an abundance of events, shall omit
not a few of them" (vol. III, pp. 259–260).

This is a curious excuse. The magnitude of the subject, instead of demanding greater attention [as it should], justifies
him in sketching it hastily. What really happens is that the
good Dean of [the Cathedral of] Granada is swamped, and
that his eternal haste gives him no time in which to wander
about in a quieter and more serene study. In this he was honest,
to be sure, for in another passage he tells us: "I write down
everything in haste and almost in confusion, as the opportunity offers, and I cannot observe order in these things because they happen without order" (vol. IV, p. 400).

This defect of Peter Martyr, the haste and lack of consideration with which he writes, is to our benefit, for it makes his
work a mirror in which we see reflected the fluctuations of
judgment and the suspicions with which the actions of Cortés
after the conquest of Mexico are regarded in Spain.

In Peter Martyr's last two *Décadas* the contradictory opinions about the Extremaduran conqueror trip over one another.
Thus, when Peter Martyr tells us how many of the conquistadores have come to a bad end, he observes that the only one
who has retained power and wealth is Cortés, "for he rules
over many cities and princes, in whose mountains and rivers
there is an abundance of gold, and no lack of rich silver mines;
but perhaps he will exemplify the common proverb, which
says 'Of riches, fidelity, and talent there may be found pri-
vately less than their public fame would have us believe.' Time
will tell" (vol. IV, p. 134).

This suspicious opinion, unfavorable at bottom, is followed
soon afterward by one of the opposite kind, when Peter
Martyr is reluctant to believe that Cortés is displaying excessive ostentation in having two gold cannons cast. "Or the story
may have been invented by the envious, for his illustrious
deeds are the constant target of nasty attacks" (vol. IV, p. 136).

His uncertainty makes Peter Martyr insistently ask those

who return from the Indies what the attitude of Cortés really is: whether he is faithful to the crown or is in rebellion against it, as some maintain. The *alguacil* Cristóbal Pérez, companion of Francisco de Garay, the unlucky explorer of Pánuco, informs him of the kind of life Cortés is leading, and adds: "The popular suspicion of Cortés' rebellion against the Emperor, conceived by our courtiers, has no foundation in fact, for neither he nor anybody else has seen any indication of treason in him, and three caravels are being readied there to bring treasure to the Emperor, together with that cannon (called a culverin) which he declares he has carefully examined, and which is large enough to admit an orange, but it does not contain as much gold as they say" (vol. IV, p. 298).

A certain Santiago García, who had left Veracruz toward the beginning of April, 1524, "also maintains that no hint of rebellion against the Emperor has been observed in him, [contrary to what] many have been whispering out of envy. According to what he and others say, we hold that there could be no greater submission than that which Cortés gives his king, that his desire is to repair that part of the city which was ruined during the war, that he has rebuilt the aqueducts he cut at that time to deprive the stubborn besieged of water, that the destroyed bridges are now in working order and many of the ruined houses rehabilitated, and that little by little the city is regaining its former appearance, the fairs and markets are operating, and there is the same number of canoes coming and going that there were before" (vol. IV, p. 312).

Up to this point everything is fine, but what Lope Samaniego, "who is now present in my house" tells him has a very different sound. And Peter Martyr tells us that a serious plan is afoot to solve once and for all the problem of Cortés' ambiguous conduct. "With respect to Cortés and his evil tricks of seducing and deceiving [opinions are] very different from those formerly held by many; also, there is clear proof that he has accumulated unheard-of heaps of gold, precious stones, and silver, part of it brought in openly through the door of his immense palace, part of it secretly by night in packages, by the slaves of the caciques, undetected by the magistrates.

There are also [stories of] his opulent cities, his innumerable municipalities and *villas*, his mines of silver and gold, the number and size of his provinces, and many other things which I shall go into at another time. Certain remedies are being secretly discussed. It would be criminal in me to divulge anything at this time. Until the fabric we are now weaving is finished, let us leave these things to one side and speak a little of other expeditions" (vol. IV, pp. 407–408).

Time passes. Ships sail to the Indies and return. Contradictory stories come and go also. New letters from Cortés arrive, in which he complains of difficulties of building his ships for the exploration of the South Sea, and its enormous expense. But "there also arrive private and secret letters from the Contador Albornoz, secretary of the king, written in strange characters called ciphers, which had been given to Albornoz at the time of his departure, for the intentions of Cortés were already under suspicion. He wrote these letters to expose the sly maneuvers of Cortés, his burning avarice, and his almost manifest desire to take over the government. But whether these things are all true, or have been contrived only for the purpose of winning favor, as frequently happens, time will have to say, for responsible men have already been appointed who will be sent to investigate the situation" (vol. IV, p. 420).

This is the secret of the fabric that is being woven: the sending over of responsible men. But the fact is that Peter Martyr, along with the other members of the Council of the Indies, does not know what card to play. Their uneasiness mounts when it is rumored that Cortés has died in the Honduras expedition. So they send over Don Luis Ponce de León to look into the conduct of the conqueror. He is "a modest man of great intelligence, whose dispositions we hope will result in bringing the wandering imperial ship safely to port, under the happy auspices of the Emperor. He also bears orders to attract Cortés, if he finds him alive, with a thousand flattering promises, and to reduce him to the proper loyalty, although Cortés had never really been disloyal, because the name of the king and Emperor was always venerated in his words and letters. But from what he did not say, as I have already indicated at length, we suspected I know not what from the conjectures and accusations of many. Since he was a man of haughty character, he was always trying to win new honors. Some time past he obtained the title of Governor General and Adelantado of all those wide regions included under the name of New Spain; and a little while ago he demanded the habit of Santiago de la Espada, which the said Ponce is taking along to present to him. [Ponce] has already been dispatched by the Emperor and will sail with a fleet of twenty-two ships. But if he learns that Cortés has died, he will have to act differently, [for] none of the other captains will dare to rebel. Provided he finds the natives quiet, everything will turn out well ..." (vol. IV, p. 444).

With this question mark Peter Martyr no longer concerns himself with Hernán Cortés, and a little later he brings his *Décadas* to an end.

Gonzalo Fernández
de Oviedo

Few lives can have been so typical and representative of the great generation that flourished in Spain in the last quarter of the fifteenth century as that of Gonzalo Fernández de Oviedo.[1] He was born in Madrid in 1478. At the age of twelve he enters the court as a page of Prince Don Juan, the unlucky son of the Catholic Monarchs, and is sent to school with him, thus receiving the best education to be had in those days. He witnesses the war in Granada, Columbus's arrival in Barcelona to meet the monarchs, after his return from his first voyage to the Indies; he is on familiar terms with the two sons of the Admiral, Don Diego and Don Fernando, who also join the court of Prince Don Juan.

The latter dies in 1497, whereupon Oviedo goes to Italy and enters the service of the king of Navarre. There he studies the language and acquires books and knowledge. "I traveled throughout Italy, where I strove with all my might to know

---

[1] For the life and works of Gonzalo Fernández de Oviedo see the long introduction of Don José Amador de los Ríos to his edition of the *Historia general y natural de las Indias* (4 vols., Madrid, 1851–1855), vol. I, pp. ix–cxii, which I have used for my notes on Oviedo's life. My citations of volume and page refer to that edition.

and read and understand the Tuscan language, and to look for books in it, of which I still possess some that I have with me after more than fifty-five years, thinking by means of them not to waste my time entirely," he writes in 1555 (vol. I, p. xviii, note 20).

Upon his return to Spain in 1502 he marries "one of the most beautiful women of his day in the kingdom of Toledo," Margarita de Vergara, who dies within a few months. He goes to the Indies in 1514 as *Veedor* [inspector] of gold smelting in Tierra Firme, in the expedition of Pedrarias Dávila, the same expedition in which Bernal Díaz del Castillo took part.

I shall not follow him in his long and varied career. For some years he was *Alcaide* [warden or commanding officer] of the fortress of Santo Domingo. He made the Atlantic crossing twelve times under the conditions then obtaining, in voyages that forced him to keep to his bunk during the frequent storms that battered the tiny vessels. He died in Valladolid in 1557, possibly engaged there in the settlement of one of the large number of lawsuits over the government of the new lands? No. He was printing his *General y natural historia de las Indias*, upon which he had been working, as he tells us emphatically, "since the time these parts were discovered by Admiral Don Christopher Columbus, in the year 1492, down to this present year of 1548; and, since I have been engaged in it for fifty years, it should be believed that it is history" (vol. I, p. xvi, note 10).

We should not be surprised that Oviedo, a man of such lively and varied curiosity about notable events, should feel impelled to relate them. So we note that, apart from a couple of translations (of a romance of chivalry and a religious treatise), all his voluminous original production is in historical works, which I shall not examine in their entirety, but confine myself to those that concern the Indies. As early as 1526 Oviedo published a *Sumario de la natural historia de las Indias*, which he wrote from memory in Spain, since all his papers were in Santo Domingo. It is a brief description of the newly discovered lands, their most noteworthy flora and fauna, the customs of the natives, gold mines, and navigation.

Oviedo's historical works are well received at court, and in 1532 he is appointed General Chronicler of the Indies. In 1535 he publishes the first part of his *General y natural historia*, upon which he continues to labor incessantly, enriching it with all the data that come to his hands, until the year 1548. He did not have the satisfaction of seeing it completely published during his lifetime, because, as Gómara tells us,[2] of the intrigues of Father Las Casas, who was a personal enemy of the chronicler. So it remained in manuscript until the past century, when it was published by the Royal Academy of History of Madrid in four large volumes.

Oviedo was well aware that the discovery of the Indies was revolutionizing human thought. Just as Columbus had sailed his caravels to unknown places, thanks to new methods of navigation . . . , the human mind should now attempt to penetrate new knowledge and seek new directions, freeing itself from the trammels of authority of classical writers. The conflict in Renaissance minds (the study of which has not yet been undertaken to my knowledge) between the rediscovery of ancient culture and its veneration, on the one hand, and the piling up of new experiences on the other, would make a moving study, for they simultaneously attack [ancient] culture and shake it to its foundations. It was a serious problem for those men: the conflict between "authority" and the evidence of one's own experience which contradicts it; between the desire to digest [ancient] knowledge and the new discoveries that invalidate it.

Oviedo, therefore, trusts to his own experience despite the thousands of books accumulated by others. "The said [content of my books] has not been drawn from the two thousand volumes I have read, as Pliny remarks . . . ; but I have gathered everything I write here from two thousand millions of hardships and necessities and perils which for more than twenty-

---

[2] See the vitriolic denunciation of Oviedo in Las Casas' *Historia de las Indias* (3 vols., Buenos Aires, 1951), vol. 3, chaps. CXLI–CXLVII; also, Francisco López de Gómara, *Istoria de la conquista de México*, English translation by L. B. Simpson, *Cortés, the Life of the Conqueror* (Berkeley and Los Angeles, 1966), p. xvi. [Note amended by the translator.]

two years I have seen and experienced in my own person" (vol. I, p. 6–a).

The revolution is first manifested in cosmography, in the arts of navigation and all the natural sciences. "What I have written cannot be learned at Salamanca, Bologna, or Paris, but in the school of the binnacle, which is the place where the compass is kept, with the quadrant in one's hand, steering by the North Star by night, and with the astrolabe on clear days" (vol. I, pp. 39–40).

He feels a palpable pride in the defeat of ancient notions. "It is best to leave all this to navigation charts and the new cosmography, which, since they were unknown to Ptolemy and the ancients, are not mentioned by them."[3] Antiquity, nevertheless, still carries some weight, and fables and absurd myths are repeated, mingled with the new discoveries. . . . Oviedo had an encyclopedic sense of knowledge. He dips into everything, from a dissertation on the origin of syphilis to a description of rare plants and animals, and an account of an expedition of conquest. His history is "general and natural." It includes "natural sciences" and "cultural sciences," as we should say today, using Rickert's terms. And if in the former, observation may be repeated as often as one wishes, in the latter we know how suspect human testimony is, in Oviedo's time as in ours.

What method does Oviedo pursue as chronicler? He explains it himself. It is very simple, the only one possible when he is narrating contemporary events, which is all that interests us in Oviedo's history. "For I do not depend upon the authority of some poet or historian when I write, but upon myself as an eyewitness of most of the things I shall speak of here; and what I have not seen myself I shall relate from the accounts of trustworthy persons, never depending upon the evidence of a single witness, but upon that of many, in those things I have not experienced in my own person" (vol. I, p. 10–a).

Our chronicler gives first importance to what we should

---

[3] *Sumario*, in *Biblioteca de autores españoles*, vol. 22, p. 473–b.

now call *vivencia*, that is, to his own experience as a witness of the events he records. Hence Oviedo cannot imagine how Peter Martyr can write about the Indies without leaving Spain. "Indeed, I have seen things written in Spain about the Indies which fill me with astonishment at the boldness of the authors who, trusting to their elegant style, are as far from the truth, nevertheless, as the heavens are from the earth. And they excuse themselves by saying: 'That's the way I heard it and, although I did not witness it, I had it from persons who saw it and described it.' And they had the effrontery to write in this fashion to the Pope and to foreign kings and princes" (vol. I, p. 10–b).

[In Oviedo's view] it is fundamental to have been a witness of what one relates, and when one writes a narrative one must be possessed of the desire not to deviate from the truth, and not deliberately to allow partisanship or self-interest to distort the facts. When Las Casas complains of what Oviedo writes of the disastrous expedition [of Las Casas] to Cubagua and Cumaná to try out the Dominican's methods of peaceful colonization, Oviedo honestly replies: "In fact, when I wrote that, I had no purpose or intention of giving him pain or pleasure, but only to relate what happened" (vol. III, p. 552–a). It is to be hoped that if Las Casas' luck changes, Oviedo's account will please him more. "For if he undertakes new enterprises I shall not cease to write of the things of the Indies, so long as Their Majesties wish to have me do so, for I hope to God that He will allow him to be more successful in the future than he has been in the past, so henceforth he may be better pleased with what I write" (vol. III, pp. 552–553).

All goes well so long as he is a witness of what he writes. The difficulty comes when he has to trust to other people's accounts. Oviedo is never sufficiently certain of the fidelity of his witnesses. "I know well enough that I am telling the truth in what I write, but I confess that in the events at which I was not present I may have been deceived by my informants. I know that in my histories particular matters will be found which will please some and displease others; and to the end that I may not be blamed, and that it may be believed that neither self-interest nor prejudice has moved my pen to speak ill of anyone, the reader should bear in mind (if he is not satisfied with my words) that it is a general fault in men to blame each other. And for this reason I shall not lack detractors, any more than ancient and more learned writers lacked them; for many kinds of men and interpreters have come to these parts, of whom most were more greedy than moderate, more ignorant than learned, more envious than courteous, persons of base lineage rather than noble and illustrious. And I prefer to win favor among the virtuous by telling the truth, than to please all those who are not [virtuous] by lying" (vol. III, p. 256–a, b).

Oviedo is aware of the vast relativity of historical knowledge, in which there are many motives for distorting the accounts of the same event made by different witnesses. "But, since in some men understanding is much greater than in others, it is not astonishing that they should differ in their accounts, and even in their actions, especially in similar things, in which intent and personal interest distort the accounts that some have given of what I have not seen. And since only God knows and understands all of them, I as a man could be deceived, or not so well informed as I should be; but as I listen to many I am beginning to perceive some errors [among them], so I shall continue to correct them where it is proper to do so, the better to distinguish where I was in doubt or straying from the straight path" (vol. III, p. 547–a).

Since the learned also make mistakes—as Oviedo reminds us in his corrections of Peter Martyr—one must accept information from whatever source, even from the ignorant. There will be time to correct it later on. "Although you may think, reader, that some of the things here touched upon are superfluous, the towns and provinces also, and that the cosmography is confused in these accounts, which mark neither the towns and promontories and shores of the seas and rivers and lakes, nor mention the degrees of latitude of each province and town, nor in what climate or parallel they lie, but they are written in soldier fashion as if [soldiers] were the only ones interested, do not believe it, for if they contain these and other defects they will not fail to be useful in the future. Indeed, everything that Claudius Ptolemeus of Alexandria wrote in his *Geography*, and what Pliny gathered in his *Natural History*, or the greater part of it, has been written by others in less elegant words, which they heard from those who observed it before them, only their followers [Pliny and Ptolemy] expressed it better" (vol. III, p. 487-a, b).

One must [says Oviedo] gather the greatest possible number of data and strive to find the common ground hidden beneath their diversity. "With these two chapters, and the two previous ones, the chronicler will end the account which he gathered and heard from trustworthy men who took part in the conquest. And let not the reader think that they contradict each other because, since men are of different degrees of judgment and nature, they observe and understand things differently, and so relate them, although they all come to a general and common conclusion, even when they disagree in many details. Every day we see cases come up which have never been thought of or even remembered. And when a judge or a prince tries to get at the truth, the witnesses will swear and depose in different ways, with fewer or more words, one of them mentioning details which the other witness conceals, or which he did not or could not understand, even though he was present. So in one and the same affair there are many different kinds of testimony, which, although they agree in form and sense, are far apart, so some kinds make better evidence than others. And so, reader, with these considerations in mind, you should think over what has been said about the conquest, and what will be said. And you may take it for granted that I obtained my information from persons who deserve to be believed and who were present throughout it. From them I gathered and examined what was pertinent to the subject, although, as I have said, it may seem to you that I jump about" (vol. III, p. 506-a, b).

Oviedo maintains an exquisite scrupulosity in always giving us the source of his information, and, when he finds there are different versions of the same story, he reproduces them in their entirety. This procedure has brought down upon his head the censures of "critical" historians. Fueter, for example, says of him: "His including testimony from different sources is a proof of his impartiality, but his lack of critical judgment is apparent in his inability to select from among his various sources. His work is a mine of useful historical matter, but it is not a history."[4]

Fueter's judgment is far too unfavorable. I do not believe that the method of many modern historians, with their reconstructions done in mosaics, with bits and pieces taken from here and there, is very superior to that of Oviedo, whose accounts, taken separately, contradict each other. His method is honest and clear. And in his inability to select or make up his mind, it is possible that he showed a more critical sense than many of today's historians, who are influenced by nonhistorical sources. How can he be blamed, for example, when in his account of the first voyage of Columbus he says that some say it was the Admiral who became discouraged and wanted to return, while others maintain that it was Columbus himself who imposed his will upon the men who wanted to give up? Oviedo repeats both versions.[5] Is it a fact that today, with a whole mountain of Columbian bibliography to back us, we know which of the versions is the true one?

After these remarks, which I have made for the sole purpose of establishing Oviedo's stature as a chronicler, I shall move on to the only part of his work that is pertinent here: Book XXXIII of the *General and Natural History of the Indies*, "in which is treated the territory and government and conquest and settlement of New Spain."[6]

As Chronicler of the Indies, Oviedo had access to the royal decrees ordering the conquistadores to send him accounts of anything relevant to his work. He was very proud of these decrees and alludes to them frequently. "For I have *cédulas* and orders of His Caesarian Majesty, addressed to all governors and justices and officials of the Indies, to give me a

[4] Édouard Fueter, *Histoire de l'historiographie moderne* (Paris, 1914), p. 369.
[5] Oviedo, *Historia*, vol. I, pp. 21–25.
[6] *Op. cit.*, vol. III, pp. 256–257.

true account of everything worthy of record, signed with their names and witnessed by notaries public, who will swear to their authenticity" (vol. I, p. 10–a). Oviedo was taking no chances.

With this authority he writes to Hernán Cortés, asking him for data on the conquest of New Spain. The conqueror, it seems, does not pay him much attention, thereby wounding the feelings of the chronicler. "In addition to this, I say that I have royal decrees ordering the governors to send me accounts of whatever concerns the history of their territories for this history of mine. I wrote to the Marqués del Valle, Don Hernando Cortés, to send me his, as I had done many times before, and he sent me some letters that he had written to Your Majesty about the events of the conquest, but did not bother to send me anything else. Of them, and of what I was informed, I shall give an account in Book XXXIII" (vol. III, p. 258–a, b).[7]

Oviedo writes his narrative without departing in any respect from the *Cartas de Relación* [of Cortés], but he misses no opportunity to correct Cortés' account, including the latter's views on the beauty of Cholula. "Hernando Cortés says in his letter that this city seen from without is more beautiful than any in Spain, because it is level and covered with towers. But I would say that a city which is good to look at from without must not be level, but lofty and seated on a slope, like Granada, Toledo, Cuenca, and others, which, because they are not flat, are very beautiful seen from without; and Burgos is also a beautiful city because it is not flat. And by day they look very well from a distance, and also by night, for some of the houses are taller than others and one can see many lights in the early evening, and the view of such cities is very beautiful. Those that are situated on a plain [on the other hand] should not be viewed from without, as Cortés says, but from some high tower, from which they will look handsome, like Ghent in Flanders, and Milan in Lombardy, and Seville in Spain, and others situated on a plain" (p. 277–b).

---

[7] From this point forward all references will be to vol. III of the Amador de los Ríos edition of Oviedo, so I shall only indicate the page.

His reservation about what Cortés says is very apparent in his comments on the seizure of Moctezuma and the latter's acceptance and that of his vassals of the sovereignty of Charles V. "And in truth, if what Cortés says or wrote really happened, the good faith and liberality of Moctezuma in yielding his sovereignty and obedience to the king of Castile, acting merely on the sly words of Cortés, seems to me a very extraordinary thing for him to do. And the tears that he says Moctezuma shed when he [Cortés] made his speech and threatened him, while stripping him of his power, and the tears of those who accepted what he [Moctezuma] commanded and exhorted them to accept, it seems to me, meant or indicated something different from what he and they said; because the allegiance that is commonly given to princes is usually given with laughter and song and music and mirth, as a sign of pleasure, and not with mourning and tears and sobs, especially when he who gives his allegiance is a prisoner" (p. 297–a).

Oviedo also finds it hard to believe what Cortés says of the destruction of the idols and the willingness of the Indians to accept it. "And so on with everything that Hernando Cortés wrote to the Emperor our lord. God, of course, could have made it possible, but as for me, I consider it a marvelous thing and a very great one, that Moctezuma and the Indian nobles should view with such great patience this treatment of their idols and temples. That they were dissimulating was proved later on when they saw how few the foreigners were who had seized their land and made them tributaries, and were destroying and dissipating their temples and religion in which they and their ancestors worshiped. It seems hard to believe that they would accept it so calmly; but, as my history will relate, time disclosed what the Indians in general had hidden in their hearts" (pp. 303–304).

As we are beginning to see, Oviedo was not as ingenuous as he has been painted. He was aware that Cortés was doing violence to the facts in his desire to believe that the submission of the Indians was concluded. In this he was premature. When Oviedo is writing, he of course knows what had happened later, the disastrous end of the Spaniards' first entry into Mexico.

Now we come to the expedition of Pánfilo de Narváez against Cortés. Here Oviedo is extremely cautious, and applies the method we have already spoken of, giving equal space to the opposing parties. "What my history relates in this chapter also follows the account that Captain Hernando Cortés wrote to the Emperor concerning the capture of Captain Pánfilo de Narváez" (p. 308-a). "Bear in mind, reader, that Pánfilo de Narváez says the opposite of what Cortés says, as will appear below" (p. 314-a).

The account continues with a cloud of warnings and reservations, at the end of which Oviedo tells us: "In this instance Cortés says a great deal in support of his position. I do not deny, nor do I approve his words in the detail he gives in his letter, for, as I have said, it was written by him. But since I said above that I would deny Pánfilo de Narváez' story, I say now that in the year 1525, the Emperor being in Toledo, I saw the said Narváez there, and he was saying publicly that Cortés was a traitor, and that, if the Emperor would give him leave, he would prove it in a personal confrontation, and that he [Cortés] was a liar. And he said many other ugly things, calling him treacherous, a tyrant, and an ingrate to his lord, and had seized the land, with the men and the money, from the one who had sent him to New Spain at his own expense, namely, Governor Diego Velázquez, and he said many other ill-sounding things. And as for the way that he [Narváez] had been taken prisoner, he told it very differently from the way Cortés told it" (pp. 315–316).

We are beginning to see that Oviedo is long-winded. I shall not repeat here his extensive commentary, which may be summarized by saying he supports Cortés. "But to tell the truth, if we leave out this trifling matter of Cortés' failure to assist Velázquez, who had sent him off as his captain and substitute, in everything else he was a valorous and very successful man" (p. 316-b). Oviedo even goes so far as to say that in the deeds of men it is not only reason that decides, but also the hand of God. "I see that these changes and things of great moment do not always move in a way that seems just to men, but obey a superior decision and judgment of God that is beyond our understanding" (*ibid.*). Well then, since Cortés is the winner in his struggle with Narváez, it is apparent that Oviedo has a notion as to what side Providence is on. Later on he will tell us clearly that Cortés was called to make the conquest against all the obstacles that were put in his way.

Here follows a description of the scenes of the rebellion of the Mexicans, and the efforts of Cortés and his men to put it down. In it Oviedo displays an infantile pedantry, as when he describes the engines that Cortés ordered built to attack the barricades of the Indians. His commentary is now as favorable to Cortés as it was hostile to him in the Cholula affair. "The architects usually call these engines *testugines* or *testudines*, which Vitruvius describes at length, as does Flavius Vegecius in his treatise on *Arte Militar*. I do not know that Cortés had any knowledge of this science, but his ingenuity and skill were more than equal to the occasion" (p. 320–b).

Cortés and his companions gradually arouse Oviedo's enthusiasm as he continues his narration of their prowess, and it leaves no room for any feeling other than admiration, which becomes more and more exalted. Oviedo will now defend Cortés even in moments in which his conduct has been open to criticism. Thus, when Francisco de Garay's men arrive, Cortés and his men say they had taken care of them very well. "Others say the opposite, that they were given fine words, but were so effectively blocked that they were forced to remain in the country when their ships were sunk. But let us leave these disputes, for it is customary among men at war to employ every device to increase their forces, especially since at the time Cortés' need of men was notorious" (p. 335–a, b).

Nor does Oviedo believe Cortés to be guilty of the death of Francisco de Garay, as some were saying. "Other parties judged the sudden and unexpected death of the said *Adelantado* in different ways and senses, in which I do not share, for I consider sudden and unexpected death as natural to men as one that is long drawn out, as we have frequently seen" (p. 455–b).

This attitude of Oviedo never turns into an unconditional devotion. When Cristóbal de Tapia comes to examine the conduct of Cortés, with the purpose of remaining as Captain and

Governor of New Spain, Oviedo defends the conqueror, who prevents it, but does not completely accept Cortés' opinion of Tapia. "Hernando Cortés says in his account that the arrival of Tapia, and his lack of experience in the country and its people caused a great deal of unrest, and that if he should stay it would be a very harmful thing. And he says other things to this effect which have more to do with private quarrels than with clean history or with the pleasure of those who read it, so I shall not repeat them" (p. 432–a).

Oviedo takes a more serious view of what Cortés says about going to Cuba to kill Diego Velázquez because he was sick of all the impediments that the latter was putting in the way of the expedition. "I do not think the Emperor liked these words, for I heard important people grumbling about them and even judging them to be insolent, especially since they were addressed to His Majesty, and in view of the fact that Velázquez was in Cuba, as this history has related, where Cortés had nothing to do" (p. 469–a, b).

Oviedo cannot forgive Cortés for his opinions about the bad government of the islands. Here he feels himself directly alluded to and makes a long defense of himself. "Hernando Cortés would have been better advised to say that the islands of Cuba and Jamaica and San Juan [Puerto Rico] have been destroyed and all but depopulated because of New Spain and the discoveries in Tierra Firme" (p. 473–b).

If I have given more space to this analysis than seems necessary, it is to emphasize the fact that Oviedo is by no means an unconditional admirer of Cortés, and to allow us to appreciate better that his praise of the *caudillo's* work arises from a pure and spontaneous enthusiasm, born of his astonishment at the deeds performed by the conqueror and his men. Oviedo pronounces his first eulogy precisely on the occasion of the retreat from Mexico. "It seems to me that this deed and the defeat of the Indians, executed in the person of Captain Hernando Cortés and by the vanquished Spaniards of his company, makes them more glorious in general, and him in particular, than any captain or soldiers of all those who have wielded arms here or in the Indies" (pp. 325–326). He also praises the conqueror's decision not to return to Veracruz, despite the urgings of his men. "It seems to me that the reply Hernando Cortés made to this, and what he did in the circumstance, was the act of a man of great good fortune and valor" (p. 332–a).

The chronicler's pen soars when he describes the return to Mexico and the siege of the city. Cortés is now for him "the chosen of God," no less. "Captain Hernando Cortés, being troubled and distressed by the occurrences in Mexico, found it impossible to ignore its sufferings. His thoughts were those of a brave man, and one might apply to him the words of Plato: 'Every man resembles the thing he loves, the thing in which he takes most pleasure.' So the person of this captain, who was so fond of and inclined to war, and so fitted for such a high enterprise, can only be compared with its own greatness. And it may be believed that he who persevered in the face of so many obstructions and hostilities knew best how necessary such a captain was for the service of God in these matters and in the conquest of New Spain" (p. 336–a).

Praises, with their pompous display of classical allusions, now build up on the slightest pretext. "But since God had provided the Spaniards and their army with a Captain General, in whom were united the qualities of which Cyrus, King of Persia, said: 'The office of the prince must exceed all others in wisdom, counsel, industry, and fatigue, not in idleness, ease, and pleasure,' all these good qualities were present in the person of Hernando Cortés" (p. 340–a, b).

When Cortés makes his second march on Mexico, Oviedo likens him to Julius Caesar, save that the Spaniard is superior to the Roman. "Beyond a doubt the ability and energy and wisdom of Hernando Cortés are very worthy of being held in high esteem by the knights and military men of our day, and of never being forgotten in the future. In this regard I frequently recall what was written of Captain Viriatus, a Spaniard and an Extremaduran. And Hernando Cortés [also] reminds me of the military prowess of that glass of chivalry, Julius Caesar the Dictator, as portrayed in his *Commentaries*, and in Suetonius and Plutarch and other authors who wrote of his great deeds. But those of Hernando Cortés, performed in a new world so distant from the states of Europe, with so many hardships and necessities, with such scanty forces, among such innumerable, barbarous, and warlike people, who eat human flesh—considered an excellent and savory dish by his enemies—he and his men the while lacking bread and wine and all the other foods of Spain, and being in such different regions and climates, and so remote from help and from their prince—all these are things to fill one with astonishment.

"Caesar waged his wars in provinces and places that were well peopled and provisioned, of the best in the world, attended by his own men and by many Romans and natives and other civilized people; and Viriatus [fought] in his own country of Spain. But here in these lands the smallest danger to men may grow very big indeed, because of the adverse effect of the airs and climate and difficult regions upon the health of those unaccustomed to them, so different from those of Spain, in a strange country and under unfamiliar stars, drinking waters of many kinds and different flavors, and so with the other things by which human bodies must be sustained, alien to the foods that our stomachs were used to, in taste as well as in their digestion, lacking physicians and surgeons and beds, and other things necessary to life" (p. 360–a, b).

Oviedo's praise is not restricted to Cortés; the companions of the conqueror, worthy of such a chief, come in for their share. "I wish to say that the men led by Captain Hernando Cortés had, many of them, borne arms for a long time before going to that country, in Spain and elsewhere; and, although their action in our Indies exposed them to new hardships, they bore them like Spaniards" (p. 446–a, b).

Oviedo cannot find for these men a better qualifier than *cortesanos* [courtly], "which in truth is not an insignificant name, but a very honorable one for all those who took part in the enterprise, so let them be proud of it and the name" (p. 361–a).

What we do not find anywhere in Oviedo is a clear recognition of the admirable courage and tenacity of the Mexicans. In this respect he is much inferior to Cortés. He did not understand the Indians, toward whom he maintains an attitude of distrust and contempt, believing that they were always ready to rebel. "Especially since the [Spaniards] are political men, accustomed to obedience, and the others are savages, accustomed to vice and idleness; the former are Christians, the latter idolatrous infidels of abominable habits. These things that they have been accustomed to, learned in long stretches of time since ancient days, cannot be uprooted or got rid of so quickly and easily that the old men will forget them, and so long as they live they will indulge in their inherited vices" (p. 456–b).

Such judgments as this bring down upon Oviedo the just denunciations of Father Las Casas.

The *Cartas de Relación* of Cortés supply Oviedo with material for forty-four of the fifty-seven chapters of his history of the conquest of New Spain. The remaining thirteen are based upon various reports and letters, one of them written by Viceroy Don Antonio de Mendoza. The most interesting report is that of "several gentlemen and soldiers who had taken part in the conquest of New Spain" (p. 494)—Oviedo does not identify them—because it tells us that before the arrival of Narváez Moctezuma had begged Cortés to get the Spaniards out of Mexico, and Cortés had answered, telling Moctezuma that he lacked ships to sail away in, but was ordering them to be built.

This episode is repeated by Gómara in Oviedo's own words, so he was doubtless acquainted with Oviedo's manuscript. But why does Cortés fail to mention it in the *Cartas de Relación*? Did he perhaps believe that this was only one more of Moctezuma's vacillations, to which he had become accustomed ever since the beginning of his march on Mexico? Or could it be that he suppressed it so that he could throw all the blame of the rebellion on the arrival of Narváez? I am rather inclined to accept the first of these explanations, because otherwise it would have been an unpardonable piece of stupidity to abandon Mexico and attack Narváez, leaving the command to Pedro de Alvarado, who was not exactly a prodigy of gentleness. The account [of this episode] which Oviedo treats separately, is incorporated by Gómara in his history of the conquest. It was necessary, in view of later events, to play down the opposition of Moctezuma and the Mexicans, so that the conduct of Cortés might not be censured as imprudent and excessively overconfident. I shall return to this subject below. Not without interest are the data supplied to Oviedo by an Extremaduran gentleman, Juan Cano. Cano had gone to New Spain with Pánfilo de Narváez, and later on married Cuauhtémoc's widow, Doña Isabel de Moctezuma.* This gentleman, who was not at all fond of Cortés, passed through Santo Domingo in September, 1544, and was there interrogated closely by Oviedo on several obscure points in the conquest of New Spain. Faithful to his resolution not to compromise himself by accepting the testimony of others, in his *History* he reproduces his conversation with Cano in dialogue form.[8] The latter's testimony does not entirely clear up the obscure points. Asked by Oviedo the causes of the Mexicans' rebellion during the absence of Cortés, he replies: "Señor Alcaide, what you ask is a thing that few of those in the country could answer, although it was very notorious and the wrong done to the Indians very evident. And because of it they conceived such a hatred for the Spaniards that they never trusted them again, and many evils arose from it afterward, including the rebellion of Mexico." He then blames Pedro de Alvarado for it. Cano's dislike of Hernán Cortés is manifest in everything he says, as, for example, during the Noche Triste [he says] 270 Spaniards were left behind because they had not been told of the retreat, and that the losses Cortés admits on that occasion are much fewer than the true ones, and that it is not a fact that Cortés had lost his left hand. In all Cano's replies, true or false, he displays a fierce animosity toward Cortés—which, naturally, has caused many historians to regard his testimony as extremely valuable. But Oviedo merely registers Cano's words without comment. He must, nevertheless, have had some doubt in his mind, for he ends his narrative of Cortés' enterprise on a note of hesitation, where formerly he had been carried away by enthusiasm. "I am now in Spain, in this year of 1548, and I shall add only two things to bring my book down

---

* [Juan Cano and Isabel Moctezuma were granted the encomienda of Macuilxóchitl (in modern Hidalgo) and Tacuba (Federal District). In 1560 it was yielding them the respectable income of about 4,000 pesos a year. The Cano-Moctezuma family was an important element in colonial aristocracy.—*Tr.*]

[8] Oviedo, *Historia*, Book XXXIII, chap. liv, pp. 547–553.

to the present: one of them is, as all learned men must know, that for what the historian does not see he must depend upon various informants; and in what concerns New Spain I have said what I learned from persons worthy of credence; nor have I failed to relate what Hernando Cortés himself wrote to the Emperor our sovereign, in his letters and reports" (p. 553-a, b).

Oviedo observes the same caution, the same low key, when he tells of the death of Cortés. "I wish briefly to relate the end of Don Hernando Cortés, first Marqués del Valle. My pen will be summary in this, because I have seen several memorials and observations written by his admirers, whom he had urged to write in praise of him, or they did so by his order to please his successors, or for whatever reason they may have had. But my purpose is other, to say what is fitting for my *History* and nothing else" (p. 554-a).

Did Oviedo think that López de Gómara, to whom he was doubtless alluding in the preceding paragraph, was indulging an exaggerated praise of the conqueror? Or was he, in his official capacity as Chronicler of the Indies, afraid openly to oppose the current of opinion that was running against the Extremaduran *caudillo*? What has become of his shamefaced commentary, in which he makes comparisons with Julius Caesar, Cyrus King of Persia, and the long parade of eulogies that Oviedo presents to us?

"May God keep the Marqués in His glory, for in truth he is very worthy of being remembered. He was the originator and founder of his house and estate, which he acquired in his person and by his great merit, as the present *History* has related, though summarily" (p. 555-b).

Of all the glory of Cortés Oviedo retains only the Marquesado. He does not provide us with testimony as precise as that of Peter Martyr, to justify his frank attitude of suspicion of Cortés. There is an open contradiction between the content of his book and the way he ends it. How much was Oviedo influenced or coerced by the feeling of the time? If his opinion of Cortés had really undergone a change, why did he not correct what he had written? We do not know.

Ferdinand Columbus

The biography of Christopher Columbus, commonly known as *La Historia del Almirante*, by his son Ferdinand, among the many complicated historical problems concerning the discovery of America, has given rise to a long series of controversies and daring hypotheses. Although of late years healthier winds have been blowing in the historiography of the discovery and many things are now accepted which the past century had cast doubts upon, Don Marcelino Menéndez y Pelayo's observations in his study of the historians of Columbus are still valid: "An eagerness to embrace novelty, a love of paradox, and a desire perhaps to make oneself conspicuous and famous among men by pursuing a course contrary to that of common sense, have usually been followed by exaggerated and dangerous reactions, upon which historical truth is again wrecked."

In these few lines it is not easy to guide the reader in a subject upon which the specialists have failed to agree. A very

[Introduction to *La Vida del Almirante Don Cristóbal Colón*. Translated and edited by Ramón Iglesia. (Fondo de Cultura Económica, Mexico-Buenos Aires, 1947.)—*Tr.*]

great deal has been written about Ferdinand Columbus and his biography of the discoverer. I shall limit myself here to recapitulating and putting into some kind of order the results of other men's investigations, without claiming that my opinions are "definitive" and unchallengeable, but merely trying to give the reader some guidance in the perusal of a text which, despite everything that has been said against it, is still basic to the history of the discovery.

Ferdinand Columbus was born in Córdoba, Spain, in August or September, 1485. There is some disagreement over the exact date, but we may accept the one that is commonly given, August 15. To provide the reader with a familiar point of reference, I may remind him that Ferdinand Columbus belongs to the same generation as his namesake, Hernán Cortés, who was also born in 1485.

Before the years 1487 and 1488 Christopher Columbus, father of Ferdinand, had not discovered anything. Squares were not yet filled with his statues, nor libraries with the books destined to scrutinize the smallest details of his life. He was a poor foreigner in Spain, a Genoese who wandered about trying to get someone to listen to the plans for discovery with which his mind was filled, and which the important men did not take seriously. "Since his cape was threadbare and poor, they took him to be a wild dreamer in everything he said or talked about," as Fernández de Oviedo, one of the first chroniclers of the Indies, was to write years later.

The man in the threadbare cape had come to Spain at a bad time to get anyone to listen to him. The Catholic Monarchs, Ferdinand of Aragón and Isabella of Castile, were extremely busy destroying the Moorish kingdom of Granada and had little free time. Christopher Columbus wandered about Córdoba, his general headquarters. A widower of thirty-odd, he lived with a girl named Beatriz Enríquez de Arana, who bore him a son, Ferdinand Columbus. There is no justification for the great amount of ink that has been spilled in romantically idealizing this love affair, or in trying to legalize it in an attempt to canonize the discoverer of America. Beyond any doubt whatever, Columbus was not worried about his love life, as his apologists have been, and I think that Morison's view of it makes sense, that is, that the discoverer did not marry Beatriz Enríquez because her modest position did not suit him. Ferdinand was even more indifferent than his father, for surely his position as a bastard son would not have bothered him if his mother had been a lady of rank. Since she wasn't, he hardly ever mentions her.

The reason for it was that the situation of the Columbus family changed very abruptly. While Ferdinand was still very young, his father succeeded in realizing his plans. He made the great voyage of 1492, and all doors, including those of the court, were opened to him and his sons. Ferdinand and his elder brother Diego were accepted as pages of Prince John, heir of the crowns of Aragón and Castile. If, as seems probable, Ferdinand began his court life in 1494, when he was five or six years old [*sic*, for eight or nine], this fact must have been basic in the formation of his character and the direction of his life.

Being an intelligent lad, very early devoted to books, he greatly profited by the cultivated Renaissance circle that Isabella gathered around her, as had her father, King John II of Castile—a circle which has perhaps been too much idealized, for the Italian humanists who frequented the Spanish court wore an air of stiff-necked pedantry and created a hothouse culture of bookishness, traces of which are evident in the life and works of Ferdinand Columbus, a great traveler who says nothing about the places he sees, and about whom we should know very little if he had not noted in his books the place and date of their acquisition.

Ferdinand interested himself in a number of things before taking up the career of his father. Notwithstanding his having accompanied the discoverer in his fourth voyage (May, 1502, to November, 1504), notwithstanding a stay of several months on the island of Santo Domingo, notwithstanding his petition to continue the discoveries of the Admiral, made in 1511 and not accepted, Ferdinand was a man of the Old World, a European of the Renaissance, completely so. The major part of his life, the thirty years between 1509 and 1539, was spent in Europe.

His interest in the new lands of America was confined to his library and his writings, as he studied geography and cosmography, and took part in meetings in which lines of demarcation were traced and disputes with the Portuguese took place, for at the time they were rivals of the Spaniards in the race for discoveries. Or he advised Charles V, the grandson of Ferdinand and Isabella, of whose entourage he formed a part when Charles left Spain to accept the crown of Emperor of Germany.

We do not know that Ferdinand ever loved a woman. His great love was always his books. In his early youth he laid the foundations of his library, which he conceived on a grand scale and installed in Seville, a library which even today is kept up and to which he gave the name of *Fernandina*. The only thing we know of his travels in Italy, France, Germany, and the Low Countries we learn from the notes he made in the books he collected. A man obsessed with detail, a scholar in his study, his greatest care was to assure the conservation and increase of his bibliographical treasure. He was not as selfish as many book lovers are, but opened his library to all students. He was, however, a jealous lover, for in his will he carefully provided that readers should be separated from his books by a grating which would allow the reader only to reach his hand through in order to turn the pages.

We should bear in mind the surroundings in which Ferdinand moved. It was not for nothing that he wanted his library to be called the *Fernandina*, rather than the *Colombina*—as it was called later on—so that his name might not be lost, for he had that typical lust for fame and terrestrial glory which was the axis of life for the men of the Renaissance: Renown, Fame. Everything else perishes with death, as we are told by López de Gómara, another prime example of the humanist. For this reason Ferdinand set about writing the life of his father, when he saw the fame of the discoverer, and hence his own, placed under an interdict. Most probably he would never have written it if he had not been influenced by the atmosphere of controversy surrounding the lawsuits of the discoverer's family with the Crown, and by the statements of certain writers who concerned themselves with the discovery.

The Crown had granted Columbus a number of extravagant concessions before he undertook his discoveries—privileges that were confirmed upon his return from the first voyage, giving him and his descendants the titles of Admiral, Viceroy, and Governor of all the lands discovered or to be discovered in the Indies. We do not know what would have happened if Queen Isabella had lived; but her husband, Ferdinand, was not a man to worry about breaking his word whenever he considered it necessary. It should not be forgotten that the Catholic monarchs, as [Emiliano] Jos reminds us, had made war in their kingdoms upon an unruly and anarchical nobility, and could hardly allow a new and exorbitant power to arise on the other side of the Atlantic. It would not be necessary for the court to wait for the great conquests of Mexico and Peru, to clip the wings of the descendants of the first Admiral, Christopher Columbus. As early as 1511 their viceroyalty was limited to the Antilles. This does not imply by any means that Diego and Ferdinand Columbus were left in poverty, but it became clear that the capitulations made with their father in 1492 and 1493 were not to be honored. So the descendants of Columbus sued the Crown for privileges that could not be allowed without making them more powerful than the monarchs themselves. According to Altolaguirre, who has most closely studied the matter, Ferdinand was the most intransigeant defender of the original privileges. He spent years and years in the suit, first as attorney for his brother Diego, who died in 1526, and then for Diego's widow and his son Luis.

It is unfortunate that the records of the suits have been only partly published, up to 1527; but we learn enough from them to know that the Crown, badgered by the descendants of Columbus to fulfill its undertaking, was obliged to have recourse to a series of subterfuges, to the extreme of having its attorney-general, Villalobos, discrediting Columbus in every possible way, playing down his part in the discovery, and by so doing, supplying magnificent materials for the hypercritical writers of the past century.

All this would surely have induced Ferdinand to take up his pen in his father's defense; but there was more to come. Gonzalo Fernández de Oviedo, in the first part of his *Historia General y Natural de las Indias* (Seville, 1535), came out with the stunning news that the Indies had belonged to the Crown of Spain since very remote times. This statement, which we can smile at today, was a very grave matter in those times, for it might dash to the ground all the claims of the Columbus family. A good proof of it is that the Emperor Charles V was very interested in having Oviedo pursue his findings, even before the book was published: "I have also seen what you say you have written and expect to prove by the testimony of five authors, to the effect that the islands belonged to the twelfth king of Spain, counting from King Tubal, who seized certain kingdoms after [the time of] Hercules, 1,558 years before the birth of Our Redeemer, so that, including the present year [of 1533], those lands have belonged to the royal scepter of Spain for 3,091 years; and, not without great mystery, after the passage of so many years, God has restored them to their owners, so I shall be glad to see what foundation you have for it, and command you that, if you have not sent it by the time you receive this letter, you will send it by the first ship that sails for these kingdoms, and in duplicate, in case you have already sent it."

As if this were not enough, in 1537 there appeared the *Castigatissimi Annali* of the Genoese Agostino Giustianini, in which he tells us that the family of Christopher Columbus was of humble condition, a true statement, but one which was most untimely for those who were demanding admiralties and viceroyalties.

Ferdinand's book, in which he proposes to refute all this testimony, is basically therefore a brief in defense of his father, a polemic written for the occasion. He has been reproached for haste, whether justly or unjustly we do not know, but the fact that he was refuting writings that appeared in 1535 and 1537 does not necessarily mean that the idea of composing his book first occurred to him at that time. The controversies about the suits had been going on for a long time, and perhaps it was the works of Oviedo and Giustanini that filled his cup to the brim. However it was, Ferdinand had time during his last years to put his notes and recollections into shape, emphasizing at great length the points that interested him and passing rapidly over the others because, as he tells us several times, he is afraid of wearying his readers—a salutary fear that the majority of today's historians have completely lost.

Ferdinand, to be sure, was not a biographer of exceptional stature, but this does not justify the attacks made upon his book, some of them quite gratuitous. Today we know a good deal more of the enterprise of Columbus than Ferdinand tells us; we can point out errors in his narrative, but they are not so many or so grave as the innocent reader might suppose when he comes across a string of severe censures of Ferdinand in authors who, whether they are aware of it or not, have had to use his biography for their own accounts of the discovery.

There has been a tremendous lack of historical and psychological sense in many historians of the past century who, with their frantic obsession for exact detail, have often lost sight of their goal, going to the extreme of scolding Ferdinand Columbus for neglecting to prepare a good "critical" edition of his father's writings. We may pass over what they have said of his "prejudices," of his injustice toward the companions of Columbus, of his hatred for everything Spanish, and the like. This psychological poverty, a serious failing of many dehumanized historians, has led them to speak of "a wounded soul," "a cry of protest," "rabid hatred," and other things of the kind. If one recalls all that Columbus had to put up with in his last years from the indiscipline of his companions—whether or not he was to blame is another question—and from the attitude of the Crown in his suits, even after his death, Washington Irving's verdict on Ferdinand Columbus is still valid: "He was a man of probity and discernment, and writes more dispassionately than could be expected, when treating matters which affected the honor, the interests, and the happiness of his father."

Those who accuse Ferdinand of being "partial" ascribe it
all to his being "the son of his father," but they forget that not
all periods have had the same idea of history that they have.
The historiography of the Renaissance, as I had occasion to
emphasize when I spoke of the biographers of Cortés, was inspired by the cult of the hero; it practiced hero-worship, and
was written quite contrary to the levelling and demagogic,
rather than democratic, tendency of our day, which is forever
on the lookout for unknown soldiers and forgotten men. The
hero was the elect of Providence, and those who surrounded
him counted for little or nothing.

For a proper understanding of Ferdinand's book, I must
insist upon this last point, because the silhouette of the discoverer traced in it would have been the same even if the
author had not been his son, for Ferdinand was a humanist
of the Renaissance, and as such he would in any case have
raised the level of the protagonist, emphasized his virtues and
suppressed his defects, making him a central and unique figure
who struggles against adversaries of all kinds.

We do not know that Ferdinand sickened and died before
he could have his book published. In any event, there was in
it sufficient material to prevent its appearance in Spain. It
was left for a learned Argentinian, Torre Revello, an expert
in these questions, to call attention to such an obvious thing.
In those days there was an effective censorship, which acted
against López de Gómara and other historians, and which
would have acted with greater motive against Ferdinand Columbus, who was involved in a suit with the Crown. Perhaps
Ferdinand himself thought it desirable to have his book printed
outside of Spain, because of his reflections on the conduct of
Ferdinand the Catholic toward his father.

If he did not do so himself, someone else did, possibly his
nephew Luis, grandson of the first Admiral, who was more
interested in women than in books, since he was condemned as
a trigamist. We do not know what happened to the manuscript
of Ferdinand Columbus after 1539, the year of his death, until
1571, when it was published in the Italian translation of Alfonso
de Ulloa. A great deal of ingenuity and erudition has been

spent in demonstrating that the Venetian text could not have been the work of Ferdinand, and more ingenuity and more erudition in attributing it to a different author. It is an interesting debate, because it is a good demonstration of the excesses which a hypercritical attitude can lead one to commit.

It was Henry Harrisse (1830–1910) who did most to demonstrate that the biography of the Admiral could not have been written by his son. This man of violent character, extremely opinionated, as he is depicted in various anecdotes in Gustave Flaubert's correspondence, spun truly erudite filigrees to prove that the book was not the work of Ferdinand Columbus; but he fell into the trap of so many hypercritics, that is, he could not resist the temptation of suggesting another possible author, the humanist Pérez de Oliva. "If it were permissible in a critical work to advance an hypothesis, we should be tempted to conclude that, toward the year 1563, a copy of Oliva's manuscript was brought to Genoa by some adventurer who gave it or sold it to Baliano di Fornari, attributing it to Ferdinand Columbus to enhance its value, a piece of chicanery of which literature in all ages and countries affords thousands of examples. Ulloa must have used this original history, which consisted of only nine books, as the nucleus of the *Historie*, and added the chapters whose apocryphal nature we believe we have demonstrated." Thus Harrisse in 1872. And so great is the influence that these hypercritical exercises have upon certain writers with their detective story technique that even today their opinions are quoted and have their defenders—which shows they have little knowledge of the author of the *Bibliotheca Americana Vetustissima*, for in 1884 he had to retract what he had affirmed in 1872. His thesis, so elaborately contrived, was destroyed by the discovery of the manuscript of the *Historia de las Indias*, by Father Las Casas, in which the author states on several occasions, including a direct quotation, what Ferdinand Columbus says in the Life of his father. Harrisse had reluctantly to admit his mistake, although he covers himself by resorting to the device of the fox in the fable: "While we await the corrected text that criticism demands, we have aimed to compose our work without borrowing anything whatever from that book

[Ferdinand's], the importance of which has been exaggerated."

Harrisse's retraction did little good, for even today, it seems, there are people who devote themselves to refuting it, and others to supporting it. And, since the tendency toward hypercriticism dies hard, there has recently appeared the thesis of the Argentinian professor, Rómulo D. Carbia, a conscientious scholar, but terribly fond of advancing startling theories, according to one of which the author of Ferdinand's biography was none other than Father Las Casas himself. "In my view," he tells us, "there are self-evident indications that allow one to think that it was the said priest who, making use of a literary fraud, forged the book that has been attributed to the pen of the Admiral's son." Carbia rests his thesis upon the tone of the book, in which he believes he detects the combative style of the Dominican, and upon the attacks that appear in it against the theory of Oviedo, that is, that the Indies had anciently belonged to the Crown of Castile.

Not satisfied with one attribution, Carbia gives us another: "Finally, the hypothesis that the biography attributed to Ferdinand is an arrangement based upon the lost narrative of Pérez de Oliva is something well worth considering."

Here also the hopes of the stubborn searchers for new authors of the biography have been frustrated, for recently a copy of Pérez de Oliva's book turned up in New York, and Leonard Olschki, who examined it, roundly states: "There is not the slightest evidence that the author drew any information whatever from his fellow-countryman, Ferdinand Columbus. There are, of course, some similarities in the report of fundamental events, but the divergence between Ferdinand's *Historie* and Pérez de Oliva's narrative is so deep in every respect that the two works appear irreconcilable at first sight." Pérez de Oliva's book, which had been so longed for, is a simple extract of the first *Década* of Peter Martyr. This is nothing to be surprised at, for the learned Andalusian [Pérez de Oliva] had done the same thing in his account of the conquest of Mexico, in which he merely repeats one of the *Cartas de Relación* of Hernán Cortés.

The list of attributions to possible authors of the Life of the Admiral does not stop here. Alberto Magnaghi, otherwise a serious enough scholar, goes to the extreme of thinking that Luis Columbus, that light-hearted trigamist, was the author of the biography.

In the face of this proliferation of misguided and picturesque theses, which lead their authors to abandon all contact with the reality they should have studied in the first place, I shall again appeal to the solid opinion of Menéndez y Pelayo about the Life of the Admiral: "Whether it is by Ferdinand, or by Pérez de Oliva, or by anyone else, is immaterial for the value of almost everything it contains, for it is in substantive agreement with the diaries, letters, and other writings of the Admiral which we luckily possess, and which the author, whoever he may have been (and who more likely than the Admiral's son?) had at his disposal, making abstracts of them and utilizing them, as many others have done before and since."

I believe there are enough of us today who think that the book in question could have been written only by Ferdinand, as the reader may see for himself, especially in Ferdinand's account of the fourth voyage of Columbus, in which he accompanied the Admiral. It has the indelible stamp of the eyewitness. The reader may also consult Father Las Casas' *Historia de las Indias*, in which whole paragraphs of Ferdinand's biography are copied, and he cannot doubt for a moment that their author was none other than Ferdinand. And if, in spite of everything, the reader is still troubled by misgivings, I am listing below a number of works in which he will be able to follow more closely the denouement of this comedy of errors.

For my edition I have utilized the Venetian text of 1571 and that published by Rinaldo Caddeo, and compared the translations of González Barcia and Serrano y Sanz. The unlucky González Barcia suffered from the snowballing process so common in this kind of study. One critic pointed out errors in his translation; another said that it was exceedingly bad; a third, that it was lamentable. It is really not so bad as all that. It does contain errors, which Serrano y Sanz unmercifully lists; but that of Serrano y Sanz also contains a few, which I have not bothered to note, considering it a sterile and pedantic exercise. For this same reason, perhaps, I may be forgiven for the errors I may have committed, for the Italian text is not always clear and offers difficulties that may never be resolved because of the loss of the Spanish original. Father Las Casas' *Historia de las Indias* has made it possible for me to restore certain passages.

The student should consult the Italian text of Caddeo's edition, which is copiously annotated. In this one of mine, intended for the lay reader, I have reduced to a minimum the notes I believe indispensable for the best understanding of the text. I have altered the title, for the traditional *Historia del Almirante* is a bad translation of the Italian. In its place I suggest *Vida del Almirante Don Cristóbal Colón*.

BIBLIOGRAPHY

Altolaguirre y Duvale, Angel de. *Cristóbal Colón y Pablo del Pozzo Toscanelli*. Madrid, 1903.

Ballesteros Beretta, Antonio. *Cristóbal Colón y el descubrimiento de América*. 2 vols. Barcelona, 1945.

Caddeo, Rinaldo (ed.). *Le Historie della vita e dei fatti di Cristoforo Colombo per D. Fernando Colombo suo figlio*. 2 vols. Milan, 1930.

Carbia, Rómulo D. *La nueva historia del descubrimiento de América*. Buenos Aires, 1936.

Colón, Hernando. *Historia del Almirante Don Cristóbal Colón por su hijo Don Fernando*. Translated by Manuel Serrano y Sanz. 2 vols. Madrid, 1932.

Gandía, Enrique de. *Historia de Cristóbal Colón. Análisis crítico de las fuentes documentales y de los problemas colombinos*. Buenos Aires, 1942.

González Barcia, Andrés (tr.). *Historia del Almirante de las Indias Don Cristóbal Colón por Fernando Colón, su hijo*. Madrid, 1749.

Harrisse, Henry. *Fernand Colomb; sa vie, ses oeuvres. Essai critique par l'auteur de la Bibliotheca Americana Vetustissima*. Paris, 1872.

Harrisse, Henry. *Christophe Colomb. Son origine, sa vie, ses voyages, sa famille et ses descendants*. 2 vols. Paris, 1884.

Irving, Washington. *The Life and Voyages of Christopher Columbus*. 3 vols. London, 1877.

Magnaghi, Alberto. *I presunti errori che vengono attribuiti a Colombo nella determinazione delle latitudini*. Rome, 1928.

Menéndez y Pelayo, Marcelino. "De los historiadores de Colón." In

Estudios y discursos de crítica histórico y literaria, vol. 7. Santander, 1942.

Morison, Samuel Eliot. *Admiral of the Ocean Sea. A Life of Christopher Columbus.* 2 vols. Boston, 1942.

Olschki, Leonard. "Hernán Pérez de Oliva's 'Ystoria de Colón.'" In *The Hispanic American Historical Review*, vol. 23, No. 2, May, 1943.

Torre Revello, José. "Don Hernando Colón. Su vida, su biblioteca, sus obras." In *Revista de Historia de América*, No. 19. Mexico, June, 1945.

Ramón Iglesia

University of Wisconsin
December, 1946

Part Two:
CRITICAL REVIEWS

Admiral of the Ocean Sea [*]

The first bull's-eye scored by this new biography of Christopher Columbus is its title, which clearly indicates the nature of the book, the fundamental purpose of which is to study Columbus as a navigator.

Morison is a scholar, but he is also a sailor and has followed all the voyages of the great Genoese, in expeditions in sailing vessels financed by Harvard University. This fact gives him the greatest confidence in settling the many disputed points in the voyages of the discoverer of America and makes his book a solid contribution to Columbian literature.

Morison's study could hardly have been more thorough. He begins it with a few notes in navigation by sail which the author thinks are indispensable to keep the reader on course. Even so, the book turns out to be hard going for laymen in nautical matters, at whom Morison continually aims his shafts.

The confidence of the author in recounting the four voyages of Columbus is manifest, for he has analyzed the writings of Columbus and keeps them before him in his own voyages,

[*] Samuel Eliot Morison, *Admiral of the Ocean Sea; A Life of Christopher Columbus* (Boston, 1942).

which he makes in circumstances analogous to those of the Admiral—hence the great value of the book for the history of geography.

Morison has the gifts of a great historian, and has sufficient life and force to handle confidently an astonishing mass of material, and to give us a vigorous feeling of immediacy, of being present at the events described. The best part of the book is doubtless his account of Columbus's first voyage, his full description of the caravels, their sailing qualities, and life on board in all its many aspects. On numerous occasions he tells us that what he is most interested in is Columbus as a man of action: what he did, not what he intended to do. Morison is glad "to leave his psychology, his 'motivation,' and all that to others." He has a sane common sense which makes him reject all the fantasies and inventions that have been woven about the life of the discoverer. His biography, taken as a whole, is completely conservative and traditional, and Madariaga is not the one who comes off best in his intelligent criticisms.

Morison's good sense and his simplicity of spirit, on the other hand, weaken his psychological analysis of Columbus. In the chapter he devotes to Columbus the man he hardly does more than repeat a few pen-pictures drawn by contemporaries, eulogistic stereotypes. His virtually unconditional admiration of the Admiral forces him to take up the defense always, even when his own observations do not agree with those of the Genoese. This is the weakest part of the book.

But let's not be carried away by a preference for psychological biographies. Morison tells us clearly enough that his purpose is different. Certainly his purpose of studying thoroughly the work of Columbus the navigator is fully and conscientiously achieved.

Revista de Historia de América. Mexico, December, 1942.

A Comedy of Errors*

The last book of Stefan Zweig, the great Austrian writer, who died recently, is a short work, full of wit and freshness. He does not narrate the life of a man, but the history of a word, America. Zweig is amused by the chain of errors that caused the New World to be named as it is, and he describes the process with ironical delicacy.

The present-day reader can hardly imagine how much he is in debt to the author for treating such a tangled and arid subject in such a suggestive way. Zweig moves very easily through a mountain of materials which, by and large, he handles well. One could point out a few errors, but why do it? When one thinks of the innumerable solid and well-documented works that are totally unreadable, one is inclined to pardon Zweig, not only for the few errors he falls into, but even for the others he might have committed, thanks to the beauty of his style and the life he manages to infuse into historical subjects.

Zweig begins by briefly describing the rise of Europe since

---

* Stefan Zweig, *Amerigo, A Comedy of Errors* (New York: The Viking Press, 1942).

about the year 1000, with its terrors and its stupidity, with its vague memory of a world that had been better, more beautiful, more full of color, and with the obsessive hallucination of cataclysm, of an immediate end. But the world doesn't come to an end, despite all the predictions, for which one must thank God. Great cathedrals are built, and the desire to rescue the Holy Sepulchre arises. It is rescued; it is lost. With the Crusades Europe acquires a new vision of the world. The despised Orientals make the Europeans ashamed of themselves. Then comes an urge to create, to know, to comprehend, and possibly to surpass the models of Classical antiquity. Universities are founded. Impatience with the ignorance and narrowness of the inhabited world becomes greater and greater.

Years pass. Toward the end of the thirteenth century Marco Polo returns with the stupendous story of his long voyages to the far corners of the earth, the Orient, where a new ocean appears. He has traveled to the most remote places, of incalculable riches. The incredulous have to be convinced by the sight of the treasures and jewels that he has brought back from his fantastic journey. The news flies over the whole west and shakes it to its foundations.

A Portuguese prince, Henry the Navigator, gathers about him astronomers, cartographers, and pilots, and, in the farthest corner of Europe, they avidly study the possibility of reaching the Spice Islands by sailing around Africa. During the fifteenth century, Madeira, the Canaries, and Cape Verde are discovered; the Equator is crossed—a deed that had been considered impossible—and, in 1486 Bartolomeu Diaz doubles the Cape of Good Hope. There is nothing to do now but steer to the Orient.

Spain does not wish to be left behind in the race for discoveries. The astonished Portuguese hear that a certain Columbus, sailing to the west instead of around Africa, has reached India! Everybody wants to have a finger in the discoveries. England sends out Sebastian Cabot, who also finds land. The *Mare Tenebrosum* shrinks more and more. Cabral, who gets off his course to the west, finds new lands farther south than those discovered by Columbus.

By the end of the fifteenth century so much has been discovered in its last ten years that people get confused and disoriented. They can't find enough saints in the calendar to baptize all the new islands. Columbus announces that he has seen a river that must have its source in Paradise. Is the terraqueous globe larger or smaller than had been believed?

And lo and behold! In the midst of this chaos a letter is published simultaneously in Paris and Florence, written by one Albericus Vespucios, or Vesputios, informing Lorenzo de' Medici of a voyage he made in the service of the King of Portugal, in the course of which he reached lands unknown up to that time. Epistolary accounts of this sort were very common at the time, for the great commercial houses maintained agents in Seville and Lisbon to keep them abreast in the matter of expeditions. Copies circulated from hand to hand, and were occasionally printed, to satisfy the craving for news in a day when there were no newspapers.

The letter of Vespucius [Vespucci, of course] enjoys an immense vogue, for he writes agreeably and draws an idyllic picture of countries he claims to have seen: countries of prodigious fertility, of a delightful climate, whose inhabitants live in a state of perfect innocence, happy, naked, without moral trammels of any kind. "If Paradise exists anywhere," says Vespucci, "it cannot be far from here." This by itself was enough to excite interest, but there was another item in the letter which aroused even more interest, the words *Mundus Novus*.

A New World! Up to that time Europe had believed that the newly discovered lands were part of Asia. Columbus's insistence in clinging stubbornly to this notion is well known. The author of the letter, on the contrary, claims to be speaking of a continent to the south of the Equator, parts of which [he says] are more densely populated with men and animals than Europe, Asia, or Africa. Vespucci's letter enlarged the world, while Columbus was trying to make it smaller. Zweig gives Vespucci the credit for giving meaning to the discovery of Columbus. His announcement that the newly discovered lands are a new world is "the first Declaration of American Independence."

Everyone waits impatiently for Vespucci to keep his promise

made in his first letter, that is, to give a further account of his explorations and voyages. Their curiosity is soon satisfied. Another letter, signed by Amerigo Vespucci in Lisbon in 1504, is published in Florence. In it the author gives a few details about himself and four voyages he has made in Spanish and Portuguese vessels, between 1497 and 1504. Its content is the same as that of his first letter of 1503.

And here begins the long chapter of errors which Zweig summarizes with great skill. In 1507 a printer of Vicenza publishes an anthology of travel pieces, including Vespucci's *Mundus Novus*, to which he gives the ambiguous title *Mondo Novo e paesi nuovamente retrovati da Alberico Vesputio fiorentino*, a title that might lead one to believe that the new lands have not only been named by Vespucci, but that he is their discoverer. This is the beginning of the Florentine's rise to immortality, "perhaps the most grotesque ascent known in the history of fame," although Vespucci himself had not the least knowledge of it.

At St. Dié, in a remote corner of Lorraine, there is a group of humanists under the protection of Duke René II. The letters of Vespucci are known there. A young cosmographer, Martin Waldseemüller, no doubt honestly, believes that their author has discovered the new lands, and in his *Cosmographiae Introductio*, published in 1507, he proposes that they be named after their discoverer: "Since Amerigo discovered this land, let it be called henceforth the land of Americo, or America." He repeats the suggestion elsewhere in his book and places the name on the accompanying map.

America, says Zweig with feeling, is a magnificent name. It is strong, full, easily remembered, and well suited for a battle cry, proper for a young land. Waldseemüller's error takes hold rapidly, and the name keeps on spreading over more and more territory, until Mercator, the great geographer, in 1538, applies it to the two parts of the continent, which by this time are recognized as a geographic unity. So within thirty years Vespucci has made himself immortal without being aware of it himself, an episode without parallel in history.

Now Zweig plunges bravely into an account of the tremendous controversy, which has been going on now for centuries, over the character of Vespucci and the nature of his work. I shall not repeat in detail what he says, for I do not intend to render unnecessary the reading of his book, but rather to encourage it. Columbus and Vespucci have been made to appear as rivals, although in fact they were friends during their lifetime. The vigorous attacks of Spanish historians such as Las Casas, Herrera, and others, in whose eyes Vespucci was nothing but a miserable impostor who tried to rob Columbus of the glory of the discovery, have been countered passionately by the compatriots of the Florentine. Archives have been diligently searched, new documents unearthed, which only complicate the question, until finally light is shed on it by the thesis of Professor Magnaghi, which Zweig accepts fully. [In it] Vespucci is shown not to be the author of the letters attributed to him; his name is attached to them; the content of some letters of his are used—discovered much later—altered to suit the whim of their publishers. This is the only way in which the contradictions in the Florentine's writings can be explained.

The irony of this comedy of errors reaches its climax. The man who gave his name to a continent, to a fourth part of the world, is not even the author of the few pages ascribed to him. And finally, Zweig concludes, the name of an obscure man, as Vespucci was, is more appropriate for a democratic country than that of a king or a conqueror.

Cuadernos Americanos, Mexico, May–June, 1942.

Chronicles of the Conquest[*]

Imagine the surprise of a Hispano-phobe like Genaro García, author of the *Carácter de la conquista española en América y en México*, if he could raise his head today and leaf through the book of Agustín Yáñez which is here being reviewed. Those ferocious assasins, those pitiless fanatics who wrote the first accounts of the conquest, are boldly placed by Yáñez among the exponents of *mexicanismo*.

This striking affirmation of Yáñez may perhaps come as a shock to the Spanish reader, made without evasions in the beautiful preface to his selection of chronicles of the conquest. Just imagine: the first chroniclers of New Spain as exponents of *mexicanismo*. This may possibly surprise the Spanish reader, but it will surely not offend him. It is altogether fitting that the desire felt by those men to incorporate these lands within the bounds of their culture, those men who, like Cortés, felt their charm so deeply, should be answered by a Mexican of today who claims such men as his countrymen.

---

[*] Agustín Yáñez, *Crónicas de la conquista de México* (Mexico, *Biblioteca del estudiante Universitario*, 1939).

In Yáñez' book, in his introduction and in the notes that precede the selected pieces—all of it as brief as it is pregnant with content—the love and understanding that the author feels for the work of the conquistadores, and for those who wrote of it, is fully expressed. "Throughout these documents," Yáñez tells us, "there spins a whirlwind of passion. The authors admire but can hardly believe their own exploits. They are still possessed and bewitched by the hot fever that impels them to penetrate an unknown country, so mysterious and full of wonders. Across the centuries they invite us to share in their exaltation of spirit, and they do so with imperishable vividness. We hear their steps and their voices; we reconstruct their gestures and attitudes; we participate in their astonishment at the cultural and natural magnificence of the lands they explore and conquer; we share their anxieties, hopes, and successes. We hear the beat of their horses' hoofs, the clash of their arms; we feel the fire of the sun, the endless rains; we see the rivers in flood; we sense the breath of the mountains; we hear the murmur of village life and the small noises of the night watches. It all comes to life in these pages."

This beautiful paragraph makes it evident that Yáñez is not the typical specialized historian, detached and cold, such as we are abundantly acquainted with today. In him are gathered attributes that are rarely found in one person: he is a humanist, and neither philosophy nor literature is foreign to him. So he succeeds in these brief pages in giving us a much more comprehensive and much denser vision than we are accustomed to find in publications of this kind.

Yáñez proposes in his book to present "a chronicle of the conquest made up of selections from different chroniclers, in strict chronological order, all written by witnesses of, and actors in, the events." This is his purpose, and he succeeds surprisingly well, given the necessary limitations of his volume. In this fashion he manages to give us a book much more valuable than any one of the modern rehashes—the number of narratives of the conquest published in English alone is overwhelming—which, while raiding the ancient chroniclers, succeed only in distorting or killing them.

It is unfortunate that the criterion of the anthologist—just as it is in principle—finds no room in his pages for anyone other than "witnesses of, or actors in, the events," thus leaving out a writer as notable as Francisco López de Gómara, the chaplain of Cortés, who was the first to publish a history of the conquest of Mexico. In Gómara we see a miracle, that is, that one who was not present at the events he relates succeeds in making them live for us as if he had been present. Cortés is the real author of this miracle, so deep was the impression he made on the spirit of his chaplain and chronicler.

Yáñez' volume ends, so to speak, with a tremendous question mark, the Maya chronicle of Chac-Xulub-Chen. For there is still much to be done in the field of Mexican historiography, and one of its most arduous tasks will be to bring to light the content of the native chronicles, or those based on native testimony, and it should be done with the light of affection and understanding that shines forth in the pages that Yáñez devotes to the Spanish chroniclers. The drama of native culture, apparently buried, but struggling to survive, can be written only by a Mexican who, like Agustín Yáñez, feels the heart beat of his people: "the drama of *mestizaje*—the heterogeneous—which is trying to annul the negations, to search out its spirit and center it on the magnificent stage of nature."

Letras de México. Mexico, July 15, 1940.

Hernán Cortés[*]

The pleasure we feel upon reading this biography of Cortés that Salvador de Madariaga has just published is like the pleasure we experience when we hear again an old song that we know by heart. It was written for the general reader, so we find in it little that is new; but the author makes good use of traditional sources to put together an agreeable life of the Extremaduran hero.

The narrative is slow at times, prolix at others, for the author sometimes abandons himself to the joy of telling a story, even secondary episodes in which Cortés has no part, such as the Nicuesa-Ojeda expedition, in which it is difficult to see why "it deserves some study, even if it is only because it increases our understanding of not a few aspects of the conquest of Mexico."

The tone of the book is dignified, although it suffers from a too-frequent use of irony, which becomes a bit tiresome. In this I suppose the author is trying to give his narrative an air of ease and amenity, which makes him prefer sources richest in picturesque detail. For example, he uses Cervantes de Salazar

[*] Salvador de Madariaga, *Hernán Cortés, Conqueror of Mexico* (New York, 1941).

beyond any need, even going so far as to reproduce the innumerable discourses that the chronicler puts into the mouths of his characters—this despite the fact that Madariaga himself tells us that Cervantes de Salazar was "always ready to improve with his own eloquence that of the personages of his chronicle" —ready to improve and even to invent, and the discourses were not the only things he invented.

Madariaga also leans heavily on Bernal Díaz del Castillo, but fails to probe deeply enough into his character, for he detects in him "a touch of envy, but only a touch. . . . But there were others in Cortés' company whose envy lacked [Bernal's] lightness and good humor." I could expatiate on this subject but shall not, for later on Madariaga remarks that Bernal "never omits a shadow in his portrait of Cortés."

In general Madariaga makes proper and abundant use of chroniclers contemporary with the conquest, and reduces to a minimum the use of later accounts—those of Alamán, Prescott, and Orozco y Berra—which appear occasionally in the notes when some doubtful point comes up for discussion.

Madariaga's portrait of Cortés is colored by an unqualified admiration and enthusiasm. Cortés is the greatest and ablest man of his time, the typical Renaissance man, a man of arms and a man of letters, a great captain, a great statesman, a great governor. Madariaga sees in him all the characteristics of the god Quetzalcoatl, with whom the Indians were to identify him —the Eagle and the Serpent. "Although he was capable of falling upon his prey like an eagle, he preferred to coil about it like a serpent." Madariaga continually stresses Cortés' gift of getting along with people, his capacity for taking decisions which he had already decided upon in the solitude of his command, and giving them the appearance of coming from his companions. "From the first moment we sense in Cortés a continuous interchange of influences, which flow from the chief to his men, and from his men to the chief, so that the army begins to take on the character of an organized community."

A basic element in the character of Cortés is his profound religiosity, an ingenuous and simple faith, "the only ingenuous and simple trait in that artful character." But Cortés, that cautious, foresighted, most able man, can throw everything to the winds when his religious faith is involved. "His religious impulse was the only one strong enough to come to the surface, breaking through the steel armor of his self-control and obscuring his usually clear vision of immediate or distant realities." Madariaga sees as high points in the life of Cortés two moments in which he affirms his faith: one, when he attacks the god of war in the great temple; the other, when he kneels before the first Franciscan friars upon their arrival at Mexico City, "an act in which the conquistador, the strong man, places his strength at the feet of the spirit."

The faith of Cortés "was the source of his strength and the cause of his weakness." The conquistador was about to confront in his enterprise another man whose faith was as deep-rooted as his, Moctezuma, whose religiosity plays a decisive part in his conduct toward the Spaniards. "It so happened that religious faith was also a predominant passion of Moctezuma, which brings out a curious parallel between the mental patterns of conqueror and conquered, for we can see now how Moctezuma's religious zeal interferes with the logic and harmony of his attitude."

For Madariaga, this conflict between the two worlds, the Spanish and the native, is exemplified in the conflict between the two faiths, of which the stronger is the Spanish, and it prevails for that reason. The apparently ambiguous conduct of Moctezuma is explained by the fact that from the beginning he had believed that all his misfortunes had been ordained by the gods, and later on the psychological fabric he had erected in his imagination fell to the ground when he saw that it was Cortés himself who destroyed the idols. Moctezuma was neither a weak and luckless king, nor a traitor. "He was the high priest of a magic religion, facing events as they occurred, acting in agreement with his colleagues in the service of the gods."

Madariaga clearly sees the inevitability of the conflict, and frequently observes that Cortés "had that aversion, instinctive in every superior man, to do no more than was strictly necessary in each case." But all Madariaga's sympathies are on the side of the Spaniards, and he is always able to justify Cortés' acts of cruelty, as, for instance, when he ordered the amputation of the hands of the suspected Tlaxcalan spies; or [the massacre at] Cholula; or the execution of Cuauhtémoc. He even goes so far as to justify the slaughter ordered by Alvarado during the absence of Cortés. "It is evident that we must excuse Alvarado for having *imagined* a conspiracy, but we must also praise him for having *thought* there was one and that the danger was imminent."

Madariaga is completely and consistently sincere in his partisanship. He has no sympathy for the Aztecs, although he does admire their heroism, symbolized in Cuauhtémoc, whom he praises. "In Cuauhtémoc the Mexicans had found a leader, one not only of an indomitable spirit, but one of keen military ability, one, in short, worthy of a place beside his Spanish rival."

Madariaga does not, perhaps, give sufficient space to the most remarkable aspect of Cortés, that of the conqueror conquered, but he realizes it well enough. After the destruction of the Aztec capital, for example, he tells us: "Cortés was not a man to take pleasure in a victory won at such a price. During the night of his second attack on Mexico, he must have dreamed regretfully of his first entrance, in which, surrounded by the splendor of gold and featherwork of Moctezuma, and bathed in the clouds of incense and copal, he had been the incarnation of the god of the Plumed Serpent."

Here [according to Madariaga] lay the greatest merit of Cortés: his nostalgic memory of that first march into Mexico, his dream of the peaceful annexation of the domains of Moctezuma to those of Charles V, his work as explorer, settler, and governor, which he finished after the submission of Tenochtitlán. "Even though Cortés should not occupy his place in history as the conqueror of Mexico, he would still have it as the man who organized the systematic and scientific exploration of the Pacific coast from Panama to California."

It is a great pity that Madariaga saw fit to close his book with what might be called his out-of-date and ill-considered remarks about the Aztecs' attitude toward Cortés—remarks that only open again the old wounds that are on their way to being healed. He is as vehement and passionate as those he censures.

The book would have gained a great deal if he had ended on a different note, if he had suppressed the few sentences, which I prefer not to discuss, because it would merely reawaken an ancient and painful polemic, now sterile and outmoded. Things have changed in Mexico more swiftly than Madariaga thinks, and we need only a little time to arrive at juster appraisals of Hernán Cortés, concepts now harbored in the spirit of many Mexicans.

Filosofía y Letras. Mexico, April–June, 1942.

The Official Chronicle
of the Indies*

Professor Carbia's notion of the official Chronicle of Castile, and of its derivative, the Chronicle of the Indies, may be summarized in the words of Luis Cabrera de Córdoba, historian of the reign of Philip II: "The purpose of history is not to write things down to the end that they be remembered, but to teach men how to live by experience. The purpose of history is to promote the public good." The whole tone of Carbia's book, indeed, is typical of the pious and counterreformist days of Philip III, when Cabrera de Córdoba wrote. Professor Carbia does not show the slightest interest in knowledge of the past for its own sake, or even a desire to depict high human qualities, enviable and worthy of imitation: "One always notes in them [the chroniclers]," he tells us, "something of a spiritual inspiration which I am inclined to call ascetic. . . ." "The official chronicle had, essentially, a basic Christian asceticism, a severe introspection that analyzes, with objective austerity, the very foundations of our soul."

Professor Carbia sprinkles his pages with words like "mystic"

---

* Rómulo D. Carbia, *La crónica oficial de las Indias occidentales* (La Plata, 1934).

and "ascetic" as he writes of our chronicles. And, although it is true that in the quoted passages he blunts the edge of his asseverations with a few grayish "somewhats," it is also true that in general they are shattering. He even goes to the extreme of telling us that the invocations "that appear frequently at the beginning of such works correspond to everything in the vocabulary of mystic asceticism which is called putting oneself in the presence of God." He suggests parallels with *The Imitation of Christ* and the *Spiritual Exercises* of St. Ignatius. I really think this is carrying things too far.

Faithful to his narrow interpretation of the purpose of our medieval chroniclers, Professor Carbia necessarily has to omit many names from his study, authors he calls official or semi-official, whose works lack a sacerdotal or austere character, but are "nationalistic and epic."

The question of origins is always a delicate one. The official chronicle, according to Carbia, originates in the days of Ferdinand II and his mother Doña Berenguela. It has nothing to do with the *cronicones* [the primitive short chronicles]. We must go back to the remote days of Biblical literature to find an antecedent for the Castilian chronicles, since "only among the Semites were these accounts of the past known and written, for a frankly religious purpose."

Evidently, then, our first historian, the Chancellor Pero López de Ayala, was unaware of the changes that had taken place in the purpose of history, for he tells us in the foreword to his chronicles: "The memory of men is very weak, and cannot recall everything that happened in the past." Thus, in Castile, "A written record was made of all the great exploits and conquests of the aforesaid Gothic kings, and of all those who reigned after them, from the time of King Pelayo down to that of the said King Alfonso, who won the battle of Tarifa. Wherefore I, Pero López de Ayala, with the help of God, intend to continue it in this fashion as truthfully as I can."

So much for the introduction, the thorniest and most dubious part of Professor Carbia's book. Then he takes up the official chronicle of the Indies, which grew out of the desire of the Spanish monarchs to know everything that happened in the new possessions of the Crown, about which so much nonsense had been written, both in and out of Spain. He details minutely the vicissitudes suffered by the office of principal chronicler, which had been incorporated in the Council of the Indies in the time of Philip II, until Antonio de Herrera was appointed to it. "The great chronicle," [writes Carbia], "had anything but a happy history." The only one able to finish his work, apparently, was Herrera. . . . . In the eighteenth century, after the Academy of History was given the job, that learned body could not complete it and was obliged to turn it over to Don Juan Bautista Muñoz. Professor Carbia describes accurately enough the scanty results achieved by the Academy, until the loss of our colonies relieved it of the onerous duty of Chronicler of the Indies.

Throughout Professor Carbia's book the documentation is solid, although at times excessive and redundant. It is a pity that the idea behind it is so one-sided. Against Professor Carbia's interpretation of history, it may be well to consider the words of [the sixteenth century Spanish historian] Fox Morcillo, in his *De Historiae institutione*:

"The writing of history, it seems to me, had its origin in a lust for honor and immortality, which Nature implants in all men. I have known men to practice it, not to exalt their own fame, but that of their ancestors."

History, therefore, is an enhancement of living values, a desire to achieve immortality on earth.

Tierra Firme. Madrid, 1935, No. 2.

Institutions of the Indies[*]

In this book Professor Ots brings together the works he used in his short course on the "Social Institutions of Spanish America during the colonial period," given at the University of La Plata.

It begins with a survey of the legislation governing the Indians' working conditions. The view he presents is necessarily one-sided, since, according to the *Recopilación de Leyes de Indias*, the condition of the Indians turns out to be decidedly superior to that of the European workers of the time [1680]. So benign are the laws that their application is sometimes impossible, owing to the fact, observes Ots, that the Spanish legislator was working from a false premise, generously considering that all the Indians were free vassals of Castile, which "produced a profound gulf between law and fact."

Professor Ots then gives us a broad panorama of the social classes of colonial America, and makes some keen observations on the new nobility thus created, thanks to the excessive privi-

---

[*] José Maria Ots [Capdequí], *Instituciones sociales de la América española en el período colonial* (La Plata, 1934).

leges granted in their capitulations, at a time when, in Europe, such privileges were considered contrary to all noble, territorial, or personal rights.

When he speaks of the Creoles, he gives proper emphasis to the defense made of them by our Solórzano [y Pereyra], in his *Política Indiana*. The Creoles, legally the equals of the Spaniards, suffered when they saw themselves always discriminated against. The Dominican Thomas Gage, who about 1630 traversed part of our American possessions, frequently observes how the Creoles could be counted on to [help] expel the Spaniards. Solórzano wisely recognized the evil and suggested its remedy. In his opinion, given equal merits, posts should be given to those born in the Indies, because of "the greater love they will have for their country and fatherland where they were born." Unfortunately, his advice was not heeded, and the Creoles, thus left behind, later on stoked the wars of American Independence.

After the third chapter, the book flows through narrower juridical channels, and in them Professor Ots surely makes his most valuable contribution, minutely analyzing the problems arising from the condition of the Indian, his liberty or slavery, and the encomienda. His exposition of those passion-ridden polemics which gave rise to an astonishingly prolix legislation, is brief and clear.

The author is exceedingly cautious when he tackles the thorny subject of legislation and the so-called "leyenda negra." We don't have enough facts, he says. It may be well to add that the facts themselves obscure and distort the issue, always in one direction or the other. Will today's critics be able to untangle the immense mass of anathemas and apologies that have gone on piling up through the centuries?

In his chapter on family law, in the midst of the great number of regulations governing matrimonial obstacles, forced marriages, and the like, the complications arising from obliging Indians to have only one wife turn out to be picturesque, for hardly ever do they remember which of their wives was the first, that is, the lawful one.

Finally, when Ots takes up the subject of women in the Indies, the tragic gap between law and reality stands out more strikingly than in the rest of his book. Indian women, who could not in any circumstances be legally enslaved, were forced to work in the mines, were bought and sold, and suffered frequent abuses, which the authorities continually tried to prevent. In contrast, his notes on the work done by Spanish women establish the existence of a modern attitude on the part of the colonists.

The book, as we have seen, tackles a series of problems of high interest to students of American history. Although in its nature the book is concerned only with the legislative aspect of American colonization, it has the great merit of bringing together materials which heretofore have been widely scattered. It also gives us a clear picture of our laws of the Indies, so frequently quoted and so little known in detail.

Tierra Firme. Madrid, 1935, No. 2.

The Commerce of the Indies[*]

The reading of this massive volume by Professor Haring leaves me with a bitter taste in my mouth. As I turn its pages it seems to me that I am moving through an empty or badly cluttered hall, and it gives me the painful feeling of witnessing one of the most fundamental aspects of the wrecking of the enormous state machine of the Hapsburgs. The pain is all the greater because the author faithfully and objectively piles fact on fact, with few or no commentaries, which gives his account an air of fatalism, of implacable catastrophe.

Professor Haring's book, as its title indicates, is divided into two major parts: the one concerned with commerce, the other with navigation between Spain and the Indies. There is a brief introduction and an excellent annotated index, which is not only indispensable to the economic historian, but very useful to every student of American history in the sixteenth and seventeenth centuries.

In the first part he explains the development and functioning

* Clarence H. Haring, *Comercio y navegación entre España y las Indias en la época de los Hapsburgos* (Mexico, Fondo de Cultura Economica, 1939).

of the complicated bureaucratic organization that grew up around the commerce of the Indies. A Spaniard of today is pleased when he begins this reading, when he sees how the Casa de Contratación of Seville becomes a center for maritime and geographical studies of the first importance, studies which are quickly translated into other languages and used as texts by foreign institutions of the same kind. He is pleased to see the wide scientific collaboration, as the eminent men of other nations are called in to participate in the work of the Casa de Contratación—all this without taking into account its commercial and juridical functions.

But how long does his pleasure last? His vision of the encouragement of studies, of the enthusiasm for systematizing the results of the new discoveries, could hardly be more fleeting. In the third chapter, "Organization vs. Efficiency," we learn that the love of hierarchy and the ankylosis of Spain during the reigns of the last Austrian monarchs weigh heavily upon all the organization and commerce of the Indies and their institutions. The evil is not that the country was ruined, but that its governors were incapable of finding the means to rescue it from ruin. On the contrary, they contributed with their foolish measures to make the ruin daily more total and irremediable.

This terrible progressive paralysis of the springs of Spanish life is the note that is struck throughout the pages of Haring. Everything that at the beginning of the sixteenth century is audacity, impulse, originality, is soon converted into sluggishness, routine, and emptiness. Places in the Casa de Contratación are bought and sold, and delivered to the highest bidder, however incompetent he might be. The number of officeholders is increased beyond measure, and the dispatch of business is benumbed. And in the face of the excessive monopolistic tendency, in the face of the suspicious attitude of the Crown, whose only salvation lies in the lucky arrival of the *flotas* with their cargoes of precious metals, there is fraud and deceit and bribery on all sides, practiced by Spaniards and foreigners, in that monstrous and unintelligible work of rapine which was for so many years the exploitation of the Indies.

In the time of Charles V the most gigantic enterprises seemed feasible to the Spaniards, but only a little later they were incapable of solving the slightest problem. This sudden change can be appreciated in all its violence in the chapter on the Isthmus of Panama and the proposals to cut a canal through it. As Gómara exclaims triumphantly: "There are mountains, but there are hands. Give me a man who wishes to do it, and it can be done!" Philip II orders, on pain of death, that no one shall speak further of constructing a canal, and the Jesuit Acosta warns that to correct the work of Providence by establishing communication between the two oceans would meet with certain punishment.

Equally instructive and despairful are the chapters in the second part in which Haring discusses the convoy system, the make-up of the *flotas*, the struggle with pirates, and all the vastly minute legislation concerning the ships and navigators of the Indies. There is always the same contrast between an excessive codification [of rules] and their total ineffectiveness. The vessels are overloaded beyond reason, so that when the occasion arises, their guns cannot be fired. The sailors, recruited from among the undesirables, are fantastically incompetent, and shipwrecks occur with terrible frequency. In Seville efforts are made to improve their training, but are rendered fruitless by the systematic jealousy of the Crown, which goes to the extreme of forbidding the publication of such works as the *Itinerario de la Navegación* by Juan Escalante de Mendoza, because in it one may find information that might be of use to foreign sailors, enemies of Spain.

This book of Haring's makes dismal reading for Spaniards, but it is fundamental, not indeed for specialists, but for all readers of today. Looking beyond the minute and impersonal analysis, one can see only too plainly the unhappy results attendant upon an intransigeant autocracy and a rigid and corrupt bureaucracy, which will not admit criticism or reform of any kind, but does admit fraud and mockery. This is the fatal experiment that the present neo-imperialists of Spain, who lack its greatness, wish to repeat.

España Peregrina. Mexico, April, 1940.

Father Acosta's *Historia**

With the publication of this book, the Fondo de Cultura Económica has performed a splendid service for people of Spanish speech. Father Acosta's work was first published in Seville in 1590, almost coincident with the first centenary of the discovery of America. There could be no greater tribute to the glory of the discoverers than this book, in which, collected and systematized, are all the facts we have about the New World at the end of the sixteenth century.

What in other authors writing of the New World had been merely a hodgepodge of odds and ends, unformed and picturesque, in Acosta is organized in a severe and logical harmony, with an equilibrium and proportion that are, perhaps, the greatest charm of his book.

Acosta's *Historia* is dedicated to a woman, Princess Isabel Clara Eugenia [daughter of Philip II]. In it the author undertakes to explore an astonishing number of subjects, as diverse as they are numerous. And he succeeds, thanks to his marvelous style and the fluidity and animation that appear on all his pages.

* P. José de Acosta, *Historia natural y moral de las Indias* (Mexico, Fondo de Cultura Económica, 1940).

It was a happy time, that of Acosta. In those days it was not held that learning was the private domain of a few specialists, nor was it held that a book lost prestige by being made accessible to a wide public. The author treated his varied themes with a humane and loving understanding, in the most disparate fields, and fused and unified them in a way that now seems magical and prodigious.

This is the air that circulates freely throughout Acosta's pages, humane and cosmic, making them as comprehensive as they are beautiful. The Jesuit's love of nature has a high poetic quality, a serene and restful love that does not get out of hand, not an overpowering love like that of the romantics, but harmonious, subject to the laws of Divine wisdom, which Acosta sees in operation even in the smallest details.

Among the Spaniards of his day, few felt the beauty of the New World as deeply as Acosta. By comparison he considers the most perfect of human creations to be trivial. "In fact," he tells us, "the works of Divine art contain I know not what of grace and elegance, hidden and secret, so to speak, which seen once or many times always give us new pleasure. Unlike human arts, however cleverly designed, which, if frequently contemplated, are not held to be worth anything, be they very pleasant gardens, or most elegant palaces and temples, or fortresses of superb architecture, or paintings, or sculptures, or precious stones of as exquisite a workmanship as one could desire, it is a certain and established fact that if you see them two or three times you will hardly be able to fix your attention upon them, but your eyes will wander off and look at other things, as if tired of the sight. But if you will gaze upon the sea, or fix your eyes upon a tall cliff that juts out strangely, or upon the countryside when it is dressed in its natural greenness and flowers, or upon a river in flood that runs furiously and charges at the rocks, as if bellowing in combat; and finally, whatever works of nature you contemplate, no matter how often, they will always give you new pleasure and never tire your eyes, for it seems they are like an abundant and magnificent feast that Divine wisdom silently and ceaselessly spreads before us, delighting our senses."

This man, who always felt himself so small beside the marvels of nature, nevertheless lends such a human warmth to all creatures and phenomena in it that he brings them to life and gives them the quality and grandeur of humans. He says of the winds: "There are winds that blow in certain regions which are, so to speak, the masters of them and will not admit competition by their rivals. At times different and even contrary winds blow at the same time and divide the way between them, and it so happens that one will blow aloft and the other down below. Sometimes they come into violent conflict, which for those who sail the seas is a great hazard." Of quicksilver he says: "The most marvelous property it has is this, that it clings to gold with an amazing affection, and seeks it out wherever it senses it. Not only this, but it becomes so one with it, and so joins it to itself, that it detaches it from all other ores or bodies with which it is mingled. Thus it happens that those who wish to save themselves from the danger of quicksilver [poisoning] take gold." "Association with such a high-spirited and short-lived creature is hazardous, for it has another property, to wit, it boils and turns itself into a thousand little drops, of which, however small they may be, no drop is lost, but sooner or later rejoins its liquid."

Acosta was a great humanist and a great admirer of Classical antiquity, which gives his book the liveliness of a dialogue and the polemic of the ancient writers. At the same time it contains a coherent body of knowledge, giving him a new and implacable weapon, that is, his own observation and experience. This is a weapon that Acosta wields tirelessly, and his stance is all the more admirable in that his solid classical education could have blinded him, totally or partly, to the direct observation of facts. But it did not blind him. Acosta's eyes are wide open, and he ably and joyfully attacks every venerable theory not verified by his own experience. Nothing is more typical of him than the passage in which he tells of his fears upon approaching the Equator, fears grounded upon descriptions of the Torrid Zone written by Classical authors. With great surprise and pleasure he establishes the fact that it is not burning, but feels cold. "Here I confess that I laughed and mocked at the atmospherics of Aristotle and his philosophy, when I observed that at the time and place in which, according to his rules, everything would be burning, I and all my company were cold."

Acosta laughs at Aristotle, a serious thing for him to do, for the Greek philosopher was one of the authorities he respected most; but it was an even more serious thing to go counter to the Bible and the Church Fathers. What intellectual vigor he displays when he attempts to enclose a whole world of new facts within such a venerable and, for him, indisputable framework! The presence of man in America, of animals that do not exist on other continents—how did they get to the Indies? Where did they come from?

It is very moving to see how Acosta is forced to cut his traditional moorings and face problems of which the ancients could have no knowledge. "And, since I have no authorities to follow, I shall be guided by the thread of reason, however weak it may be, until all [doubts] shall be removed from my eyes." And how he follows that thread! There are still many problems that modern science has not answered beyond the point where Acosta left them. He is still showing the way.

Acosta was writing in the days of the Counter-Reformation. The unlimited and joyous optimism in the possibilities of human understanding in the great days of the Renaissance had been succeeded by a feeling of renunciation, of limitation and fear, which he keeps within bounds, thanks to his serene religious faith, but which was to plunge the Spanish spirit into the abyss of disillusionment and impotence.

In this regard it is extraordinarily interesting to compare Acosta's work with that of another Spanish historian of the Indies, also a priest and a humanist, Francisco López de Gómara, who wrote about the middle of the sixteenth century. Gómara, for example, was in despair because he could not learn the name of the pilot who had died in Columbus's house after giving Columbus the first indication of the existence of land to the west. Acosta preferred to let the name be unknown. "We do not know his name yet, but such a great enterprise should be attributed to no one but God." Gómara had a magnificent confidence in the possibility of digging a canal across the Isthmus of Panama to join the two oceans. "There are mountains, but there are hands. Give me a man who wishes to do it, and it can be done."

But Acosta, on the contrary, warns that anyone attempting to do such a thing would bring Divine punishment down on his head. "No human power will suffice to level the impregnable and impenetrable mountains that God has placed between the two oceans, mountains and cliffs that are solid enough to withstand the fury of both oceans. And even though it were possible for men to do so, in my opinion it would be just to fear the punishment of Heaven if one should attempt to correct the works that our Maker, in His great wisdom and foresight, ordained when He created the universe."

Renaissance in Gómara, Counter-Reformation in Acosta. So the curiosity of the latter is not as disinterested as that of the man of the Renaissance, but his whole store of knowledge must be placed in the service of the great cause, the evangelization of the natives. "Because the purpose of my history is not only to record what is happening in the Indies, but to direct such knowledge toward the fruit that may be harvested there, which is to help these people to their salvation and to glorify the Creator and Redeemer who rescued them from their deep darkness and gave them the admirable light of His Gospel."

To convert and govern the natives one must know them thoroughly; one must know their laws and customs in order to "help them and govern them by those same laws, for, in everything that is not contrary to the Law of Christ and His Holy Church, they should be ruled by their own customs."

Acosta had a high opinion of the Indians and their cultures, especially those of Mexico and Peru. He was filled with admiration for the collectivist organization of the Inca empire. "There can be no man of intelligence who will not be astonished at such a notable and beneficent government, for, although they were neither religious nor Christian, the Indians observed after their fashion the very perfect rule of having no private property, providing everyone with necessities, and supporting generously the needs of religion and those of their lord and sovereign." He was also struck by the Mexicans' passion for flowers. "The Indians of New Spain are more fond of flowers than any other people in the world."

Although he praised the Indians, he did not on that account spare his censures of the Spaniards, not sharing the fury of Las Casas, whom he mildly disagrees with. The capital defects of the Spaniards [according to him] were their greed, which made them idolize riches more than the Indians idolized their false gods, and the lukewarmness of their faith, which made them indifferent to the task of evangelization. He makes many comparisons between [Indians and Spaniards], at the cost of the latter. "The Mexicans' way of raising their children was very wise, and if some care should be taken to build houses and seminaries where these same children might be taught, Christianity would undoubtedly flourish among the Indians. Certain zealous men have begun it, and the King and his council have favored it; but, since it is not a profit-making enterprise, it goes very slowly and is done without warmth."

It is unfortunate that Acosta, whose book is so rich in content for the natural sciences, ethnography, and economics, does not give more space to narrative history. The sketches he draws of the development of the Inca and Aztec empires, and the brief chapters he devotes to the conquest of New Spain, in which he follows native accounts, show us how great was his stature as a historian, and make us grieve that he does not treat those subjects more amply.

Letras de México. Mexico, July 15, 1940.

Paradise in the New World*

Arnold Toynbee's introduction to his monumental *A Study of History* should be required reading for many historians of today. It would be well if they read it frequently, to rid themselves of the "industrialization of historical thinking," and to meditate upon the now morbid and unrestrained search for "prime materials," which are at once transformed, or an attempt is made to transform them, into "manufactured" or "semi-manufactured" articles. . . .

This remark was inspired by the impression I got from a fruitless attempt to read the two dense volumes of *El Paraíso en el Nuevo Mundo,* by Antonio de León Pinelo, just published in Peru to celebrate the fourth centenary of the discovery of the Amazon. Such a great river surely deserves the tribute of about a thousand large pages.

That is to say, it would deserve it if the contents of the book bore any relation to its size. Unfortunately, there is none. The

---

* Antonio de León Pinelo, *El paraíso en el nuevo mundo,* edited by Raúl Porras Barrenechea, 2 vols. (Lima, Peru, 1943). [Note: León Pinelo is best known for his *Tratado de confirmaciones reales* (Madrid, 1630.— Tr.]

competent Peruvian scholar, Paúl Porras Barrenechea, in his valuable preface, fills the presumptive reader with astonishment as he says: "Tremendous erudition"; "relentless citing of sources"; "it cannot be read without a considerable dose of good will," for Pinelo, "after long and painful effort, suspended in mid-air, leaves us with the ephemeral and fragile feeling of a cobweb." If that is so, why publish the book? This is a question that might be asked by the lucky reader who is not a victim of the professional distortion that afflicts us all, more or less, in these sad days of the "industrialization of historical thought." It was not for nothing that I began this note by citing Toynbee.

Leaving to one side the question of whether the publication of a book like this one of Pinelo's is justified, if it *is* published the edition should be a good one, which this edition is not. The only useful thing about it is the introduction. The same cannot be said of the text itself. There is no call to have a superstitious reverence for the anarchical spelling of old texts, and still less when the text is merely a copy, as this one is. There is no philological reason that justifies an exact reproduction without at least properly punctuating and accenting the original. According to the system adopted in this edition, we can never know whether the errors—and errors are plentiful—are the work of the ancient copyist or of the present publishers. The text has no notes whatever, outside of the author's quotations, which are not collated with the originals or clarified. It also lacks an analytical index, indispensable in a work of this kind which is almost impossible to read today, and which, if it has any value at all, has value only in its being a collection of odd bits of information.

León Pinelo is a classical example of the scholar who makes up for his lack of intelligence and his incapacity for seeing things straight, by piling up a crushing mass of data. He never thinks he has enough of them. The learned author of disquisitions on questions of vast importance, such as, for example, whether it is immoral or not for women to cover their faces, bemoans the lack of curiosity among his countrymen: "There is no one in them [the Indies] who seeks, or desires, anything but silver and gold, or something that may be exchanged for such. He who most quickly gets rich is considered the most learned, intelligent, and curious. Natural philosophy has not come by to investigate his secrets. Medicine has not come within his ken. Astronomy has not seen his heaven, or explored his stars. Nor has geography extended the limits of his continent. These subjects are so unknown to him that he is aware only of those which, by being common knowledge, cannot be concealed."

If this complaint of Pinelo's were justified, his book would not exist, for it is based entirely on other books. Faced with any fact whatever, he can never see it with his own eyes, but must run to consult some author who has written about it. This is a serious weakness in him, as is also his inability to choose among the many authors he relies on. A remarkable consequence of this is that, as he tells us: "I am not one of the most curious persons in these matters, because, although I have traveled a good deal in the Indies, I have never seen a thing that astonished me, nor have I read anyone who does not speak from hearsay, so let what I have written pass for something curious, if not true."

And this is told us by the compiler of the most nonsensical fables: of Indians with tails, others who have their feet on backward, some who sleep under water, others who sustain themselves only with the perfume of flowers; serpents with wings and arms, springs that snore, and so on!

In León Pinelo we recognize a common phenomenon: the survival in him of a stock of notes or notions, fossilized into dogma by virtue of authority, closed in upon himself, never penetrated by reality. Like so many authors who wrote of America, he was a prisoner of Pliny, a victim of the tendency to seek "the monstrous and never-before-seen" in the Indian landscape. And even here Pinelo lacks originality. He even regresses, if we compare him with authors like López de Gómara or Father Acosta, those merciless demolishers of myths and absurdities.

Love for the fantastic, the unusual, the unique, fathered many books about America. León Pinelo is not even original in his basic thesis, the strangest of all, to wit, that Paradise was situated in the New World, a notion that was cherished by its discoverer, one that has been rejuvenated today by inverting the time sequence. Indeed, the most lyrically beautiful study devoted to the Paradise of León Pinelo is that of Juan Larrea (*España Peregrina*, Mexico, October, 1940), which is recommended to the curious reader. To me, sadly prosaic person that I am, Pinelo's *Paraíso* should have been left where it was before modern scholars unearthed it—a Paradise Lost.

Revista de Historia de América. Mexico, December, 1943.

Latin America*

The first thing one comes upon in this little book of André Siegfried's is the author's confession of incompetence. Just as it is necessary to know Latin in order to speak French well, he tells us, it would be necessary to know Spain and Portugal thoroughly if one is to interpret intelligently the Latin countries beyond the Atlantic. His pages are enlivened by his effort to understand and by his instinctive sympathy. He is quite aware of his inadequate preparation for tackling Spanish-American subjects. His fears are, however, exaggerated.

Siegfried, a great traveler, a great student of peoples, author of valuable books about England and the United States, handles the data he has gathered in his brief sojourn in Spanish America with a diaphanous—possibly a too diaphanous—Gallic clarity. He analyzes the two aspects of the continent, its two axes, the geographical, north to south, and the historical, east to west. What is separated by history is brought together by geography. The future of America will depend upon which of these two factors predominates.

* André Siegfried, *Amérique Latine* (Paris: Armand Colin, 1934).

281

According to Siegfried—and this is what interests us Spaniards especially—it cannot be said that the white man conquered the southern half of the American continent as he did the northern. In the southern half white domination is very limited, and this has been the cause of complicated problems, which Siegfried underscores acutely. Latin America [he says] has a strongly defined character. It is enough for one to cross a hundred-foot bridge at El Paso for one to find himself in a world totally different from the Anglo-Saxon.

The author describes the geographic, economic, and political aspects of this world, except Mexico, which is outside his field: "that markedly Indianized country, whose soul folds in upon itself with a terrifying and hermetic self-sufficiency." In each of its aspects Siegfried notes the analogies and differences between the north and the south of Spanish America. Economically, the Spanish American countries have the psychology of peoples in the first stage of the exploitation of their soil, peoples who make up the youthful countries of the world. They export raw materials in great quantity, and get paid for them almost exclusively in manufactured articles, and this is what gives them their peculiar psychology and way of life. They live on risk and luck; they live between improvidence and quick riches. They accept as dogma that the potentialities of their countries are limitless, and they joyfully put their capital into the hands of foreigners. Siegfried emphasizes the Andalusian in the Spanish-American character. In his opinion a map should be drawn with a line between the people who save and the people who throw their money away. The Spanish American belongs to the second group. It is curious to see how the atmosphere of a country takes hold of the European immigrants who grew up in a tradition of niggardly and obstinate saving.

This same elementary quality, according to Siegfried, is found in Spanish-American political life. The state machine, which in the old European world hides itself behind complex guises, here functions openly. Siegfried stresses the point that we should not look for overly subtle explanations. In all Spanish-American life there is a primitive barbarism, neither good nor bad in itself, something distinct from what occurs in

European countries, as the people of Spanish America should try to comprehend. A dangerous misunderstanding commonly arises when, in certain countries accustomed to consider parliamentary procedures and liberalism as the predominant political forms—although at the moment there seems to be some doubt about it—they speak of dictatorship and one-man rule as habitual and endemic forms of government. This attitude annoys those involved, and they try to demonstrate that their constitutions and parliaments are models of democracy and guarantors of liberty, which creates a violent contrast between theory and practice in political affairs, one of the most interesting aspects of Spanish-American life. Siegfried is possibly not revealing anything startling when he speaks of all this; but his pages will always have the merit of clearly explaining the ideas in the minds of all who mention them, for whatever reason, under their breath.

It is to be hoped that, once the liberal taboo is broken, the phenomenon of *caudillismo*, which is so Spanish American, and so Spanish, will be properly studied. If we are to do so, it will be well to bear in mind Siegfried's initial observation. Such things cannot be sensed or comprehended by one who does not have our blood in his veins. One of these days we shall have to begin thinking in Spanish about Spanish America.

Tierra Firme. Madrid, 1936, Año II, No. 1.

Profile of Mexico*

For those who, like the present writer, have so frequently (perhaps too frequently) bemoaned the scarcity of books designed and written in Spanish about Spanish America, this work of Samuel Ramos is a feast. To come upon a book, very well written, sober, accurate, and so full of ideas and suggestions that when one takes notes during its reading one runs the risk of copying it entire—this is not something that happens every day.

Our spiritual relationship with Mexico is very thin. The vicissitudes of her politics, the upheavals in her internal life, the self-absorption of the Mexicans and their present scorn of whatever is outside their country, doubtless make it difficult for us to receive her books and magazines promptly. I know nothing of Samuel Ramos. It seems that he is highly regarded in Mexico for his essays, and that this latest book of his—the latest to reach us, in 1934—has been passionately discussed. His brief pages stir us like the alarm bell of an America which we have always been aware of, but which does not always emerge be-

* Samuel Ramos, *El perfil del hombre y la cultura en México* (Mexico: Imprenta Mundial, 1934).

fore our eyes in the books we get from Spanish America. In this one Samuel Ramos is revealed as one of the most penetrating essayists of the Spanish-speaking world of today. The precision and economy with which he manipulates his sources, and the exactness with which he applies them to the interpretation of his country's genius, are astonishing.

Here in Spain, where self-analysis and a conviction of our inferiority vis-à-vis other countries have spread since the literary production of the Generation of '98, we are not surprised to discover similar attitudes among the Spanish Americans by which they judged their problems. This virtual identity in Ramos' book is apparent, as it is apparent in a large part of the writings of young Americans, to go no farther, when we leaf through the extracts of reviews published in these same pages of *Tierra Firme*. In broad strokes, this is what Ramos tells us:

We do not know whether there really exists a Mexican culture. Whoever tries to discover it learns that what has been written about it is based upon vague ideas. Mexican culture is a borrowed culture. The Spaniards implanted there, violently, their own culture, which was in an advanced state of evolution. Since the sixteenth century European culture has had such a strong influence in Mexico that on many occasions the most highly esteemed Mexicans have been disowned because of it. In opposition to them there has arisen a cult of what is indigenous, an exalted nationalism, which in imitation of Europe denied its failures. Mexico has been divided by this tragic duality—a duality which we Spaniards know so well. She has desperately copied European standards of culture, without succeeding in assimilating them by means of a calm and continuing effort. Hence there arose such an imbalance between reality and make-believe in Mexican life that all reality was ignored, and hence also the uninterrupted series of revolutions that fill Mexican history in the nineteenth century.

The men of Mexico after Independence did not take into account the scanty potential of the country to realize their vastly ambitious plans. The Mexican does not know, says Ramos, "that the horizon of vital possibilities is extremely narrow for each people or each man." And so, "stubbornly attempting to negate his destiny," the independent Mexican allowed himself to be hypnotized by France. "The man who took control of the situation in the past century was the mestizo. His favorite game is politics. The norm of his activity is unreflecting imitation. The one country he enthusiastically admires is France, which he considers the archetype of modern civilization." The United States, on the other hand, that dangerous neighbor with its material concept of life, is the opposite of Mexico, and is especially the opposite of Indian Mexico.

Throughout the monotonous and routine days of the colony, and the bold and ill-considered innovations of the nineteenth century, the Indian has held himself aloof, aloof up to now, that is. The passivity of the Indian is in the very bowels of his character. What Ramos calls native *Egyptism* is manifest in pre-Hispanic art, all of it immutable, all a repetition of the same subjects. The Mexican, tired of sterile imitations of a life alien to him, turns his gaze toward this native Sphynx, and in disowning Europe he discovers nationalism, which is a European idea, incidentally.

According to Ramos, this new attitude brings in its wake dangers as great as the former ones. The abandonment of European culture, advocated in Mexico today, could wreak irremediable mischief upon the country. This pretended Mexican culture, closed in upon itself, is a more foolish Utopia than the other. It is not enough to read *The Decline of the West*, which has stirred up such a storm among Mexican intellectuals, in order to write the final chapter of the death of European culture, and joyfully turn one's back on it. A balance must be established between the two tendencies, the national and the foreign, to bring about a superior synthesis. Are we speaking of Mexico or Spain? The doubt is fully justified. Mexico, ourselves, all countries that have taken over the direction of present-day culture, are facing the same problems. For that reason I have tried to bring out analogies. Many of the observations that Ramos addresses to his countrymen are completely valid for us, so the book has a double interest for Spaniards.

Tierra Firme. Madrid, 1936, Año II, No. 2.